The Industrial Heritage of Britain

The Industrial
Heritage of Britain

Brian Bailey

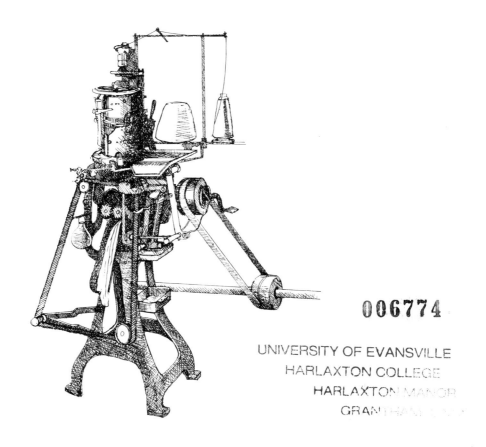

BOOK CLUB ASSOCIATES

LONDON

Contents

The Industrial Heritage of Britain was conceived, edited and designed by Holland & Clark Limited.

Designer
Julian Holland

Editor
Philip Clark

Artists
Penny Thomson
Allan Nutbrown

Maps
Martin Smillie

Picture Researcher
Sandra Assersohn

This edition published 1982 by Book Club Associates By arrangement with Ebury Press

First impression 1982

Typesetting by Tradespools Limited, Frome, Somerset
Colour reproduction by John Swain & Son Limited, London E.C.1
Printed and bound in Italy by New Interlitho, Milan

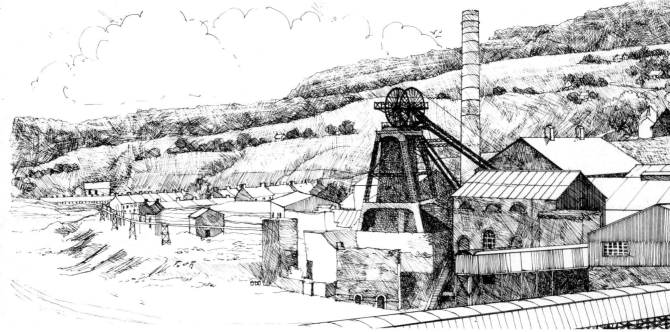

Introduction

In the days soon after the Second World War, when multitudes of schoolboys (me among them) spent much of their spare time on draughty and dirty railway platforms excitedly collecting the numbers of passing locomotives as if they were exotic plants or rare postage stamps from the farthest corners of the earth, we little realized that we were among the heralds or precursors of a new science.

For it was out of this period, and out of this sort of schoolboy passion, that a more serious attention to our industrial heritage developed, coinciding with the nationalization of the railways and the gradual disappearance of the steam locomotives which have excited so much interest and activity in recent years.

The Industrial Archaeologists

Since the 1950's, the interest in Britain's industrial past evinced by a number of specialists – mostly men with an engineering background – has spread by degrees to the public at large, and an impressive number of books has been published on the subject. The majority of them have dealt with particular regions of Britain in some detail, and the subject has acquired the dignity or the indignity of a generic misnomer – 'industrial archaeology'.

Even among those who practice it there are many who are unhappy about the name. It seems to have been coined in Manchester, and its first use in print occurred in 1955 in an article in The Amateur Historian. All writers have adopted it since—if a little uneasily in some cases.

Classical archaeology is the study of ancient human cultures through the discovery and interpretation of their remains. It is a noble science which helps man to know himself by revealing more of his past. In the same way that psycho-analysis exposes hidden individual depths, archaeology reveals hidden collective practices.

Industrial archaeology, at least in its present state, has no such aim. It is not primarily concerned with how people lived, but with how machines worked. Its incentive is a technical, not a social one, and it is possible to read one or two books on the subject and come away with the uneasy feeling that

human beings had become superfluous in the time and place to which most such books are almost entirely dedicated – the eighteenth and nineteenth centuries in Great Britain.

Here there is further cause for questioning. For if 'industrial archaeology' means what it says, why should it be confined to the Industrial Revolution? It is as if classical archaeology were confined to the study of the Roman Empire and had no interest in the civilizations of Greece and Egypt.

Industrial archaeology is riding on the crest of a wave at present, and as a science it has reached the status, in a relatively short time, of university recognition. But I suggest that if the subject does not acquire a broader base, and preferably a more appropriate title, it is destined to be short-lived. Even in the eighteenth century they knew the value of records, and more recent times have been documented by photographs. In the near future there will be nothing left to 'dig up' or to sustain the science's claim to interpret industrial development.

What industrial archaeology badly needs, if it is to expand and have any relevance to the modern world above the level of a passing hobby, is an injection of what the Germans call by that untranslatable word *Weltanschaaung* (literally 'world-view' – perhaps 'overview' is the closest we can get). After all, 'industry' is *useful labour*. It is for the people, by the people, and about the people. Its only purpose is to improve people's lives.

The neglected industries

Machines are not ends in themselves, and there is no value in the history of machinery and industrial architecture if it is not related to the social circumstances in which machines and buildings arose, and the social consequences of their creation. The only human beings mentioned in most books on the subject are the engineers who invented new machines, built new canals, or designed new locomotives. Engines are the unques-

Right: GWR's 4–6–0 King Class locomotive No. 6024, seen near Westbury, Wiltshire – a scene that was the very stuff of train-spotting in the years after the Second World War, when industry began to take on a new romantic image.

tionable heroes of these epics.

Agriculture and fishing, for example, which are the oldest industries on earth, receive little mention in the subject's literature up to the present. The argument that these industries do not have buried remains waiting to be rediscovered and interpreted only shows the weakness of the subject as it is presently conceived. In contrast, the present volume attempts to take a much broader view of Britain's industrial past than the traditional one (if one may use the word 'traditional' of something which is hardly thirty years old!), and it makes some effort to relate the development of man's machinery to his self-interest.

No one volume can cover even a single period of British industry comprehensively, of course, and some explanation of the very selective contents is perhaps necessary. I have divided the country up into eleven regions, and included in each region industries which are especially characteristic of the area, and which help to form the kind of landscape that visitors may expect to see and might wish to understand. Certain major industries, such as iron working, railways and textiles, occur in more than one region, and a technical term or a process may be referred to in one place but explained in another to save space and avoid repetition.

Apart from agriculture and fishing, several other industries are included which will not usually be found in books by industrial archaeologists, such as cider making and the manufacture of carpets, cottage industries like straw plaiting, widespread 'crafts' such as thatching, and very localized industries such as Swithland Slate working and 'wadd' mining.

The Industrial Revolution
Furthermore, although the Industrial Revolution must play a very large part in any story of British industry, I have not allowed it to dictate the shape of the book. Britons were industrious long before mass-production brought a new meaning and a new image to the word 'industry', and the volume reflects this fact in dealing with subjects that were already very ancient, and in some cases totally extinct, centuries before the age of machines and factories.

Besides, it is arguable that the words 'Industrial Revolution' are as much a terminological near-miss as 'industrial archaeology'. The prehistoric transition from Stone Age to Iron Age was a greater technological revolution for humanity as a whole than what happened in Britain in the eighteenth and nineteenth centuries. After all, the modern 'revolution' did not produce a new animal that bore twice as much wool as a sheep; it did not give birth to the idea of a railway; it did not invent bricks. It merely evolved faster and more efficient means of mining, transporting or manufacturing materials or goods which had already been mined, transported or manufactured long before it happened.

Industry and the landscape
I have followed the archaeologists in not entering into discussion of industries which do not have venerable origins. Aircraft engineering, plastics, electronics and nuclear power are too new to be regarded as part of our industrial heritage, and too immediately topical to have any kind of romantic or nostalgic associations. Environmentalists wish most of them did not exist. But today's environmental monstrosities are tomorrow's reverently preserved relics, and future generations will probably write heady aesthetic prose about Spaghetti Junction and the Fylingdales Early Warning Station.

Every reader will think of other industries which could have and perhaps *should* have been included in this book. I am only too well aware that the manufacture of boots and shoes is important to the East Midlands, for instance, and that public services other than transport are omitted altogether.

My chief aim in this book, however, has been to put human beings into the industrial landscape, and I have tried to represent as wide a variety of industrial activity as possible within the limitations imposed by the size of the volume. Everyone knows about North Sea Oil. It is in the newspapers every day, and is bringing great changes to life in Scotland and the Shetland Isles as well as to the nation's economy. But the quarrying of building stone, for instance, is gradually and sadly passing into oblivion because of the high cost of the material compared with

Right: The Nuclear Power Station at Wylfa Head on the island of Anglesey, is one of the world's largest. Building began in 1963 and the station was opened nine years later, with an output capacity of 840 MW. Will the ruins of this fortress-like power house be an object of aesthetic appreciation and industrial conservation in some remote period of the future, when nuclear power is as out of date as horse power and the architecture as old fashioned as a water mill?

bricks and concrete, and skilled quarrymen and master masons are among the ranks of the unemployed. *All* our lives will become so much the poorer because of that.

The chain-makers

One subject which is symbolic of the whole point I am trying to make, is chain-making. Iron working is important enough to find its way into several sections of the book already, and it would be hard to justify yet another page or two on one narrow aspect of it. But though chain-making is hardly mentioned even in detailed works of industrial archaeology, the omission seems significant. It is scarcely possible for anyone with any ordinary human sensitivity to discover how West Midland chain-makers worked at the beginning of the present century without realizing that the people were slaves in metaphorical chains themselves. One of the centres of the industry was Cradley Heath (then in Staffordshire), and old chain works are still in operation there. It was an important local industry of the Black Country, but I defy anyone to write about its techniques without being overwhelmed by the misery, squalor and sheer cruelty under which the chain-makers – young children among them – laboured. Anyone who wishes to pursue the theme of how industry affects lives should read *The Chainmakers of Cradley Heath* by Oscar Wilde's friend, Robert Sherard.

Industry and the individual

One does not need to visit South Wales or West Yorkshire to grasp the technicalities of coal mining or woollen manufacturing, but you cannot understand the people or the landscape properly without seeing them. Most travellers to a different landscape are looking for a change from their own familiar surroundings, and I hope this book might be found a useful travelling companion and a help towards better understanding and sympathy with the people whose permanent

Left: The Times coming off the press. The demands of the newspaper industry for high speed production led to vast machines which consume enormous rolls of newsprint, and produce newspapers ready for delivery to newsagents.

environment they are seeing, perhaps for the first time.

For what is the use of understanding how the machines and buildings of industry operated, if we do not understand at the same time that they often led to the growth of slums in overcrowded cities, and thus to stress, and thus to aggression, and thus to militant shop stewards? And that this is at least *partly* why the people of Cleveland and Clydebank are different from those of Somerset and Suffolk, where the industriousness of the people has been forced (by Nature, not by Man) into different avenues, and the social pressures have not been the same; so that resentment of one by the other is absurd and totally without profit to either.

I know of one book which implies that engineering and motor manufacturing grew up in the Midlands because Midland workers were born mechanics. This is quite the reverse of the truth, of course. They were *made* mechanics by Nature, which had deposited iron in the rock upon which they had settled. We read a great deal these days about how man has affected the landscape, but not so much about how the landscape has affected man.

There is no doubt that if mankind somehow manages to escape the nuclear catastrophe which seems to me inevitable at the time of writing, our great-grandchildren will understand nuclear physics and the mechanics of space travel, and take them for granted as we do radio and the motor car. But will they look back in anger at the generations from whom they inherited the world they live in, as we sometimes do at those who started the revolution in industry which changed Britain forever – and not entirely for the better? This is the danger of a too narrow devotion to machinery; it comes to rule our lives instead of to serve us in providing for the greatest happiness of the greatest number, tomorrow as well as today.

The printing industry

We should never look at any machine as if it had a life of its own, apart from the man who works it. Consider just one example from an industry which we all take very much for granted. It produced the volume you hold in your hands at this moment, but

the chances are that you had not given a thought to its printing before your attention was drawn to it. Now the invention of printing from movable types, like prehistoric progress into the Iron Age, had far greater consequences for mankind than the so-called Industrial Revolution in Britain. Not only that, but it has long been way ahead of most other industries in the degree of its automation. This was not because printing engineers were more ingenious men than railway engineers or the inventors of agricultural machinery. It was because the industry had a much greater impetus from universal literacy and the demand for knowledge. Civilization advances printing as war advances weaponry, and paradoxically, printing advances civilization as weaponry advances war. Now would you not expect printing, which goes back five hundred years in Europe, to be of some interest to the industrial archaeologist? Yet it rarely earns a mention, except for passing reference in connection with paper-making. Surely this is further evidence, if any were needed, that the 'science' of industrial archaeology is really much too narrowly based.

The man who operates a printing machine, though he may sometimes be disparagingly called a 'machine minder', has a very long tradition of pride in his craft behind him. He has been a more important agent of civilization than the coal-miner or the steel-worker. Every town in Britain has its printing works, large or small, where men use machines to spread information. If the men did not exist, none of the modern industries discussed in this book would be as advanced as they are. Labour disputes in the printing industry, which sometimes rob us of our national newspapers and provide television news with an occasional field day,

are about the balance between men and machines, and not allowing machines to be masters.

Further information

A glance at the ensuing pages will make clear, however, that this book does not neglect the mechanics of industry. In addition to the main text, each subject has an information panel which provides additional useful information for intending visitors to relevant locations, and mentions museums which have exhibits and which may be able to provide further information on industries concerned. At the end of the book, also, there is a list of museums throughout the country which have important industrial collections, not all of which are necessarily mentioned in the text pages. Many of these – chief of which is the Science Museum in London – have exhibits of industries far beyond their own localities.

There has been a remarkable recent growth of museums devoted to industry, not least of which are those such as the Ironbridge Gorge Museum in Shropshire and the Abbeydale Industrial Hamlet in South Yorkshire, where actual industrial sites have been rescued from dereliction and turned into unique and valuable public exhibitions.

It only remains to add that visitors interested in seeing industrial remains and buildings, as well as modern industry in operation, should always take care to ensure that they are not trespassing on private property. Mention of sites in this book does not imply public access, and enquiries should be made locally and permission sought before entering industrial premises. This applies especially to sites such as quarries and old mine workings where, quite apart from the question of trespass, real dangers lie in wait for the inexperienced and the incautious.

Left: The educational aspect of our industrial heritage – a scene at the Ironbridge Gorge Museum in Shropshire. Open air museums such as this tell the story of industry to young and old in exciting visual form, and the preservation of machinery and buildings has become a worthy preoccupation of many voluntary bodies throughout the land. Since this photograph was taken, the building in the background has been re-roofed and renovated, and now houses a vertical blowing engine.

South West England

The south west is so much dominated by tourism today that it is easy to dismiss it as a non-industrial region except for agriculture, but in fact the Cornish peninsula continues in a small way what were among the first industries of ancient Britain – mining and quarrying. The industries included in this section derive directly from the area's geology and from the water which almost surrounds it. Most of the coastal towns and villages which are now such popular holiday resorts began as fishing harbours or boat-building centres, and the seafaring tradition has remained important. The landscape is formed largely of granite and sandstone, the former providing some of the region's most dramatic landscapes, such as Dartmoor and Land's End, and the latter providing Devon and parts of Somerset with their rich red soil. Machinery and equipment for extractive industry and transport in other parts of Britain evolved from the south west's solutions to the problems of mining tin and copper and quarrying slate and granite.

Richard Trevithick, born at Illogan, near Redruth, was one of the great pioneers of the Industrial Revolution, and links it by his Cornish surname with the local Celtic heritage of two thousand years ago, when miners first sought the mineral treasures which lay hidden beneath the ancient rock.

DEVON

CORNWALL

Barnstaple

Bude

Okehampton

A30

Bodmin

Princetown

Liskeard

Lee Moor

Newquay

Plymouth

St. Austell

Charlestown

Truro

Camborne

Botallack

Penzance

Falmouth

Eddystone Lighthouse

AVON

Bristol

Bath

Weston-super-Mare

A38

Minehead

Bridgewater

Glastonbury

SOMERSET

Taunton

Yeovil

Tiverton

A30

Honiton

Axminster

Exeter

Haytor

Newton Abbot

Torquay

Dartmouth

| 0 | 10 | 20 | miles |

Tin and copper mining

Nowhere in England, perhaps, is there a more evocative and romantic industrial landscape than the area of west Cornwall where ivy-clad engine-houses and brick-topped chimney stacks stand, lonely and derelict, on moors where only tourists now come, to admire the 'natural' scenery. Around Camborne and Redruth, and on the Land's End peninsula, these relics stand like ruined medieval castles.

Cornwall's tin and copper deposits were worked before the Romans came to Britain. The people of the Bronze Age had discovered how to use an alloy of the two metals to make tools that were far superior to the flint knives and axes of their predecessors, whilst tin and lead together made pewter, which was in use from the Roman period onwards. Cornwall soon became the most important source of tin in Europe, and it was generally the most extensively worked ore next to iron, although at one later period copper took precedence.

The early tinners worked in the open air, 'streaming' ore from the rock face. (Streaming is the process of extracting ore by means of running water, which washes away waste sediment from the alluvium whilst the heavier metal settles and remains behind.) By the reign of Richard I, the tin industry had become so important that a charter for the 'Stanneries' made the workers their own masters, exempt from ordinary taxes and having their own parliament and courts.

Introduction of shaft mining

It was in the fifteenth century that shaft mining was introduced, and the organization of labour began on a large scale. Tin and copper were often dug from the same mines. By the time of the Industrial Revolution, Cornwall's miners were a race apart. Men, women and children worked in the mines. The men and boys descended the deep shafts on ladders, with candles fixed to their hats, to work long hours in darkness, and in a hot, damp and choking atmosphere which gave them diseases such as tuberculosis and consumption. As a result, many died before they were fifty. It is recorded that of sixty-seven miners buried during one year in the parish of St Just, only nine died of old age. The rest died of consumption or in mine

accidents, the average age of sixteen accident victims being only twenty-one years.

The ore was usually freed from the rockface by blasting with gunpowder, and the dust and particles thrown about by the explosions added to the miners' occupational hazards, making the awful conditions even worse. A thirteen-year-old boy who worked in a copper mine said: 'When I come up I spit nasty black trade. Sometimes I carry up borers and other weights which make me pant a good deal.'

The shafts were descended and ascended on relays of ladders supported on small

Above: The Botallack Mine, near St Just, around 1870 – a rare photograph taken by Archibald Coke. The picture shows dressing floors with round frames in the foreground. Engine houses can be seen down the cliff-side in the distance, from where underground workers went beneath the sea-bed to dig tin ore.

Left: Haytor granite
tramway, Devon. Rails
made of long granite
blocks once carried horse-
drawn trains of wagons.

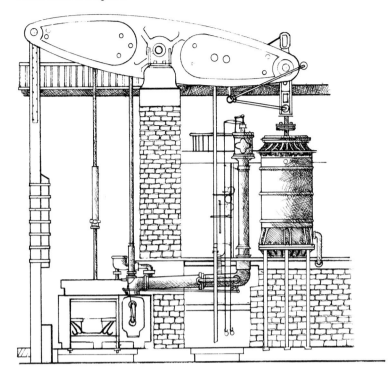

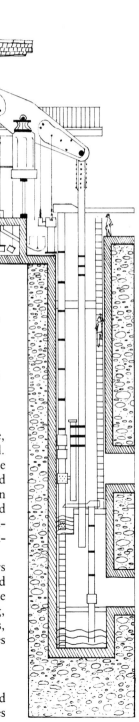

platforms down the walls of the shafts. The ladders were often made of timber taken from wrecked ships. Ore was raised to the surface in iron buckets called 'kibbles', and there it was sorted by hand – usually by women and children – from the lumps of rock.

Increasing depths and dangers
Much of the early use of steam power that gave the Industrial Revolution one of its great thrusts had its beginnings in the Cornish tin and copper mines. As the mine shafts went deeper below the surface, engines were devised to lower and raise the miners and to pump out water. Trevithick, among others, developed engines specifically for such uses, and many Newcomen and Watt engines were installed in the Cornish mines.

From the nineteenth century onwards, the demand for tin increased enormously with the growth of the food canning industry, and new mines sprouted everywhere, with names like Ding Dong, Cakes and Ale, and Cook's Kitchen. Their galleries went deep into the earth and beneath the sea. The Botallack Mine, with its particularly spectacular site on the edge of the cliffs, had galleries running a third of a mile out to sea, and the Levant Mine, nearby, had one gal-

Above: Diagram of a Cornish beam pumping engine. The principle is the same as that of a domestic water pump, the huge beam replacing the lever handle. The pump rod, left, descended deep into the earth.

Right: Diagram of tin mining shaft and engine house, showing a steam-powered beam engine used to pump out water. Ladders are shown on which miners descended to the galleries.

lery which, half a mile out from the shore, was two thousand feet below sea level. Temperatures were so insufferable in the deep mines that tinners had to be sprayed with cold water whilst they worked. In 1919, in the Levant Mine, an old engine rod broke, killing thirty-one men, and operations below the sea bed were largely discontinued after that.

Little wonder that the Cornish tinners earned the reputation of being unruly and immoral men who filled in such spare time as they had with drinking, cock-fighting, smuggling and plundering local wrecks, while the mine-owners made huge fortunes from their labours.

Influences on West Country society
Corruption spread to the Church of England clergy and laid the tinners and their families

wide open to the message of Nonconform-
ism. Wesley was a frequent visitor to these
parts, and his fiery sermons offering hope of
salvation to the poor and ignorant were
among the most powerful influences of the
Methodist Revival which still permeate this
corner of the country. There are still today
more Methodists and Methodist chapels in
Cornwall, in proportion to the total population, than in any other part of Britain.

Gwennap Pit, near Redruth, is one of the
famous places of Methodism. Originally it
was a chasm caused by subsidence above a
collapsed mine, and different tales account
for Wesley going there to preach in 1762.
One story says that it was a well-attended
cock-fighting pit. At any rate, Wesley, who
visited Cornwall more than thirty times
between 1743 and 1789, frequently preached
at Gwennap, and after his death the place
came to be venerated as a local 'Methodist
cathedral'. It was 're-fitted' as an amphi-
theatre with grassed terraces looking down
on the central circular 'Pulpit', and Methodists still hold a service in it every Whit
Sunday.

Progress and decline
Meanwhile, by the middle of the nineteenth
century, the world's most productive copper
mines were sending up two hundred thousand tons of copper ore a year, and the
Dolcoath Mine, near Camborne, was at that
time the deepest mine in the world, going
down three thousand feet below the surface.
It employed over a thousand men. Copper
took temporary precedence over tin, fetching higher prices and providing over two
thirds of the world's supply, but it was also
the first to be exhausted.

By this time, the tin-mining industry had
its own problems to contend with. Huge
deposits were being discovered in other parts
of the world, notably in Malaysia, and tin
could be imported cheaply. Gradually, the
Cornish mines started to close. Their engines wound to a standstill, their buildings
of stone were left to the elements, and one of
the most industrialized areas of Britain declined into a desolate but defiant landscape.
The men drifted elsewhere, large numbers of
them emigrating to use their skills in far-
away places, where mines were often said to

Left: Cornish tin stamps. The ores of tin oxide had to be crushed and concentrated prior to smelting, and the crushing was done by iron stamps, or pulverisors, powered by steam or water. Ore was shovelled into boxes at the base, then the heavy stamps were repeatedly raised on cams and allowed to drop.

Above: Tinners worked at one time with candles fixed to their helmets as the only source of light in the deep underground workings.

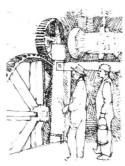

Above: The Tolgus Tin works where twelve-headed stamps, still *in situ*, were driven by a large water-wheel.

be 'holes full of Cornishmen'.

The mining of tin never ceased entirely, however. The two world wars brought some revival of activity, and tin mining still goes on in Cornwall today. Although it is on a much reduced scale, the work continues a two-thousand-year-old tradition in this corner of England, and as imported tin becomes more expensive, there is hope that Cornwall's ancient industry will make a come-back.

Remains

The derelict engine sheds and other unmistakable remains of the tin and copper mines are to be seen mainly on the Land's End peninsula and in the vicinity of Camborne and Redruth, near the A30 west of Truro.

The National Trust owns the 1840 beam whim engine of the old Levant Mine at Botallack; and also the 1854 pumping engine at South Crofty Mine. This was designed by a pupil of Richard Trevithick, whose cottage at Penponds, Camborne, is also owned by the Trust. There is a statue of Trevithick outside the town's public library.

The Tolgus works still stream tin (for the benefit of tourists) from sand and mine waste, and the only remaining set of working Cornish stamps for crushing ore is to be seen there, whilst nearby is the plant where arsenic – a by-product of the tin-mining industry – was produced.

Where to go

Botallack is off B3306 north of St Just, and South Crofty is north east of Camborne, off A3047 to the south. The Tolgus mine is north of Redruth on B3300 (Portreath Road).

At Pendeen (B3306 north of Land's End) visitors can see the tin treatment plant of Geevor Tin Mines; whilst at Wendron (north of Helston on B3297) underground levels of the so-called Poldark Mine can be visited.

Gwennap Pit is off unclassified road between Redruth and St Day to the east. Two museums with exhibits of mining are at Holman Brothers Ltd and the School of Mines, both at Camborne.

Granite quarrying

Much of south west England – most notably the Land's End peninsula and Bodmin Moor in Cornwall, and Dartmoor in Devon – is composed of granite, an ancient igneous rock formed by the cooling of molten matter after volcanic action, or by extreme heat, pressure and chemical action beneath other rocks. It consists primarily of quartz, felspar and mica, and is immensely hard and strong. Although its properties as an exceptionally durable building material were universally recognized long before the nineteenth century, it was so difficult to work that it was little used in building except in the south west.

Because it could not be cut or dressed accurately until the introduction of modern diamond-edged sawing machinery, granite was used for building the houses and churches of Cornwall and parts of Devon in the form of large irregular blocks, with rough-hewn surfaces and no ornament. One only has to travel from Cornwall to Somerset or Dorset to see the limitations of granite building when compared with the unlimited possibilities of limestone, used in the splendid ornamented church towers of Somerset.

Even so, granite was used on an increasing scale, and at one time many granite quarries were in operation, particularly around Dartmoor and the western part of Cornwall. The silvery-grey stone was carried far and wide for large building projects where strength was a major consideration. Among the famous and varied structures built of granite from Devon and Cornwall are Tower Bridge, Nelson's Column and the Eddystone Lighthouse.

Thomas Tyrwhitt's opportunism

Thomas Tyrwhitt was an Essex man, born in 1762, who became friend and secretary to the Prince of Wales and began his industrial activities on Dartmoor as a farmer. He built

Below: Convicts at work under guard in a granite quarry, about 1895. The convicts of H.M. Prison at Princetown, on Dartmoor, were not skilled quarrymen or masons. They were employed at stone-breaking, one of the most soul-destroying of jobs. Granite was freed from the rock-face with gunpowder, then broken up mainly for making roads. Granite for building purposes had to be treated with more care, by experts.

a few cottages for his workers and called his new estate Prince's Town, which soon became Princetown. He intended to cultivate large areas of Dartmoor, but reckoned without the harsh inhospitality of his ill-chosen site for both human and vegetable welfare.

Noting the government's concern about the overcrowding of French prisoners of war in prisons and rotting prison ships at Plymouth, Tyrwhitt hit on an alternative idea. He proposed to the government that a prison should be built for them on Dartmoor. Tyrwhitt's own quarries would supply the granite! The plan was eventually accepted, and Thomas laid the foundation stone in 1806. The first prisoners arrived there three years later after a building nightmare in which more than one contractor went bankrupt.

Tyrwhitt, however, was knighted for his enterprise, and lost no time in expanding Princetown, which now had a brighter future. He built a railway to it from Plymouth, and by the time the last prisoners of war had left and the gaunt buildings were deserted, he had various new schemes in mind for an imported population. Chief among them was the idea of bringing convicts to the prison, who would work as stone-breakers, producing granite which could be sold (and supplied by rail) and at the same time preparing the ground for the cultivation he still dreamed of. Eventually, the convicts came, but the fields of corn did not, though the prison is still in use after nearly two hundred years.

Reduction in use of granite

Pack-horses had carried the quarried granite slowly to canals or ports until the need for more efficient means of transporting increasingly heavier loads became urgent, and tramways and railways were built specially for the purpose. A tramway built in 1820 to carry granite from the Haytor quarries to waiting canal barges at Teigngrace, ten miles away, had long blocks of shaped granite for its rails, and was in use for more than forty years. Horse-power was still used to move the granite, but now teams of horses could pull trains of a dozen loaded wagons.

The advent of circular saws with

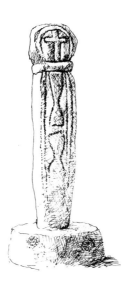

Above: A characteristic Cornish granite cross.

Above right: The church of St Michael at Michaelstow, Camelford, Cornwall. At the edge of Bodmin Moor, this is a typical unornamented Cornish church built of local granite.

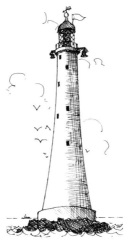

Above: The Eddystone Lighthouse. The granite structure was built in 1882, and is the fourth lighthouse on the site.

diamond-tipped cutting edges gave granite a new lease of life for building purposes, and the quarries also supplied kerb stones for roads throughout the country. But the relative difficulty of working granite, compared with the ease of other stones, made it costly, and only one or two of the old granite quarries are still working continuously today. The Haytor quarries supplied the granite for the British Museum, which was completed in 1852.

Where to go

Tourist interest in Dartmoor Prison is not encouraged, but apart from the famous buildings mentioned, Cornish granite can be seen in practically every church in the west, and many houses and cottages, as well as the Eddystone Lighthouse, which is fourteen miles out in the English Channel from Plymouth.

Best known among abandoned quarries are Haytor on Dartmoor, four miles west of Bovey Tracey, with part of its granite tramway still *in situ*; and Cheesewring quarry on Bodmin Moor, west of Upton Cross (B3254), where an industrial railway, since demolished, gave this wild locality unlikely names such as Railway Terrace. The prehistoric village of Chysauster, north of Penzance, was built of moorland granite before Christ was born.

Cider making

Cider has been produced in most parts of southern England at one time or another since its popularity grew around the time of the Norman Conquest. Herefordshire was one of the early strongholds of cider making, and well known companies, including Bulmers, still produce cider there. Much Marcle, in what is now Hereford and Worcester, has been a centre of the industry since the seventeenth century, and one local MP promoted the beverage so vigorously that he was known as the Member for Cider!

Gradually the art spread southwards, however, and it is rightly associated in most minds today with Somerset, where thousands of acres of orchards present a beautiful landscape of blossom in the spring, and seem far removed from anything we normally think of as 'industry'. British cider makers are currently producing nearly fifty million gallons a year, however – much of it for export.

The Rev. Thomas Cornish sold home-produced cider from his rectory near Taunton so successfully that his gardener (who made the cider) went into business to meet the demand, and thus the well-known Taunton Cider Company came into being. Oddly enough, H. P. Bulmer was also the son of a rector.

The pre-eminence of the West Country in the cider business is less to do with the process of making cider than with the right soil and climate for growing apples. There are about three thousand varieties of cider apple, often low in acid content, high in sugar and tannin, and of fibrous texture. They have picturesque names like Yarlington Mill, Bloody Butcher, Tom Putt, Chisel Jersey and Slack-ma-Girdle. Orchards are often owned by independent growers who are under contract to supply their crops to the cider makers.

Cider was made mainly by farmers' wives until modern times, and farmers sometimes paid their labourers partly in cider, the usual custom being to give them a 'firkin' a day in lieu of cash payments. The farmhouse process of fermenting with the yeasts found on the skins of apples produces the rough cider known as 'scrumpy'. It is low in sugar and high in acid, and can be rather powerful.

Various types of cider mill were in use for crushing the apples before the introduction

Left: An old cider press at work. The horse-driven mill first reduced the apples to pulp, which was then pressed in a 'cheese'. This consisted of a series of slatted boards between which layers of pulp were placed; pressure was then applied to extract all the juice. More efficient modern machinery can extract over 80% of the total weight of each apple as juice.

Left: A small hand apple mill and press, in which apples are first pulped by the mill and then juice is squeezed out by the screw-operated press.

Above: An old photograph of the harvest of cider apples being delivered to a farmhouse cider maker. In those days, apples were harvested by shaking branches of trees with long hooked poles and picking up the fallen fruit by hand. Nowadays, mechanical harvesting does the job in less time with less labour. Mid-September sees the arrival of the first apples, which continue to be harvested until Christmas. Farm producers often used the yeast in the skins for fermentation, producing the rough cider called 'scrumpy'.

of modern machinery. One kind was a circular stone trough, around which a horse was driven to turn a millstone which crushed the apples as they were fed into the trough. In another type, a press of stone or wood was screwed down on to the pulped apples. Old presses survive here and there in the West Country, and indeed, many farms and small cider-makers still produce the strong potion that the local drinkers call 'real' cider, which can pull your feet out from under you without warning.

Modern cider production
When the fruit has been harvested, it is delivered to the modern commercial cider factories and put in storage silos, from where it passes – sometimes through water channels – through washing and pulping machinery. Then the juice is pressed out. Modern machines can process up to five tons of pulp an hour.

Meanwhile, the juice is pumped into huge containers or tanks, where, with the addition of specially cultivated yeasts, it is left to

ferment for up to three months. After fermentation, the cider is transferred to giant vats to mature for anything from a few weeks to six months.

After maturing, the cider-maker's special art comes into its own, for cider is not brewed, like beer, but blended. The various types of apples delivered by the growers have all been pulped, pressed and fermented together, so that the contents of one vat will taste different from those of another, according to the proportions of sweet and bitter apples in each lot. The Master Cider Maker, who has learned his art during a ten-year apprenticeship, has to blend the various results together to produce consistent ciders to be sold under the many well-known brand names now available.

Where to go
A Museum of Cider has been opened at Hereford, in the old cider mills in Ryelands Street. It shows the story of cider making, from apple orchards and farmhouse production to modern factory methods, and includes a cooper's shop. The works of H.P. Bulmer in Hereford can be visited by arrangement.

One of the chief areas for growing cider apples is the Vale of Taunton Dene, between the Quantocks and Blackdown Hills. It is still possible to find smaller cider-making establishments where you can sample the products before purchasing, and see something of the equipment. One such is R.J. Sheppy & Son at Three Bridges (A38 south west of Taunton).

At Tuckenhay in Devon, three miles south of Totnes, a 19th century water-powered cider factory still stands.

Shipping

Bristol's position at the mouths of the Severn and Avon, facing the vast Atlantic Ocean, made sure of its importance as a port many centuries ago, and its people could hardly help themselves from becoming merchants and sailors once America had been discovered.

It is possible that Bristol mariners knew of the New World before Columbus, for Bristol men had been to Iceland and Greenland before John Cabot set off from the city to find a western passage to Cathay (China). Cabot found in England support for his expedition which he could not get in Spain or Portugal. Sebastian, his son, seems to have carried on the explorations where his father left off, and he was chiefly responsible for the formation of the Company of Merchant Adventurers, which, among other things, opened up British trade with Russia. Martin Frobisher sailed from Bristol a century later, still looking for a 'North-West Passage' (which did not exist) but these tales of failure that made history were only an incidental part of Bristol's maritime expansion.

Dubious path to prosperity

Sailors from Bristol exploited the Newfoundland fisheries discovered by Cabot and opened up trading with the American coast and the West Indies, making sugar and tobacco their specialized cargoes. Trading in the town was done in Merchants' Tolzey, where deals were done by the passing of money on flat-topped 'nails', like garden bird-tables. It is from this practice that the phrase 'paying on the nail' is derived.

By the end of the seventeenth century, Bristol had a profitable interest in the slave trade. More than fifty vessels were regularly occupied in seizing African men, women and children and transporting them to the West Indies to work in the sugar plantations. There was no organized opposition to the evil at that time, and Bristol became prosperous before the voices of conscience began to be heard and eventually gathered support for the abolition of slavery. Bristol fortunes then slumped, and other trading ports such as London and Liverpool prospered at her expense.

There were other obstacles to continued

expansion. The exceptional tidal range of over forty feet near the mouth of the Avon meant that ships trading with the town had to have their hulls specially strengthened, for they could be grounded twice daily, lying on the bottom at low tide. A wet dock was built in 1712 down-river at Sea Mills, but it was used mainly by whaling vessels as it was too distant from the trading centre.

William Jessop completed the Cumberland Basin in 1809, transforming the Avon at Bristol into a huge wet dock with lock gates, and this enterprise gave the port a temporary equality with Liverpool.

Changing fortunes

Men of genius and enterprise had served Bristol well before, and were to do so again, for it was from here in 1838 that Isambard

Above: An old view of Bristol docks around 1880. Note the gas lamp. William Jessop and Isambard Kingdom Brunel had carried out much improvement to the docks during the nineteenth century, but by the period of this picture, Bristol was in decline, unable to handle large modern shipping, until the building of the Royal Edward Dock early in the present century.

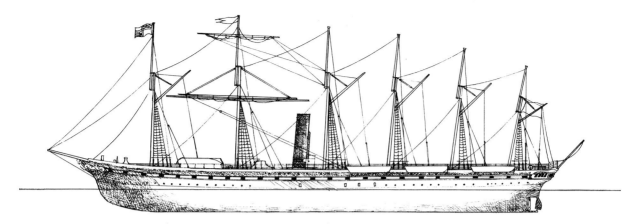

Kingdom Brunel's steamship *Great Western* sailed, bound for New York. Doubts had been voiced about the wisdom of building her at all. She would not, experts declared, shaking their unadventurous heads, be able to carry enough coal to run her engines for such a long voyage. But the *Great Western* sailed out of the Bristol Channel and opened up a new regular passenger service between the European and American continents.

Brunel, meanwhile, was still advancing – building a huge ship of iron instead of timber, to be driven by screw instead of paddles. The SS *Great Britain* was launched in 1843 by Prince Albert. It was the largest ship afloat, but it marked a turning point in Bristol's fortunes. The docks were not big enough to cope with the largest modern ships, in spite of Jessop's and Brunel's im-

Above: Brunel's screw-driven iron ship SS *Great Britain* was 322 feet long. She could carry over a thousand tons of coal and 252 passengers. The hull was constructed of overlapping wrought iron plates riveted to metal frames.

Below: A surviving warehouse beside Bathurst Basin, with ogee arches above windows which brought the name 'Bristol Byzantine' to local nineteenth-century architecture.

provements to them, and the town's greatness as a port declined as Bristol talked about the problem and did nothing while Liverpool grew bigger and richer.

Eventually, however, plans were approved for expansion, and new docks were built at Avonmouth and Portishead, which brought big ships back to the Bristol Channel. In 1908, Edward VII opened the huge new Royal Edward Dock, and the city recovered its position to a degree, importing sugar, tobacco, bananas, cocoa and wine and countless other commodities, but its days as Britain's number one trading port had passed, seemingly for ever. The city docks continued to decline in favour of the new larger docks down-river, where all the great shipping activity now takes place, and Bristol's coastwise trade is still extensive.

Where to go
The merchants' 'nails' can still be seen in Bristol outside the Corn Exchange.

The City Museum in Queen's Road has many maritime and industrial exhibits, and the Industrial Museum at Prince's Wharf should also be visited.

Nineteenth-century warehouses, locks and steam cranes can be seen at the city docks.

The most famous testimony to Bristol's maritime past is Brunel's ship *Great Britain*, preserved in the original dry dock built to accommodate her nearly a century and a half ago. The great ship was abandoned in the Falkland Islands in 1886, but has been salvaged and returned to Bristol for restoration and preservation. Visitors can go aboard, and the ship is open every day.

China clay

The St Austell district of Cornwall presents the visitor with what is certainly one of the most eerie industrial scenes in Britain – a sort of lunar landscape of white pyramids which can take on pink or orange glows in late evening sunlight and look like nothing on earth when the moon is out. These are the quarries and spoil heaps of china clay, of which Cornwall has been blessed with the most important deposits outside China.

China clay, or kaolin, as it is properly called, is produced by the decomposition of granite, which consists mainly of mica, quartz and felspar, fused together by intense heat and pressure. It is the chemical decomposition of the felspar which produces kaolin – a hydrated aluminium silicate in scientific terms, soft, white and slightly greasy when you touch it. When mixed with water, it is easily moulded and retains its shape.

Vital raw material

In England it was William Cookworthy, an eighteenth-century Plymouth chemist, who discovered that the chief ingredient of Chinese porcelain was kaolin, and since then the deposits around St Austell have been worked continuously, with some important workings on Dartmoor, too. The ghostly waste heaps are largely formed of glistening white mica washed out from the kaolin.

It seems at first sight extraordinary that the main centre of pottery manufacture should be in Staffordshire, over two hundred miles away from the source of its vital constituent, but of course that was not always the situation. The Potteries grew up near supplies of coal and the local clay suitable for earthenware before the importance of kaolin was realized. It was not long, however, before leading potters such as Josiah Wedgwood and Thomas Minton went down to the south west to work out trading deals with the owners of the china clay works, and huge quantities were soon being exported to Europe, too. Minton used clay from Lee Moor, on Dartmoor, in his factory. At that time the deposits in Devon were independently owned and operated, but in due course they all came into the ownership of the Cornish operators.

The little harbour of Charlestown on St Austell Bay was built specially in 1798 for

Above: Aerial view of the lunar landscape created by kaolin quarrying around St Austell. The white pyramids of waste consist chiefly of mica washed away from the vital constituent.

the shipping of china clay and copper from the local mines owned by Charles Rashleigh. Down the road towards Mevagissey there is a little place called London Apprentice, after an inn of the same name. The inn was so called because of the large number of Londoners who came to work in the china clay industry, which also absorbed many workers from the declining tin mines.

Extraction and uses

The early method of extracting kaolin was well described in a nineteenth-century guide, which explained that the clay was 'piled in stopes or layers, upon an inclined plane, and a stream of water is then directed over it, which carries with it the finer and purer portions, and deposits them in a large reservoir, while the coarser residuum is caught in pits placed at suitable intervals. From the reservoir all the water is drawn off, and the clay removed to pans, where it is passed under the influence of a novel drying-machine, thoroughly relieved of moisture, properly packed up in barrels, and removed to the seaside for shipment.'

Right: The wooden, 35-foot diameter breast-shot waterwheel at Wheal Martyn, used for driving pumping machinery, is seen above, while below is a 'pan kiln' in which clay from settling tanks was spread a few inches thick to dry over tile-covered flues. A 'travelling bridge' ran on rails along the length of the kiln to help spread the wet clay along it.

The basic process of extracting kaolin is still the same, but of course today's methods are more mechanized and sophisticated. It often surprises people to learn that the clay is used by other industries on a much larger scale than in pottery making. Of the two or more million tons of kaolin extracted locally each year, more than three-quarters is used by the paper-making industry. China clay is also used in paint, drugs, cosmetics and other products as well as pottery.

China Clay today

One of the major problems of the china clay industry, which occupies an area of many square miles around St Austell and is centred on Hensbarrow Downs to the north of the town, has been its environmental hazards. River pollution has killed off the fish, which found themselves swimming in milk instead of water; white dust has settled everywhere; and the ever-growing waste heaps (there are eight tons of waste to every one of kaolin) have remained useless and unsightly hills on which no vegetation could re-establish itself. Now some of these problems are being tackled and overcome, and a use has been found for the waste material in filling excavations.

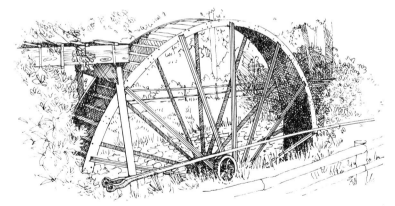

Where to go

The best view of the weird landscape of china clay working is from Hensbarrow Hill on the minor road to Roche, north of St Austell.

Visits can be arranged to the 'Blackpool' pit and plant of English China Clays at St Austell.

The Wheal Martyn China Clay Works is a museum run by the industry. Water wheels, kilns and settling tanks can be seen there, all *in situ*. The museum is just west of A391, three miles north of St Austell.

Lee Moor and neighbouring villages on the fringe of Dartmoor north east of Plymouth are a sort of industrial outpost of Cornwall, all the pits being owned by English China Clays, but one of the Dartmoor workings is among the world's largest china clay quarries.

Central Southern England

The industries of this region were determined partly by nature and partly by man. Much of the land consists of limestone, which is particularly good for building purposes, and we can see the medieval builders' joy and skill in using it in the architectural extravagance of many of the churches in this part of England. Prehistoric settlers had already established a local pattern of stone building and the transportation of materials long before Gothic architecture made its appearance. Stonehenge on Salisbury Plain is among the oldest man-made structures in Europe. At the same time, the land provides fine pasture for sheep, whose wool led to a tradition of weaving, while the timber of the New Forest helped to build the Royal Navy.

One of the pioneering sons of the central southern region was Isambard Kingdom Brunel, who was born at Portsmouth. His works, like those of Trevithick, were far-reaching indeed.

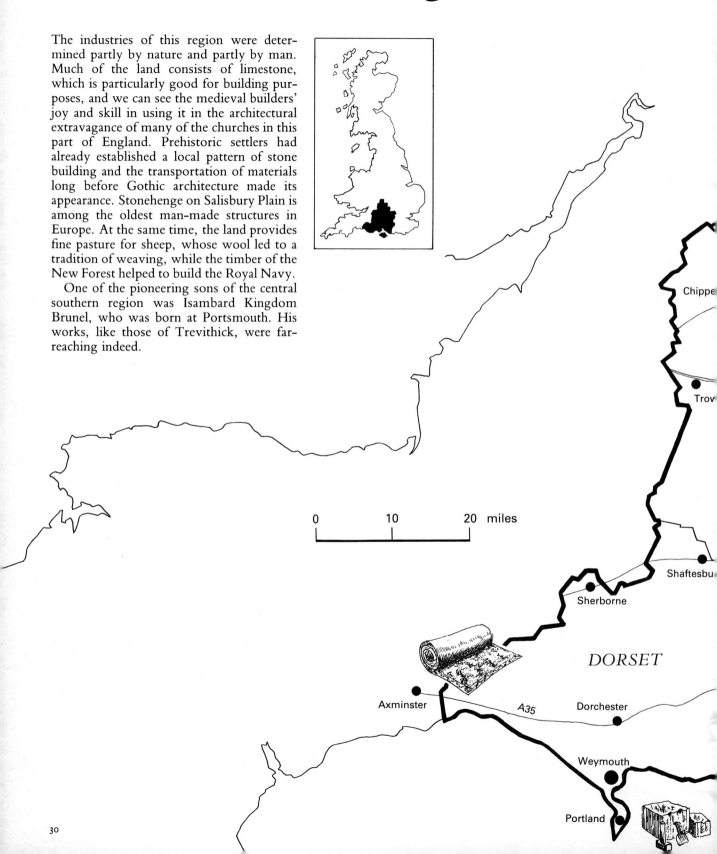

0   10   20 miles

Chippe

Trov

Shaftesbu

Sherborne

DORSET

Axminster

A35

Dorchester

Weymouth

Portland

Banbury

Bicester

A34

Oxford Canal

Witney

Oxford

OXFORDSHIRE

Swindon

Wantage

A4

Windsor

Reading

Marlborough

Newbury

BERKSHIRE

A4

Devizes

Kennet & Avon Canal

A34

Basingstoke

A30

WILTSHIRE

Andover

Alton

Chilmark

HAMPSHIRE

A30

Wilton

Salisbury

Winchester

Petersfield

A33

A3

Southampton

A31

A27

Bucklers Hard

Poole

Portsmouth

Bournemouth

Cowes

Isle of Wight

Swanage

31

Stone quarrying

The most important and extensive supply of all Britain's rock suitable for building is the belt of Jurassic limestone which runs up through England from the coast of Dorset to the coast of Yorkshire. It was formed roughly two hundred million years ago and consists essentially of calcium carbonate, originally formed beneath the sea by precipitation and from the shells and skeletal fragments of marine organisms.

Two parallel bands of stone occurring within the system provide the building material. They are known as Oolitic and Liassic limestone, the first being of fine rounded grains like miniature frog-spawn, and superior for building purposes to the other, which is coarser, softer and more shelly. Between them, these stones give us the beautiful warm-coloured stone towns and villages of Dorset and Somerset, the cooler but incomparably stylish buildings of the Cotswolds, the rich brown villages of parts of the East Midlands, where the stone is coloured by the presence of iron in the rock, and the attractive villages of the North Yorkshire Moors.

The quarrying industry has been singled out for discussion under Central Southern England for one overwhelming reason; because it is here that the Jurassic system produced what is universally acknowledged to be one of the world's finest building materials – Portland stone.

Portland limestone

The so-called Isle of Portland, which is actually a peninsula joined to the mainland by the famous Chesil Bank, is formed entirely of limestone, which rises from the sea at Portland Bill and provides the 'island' with its only industry. Portland is a bleak and treeless place, and 'the soile is sumwhat stony' as John Leland, the sixteenth century antiquary, remarked with English understatement.

The quarrying of Portland limestone has a long history. As far back as the fourteenth century it was transported by sea to Exeter for use in the cathedral and to London for use in the Tower. But the greatest period of its exploitation began in the seventeenth century, after the Great Fire of London. Portland stone is hard and fine-grained, so

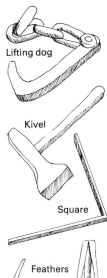

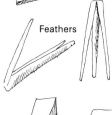

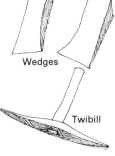

Above: An old view of quarries on the Isle of Portland, showing lifting tackle for raising huge blocks of stone from the pits below. From 1848 onwards, convicts were employed at the quarries with a system of incentives. The prison built for them accommodated 1500 men. Convicts built Portland's 1½-mile breakwater enclosing the harbour on the east side. It took twenty-three years to build.

Left: Tilly Whim Caves near Swanage, Dorset. The 'caves' were cut into the rock face for quarrying the limestone known as 'Purbeck marble'.

Above: Some tools of the quarryman. The purposes of most of them are self-evident. All sorts of hammers are used, from small 'kivels' to heavy sledge-hammers, as well as picks such as the 'twibill'. (A twibill was originally a battle-axe with a double blade.)

that it can be quarried in large blocks and dressed to a smooth surface called 'ashlar' by masons and architects. It is thus eminently suitable for large-scale public and private buildings such as palaces and town halls.

After the Great Fire, Sir Christopher Wren decided to use Portland stone for rebuilding St Paul's Cathedral, and he became 'Surveyor of the Quarries on the Island of Portland'. In the period of twenty-five years after the foundation stone was laid, fifty thousand tons of stone were dug out of this island for the purpose and carried by sea round the coast and up the Thames. Because London has no good building stone anywhere near it, Portland also became the chief source of material for a high proportion of the capital's most famous buildings – the Banqueting House, the National Gallery, Somerset House, the Bank of England, to name but a few. The stone stands up well to the smoky atmosphere of the city, it can be very effectively cleaned, and its monumental effect enhances the architectural interest of a great capital.

The quarrying process

By the middle of the nineteenth century, there were more than fifty quarries on Portland, producing nearly twenty-five thousand tons of stone a year. A quarryman's job was very tough and highly skilled. As the building stone was deep below the surface, colossal amounts of 'overburden' had to be shifted and dumped first. Then the stone had to be parted from its host rock. (The geologist's 'rock' only becomes the builder's 'stone' when it has been separated from its natural site by the quarryman, either with hammer and chisels or by blasting with gunpowder.) Freshly-hewn stone is called 'green' by the quarryman, before the 'quarry sap' has been weathered out of it by exposure, and over a period of time it changes colour. Portland stone is creamy-grey when green, as it were, but weathers to the greyish white so familiar to us.

The next stage was to split the huge boulders into blocks of workable or transportable size. This was often done with 'plugs' and 'feathers' when there was no natural fissure in the stone. A row of holes was drilled in the stone along the line of the

Right: Limestone quarry, Portland, Dorset.

Overleaf: Bucklers Hard, Hampshire, formerly an important ship-building centre.

Above: The method of splitting large blocks of stone by means of 'plugs' and 'feathers'. Holes are drilled at intervals along the line of the required split. Metal feathers are then inserted to receive the plugs, or wedges, and when these are hammered in they cause a clean vertical break right through. The plugs must be hit in sequence to apply even pressure along the line. This traditional method is still used in some quarries.

required split, into which the 'feathers' were inserted. These are curved metal pieces which, when two are inserted into a drilled hole, receive a metal plug or wedge. When the plugs are struck with the quarryman's hammer, the stone splits into pieces. A block of stone as big as a motor car can be split accurately by this method. Nowadays, however, diamond-tipped power saws can cut through stone as if it were cheese.

The hauling of heavy loads of stone from the quarries to the waiting ships was a hard job for horses, too, until a railway came to Portland in 1826. At about the same time, the idea was first mooted of using convict labour to build a breakwater and create a fine harbour which would serve military as well as industrial purposes. Convicts who would otherwise have been sentenced to transportation were brought to Portland from 1848 onwards, and they built the prison (now a

Borstal institution) and the breakwater, in what was the first penal reform experiment in using convicts for useful work.

Other local building stones

The so-called Purbeck Marble, which is not a true marble at all but a limestone which can be given a high polish, has also been quarried for many centuries on that other misnamed Dorset peninsula, the Isle of Purbeck.

The qualities of this stone are such that it was actually more popular than Portland in the Middle Ages. It had been used by the Romans as far away as Wroxeter in Shropshire, and our cathedrals throughout the country – Salisbury prominent among them – are full of this stone, which could be carved to the finest architectural detail.

Stone which is fine enough in grain to take intricate carving is called 'freestone', and the experts who work it are traditionally called 'freemasons', but although the institution of Freemasonry had its beginnings in this ancient craft, it has little connection with stone-cutting today.

The village of Corfe, where the famous castle and most of the old houses were built of the local stone, was also the headquarters of the masons who dressed and carved the material, and the Ancient Order of Marblers and Stonecutters still meets in the 'town hall' every year on Shrove Tuesday.

On the Isle of Wight, limestone has been quarried at several sites, including Quarr. These quarries were owned by the Benedictine monks of Quarr Abbey, and produced the stone for building Beaulieu Abbey on the mainland.

Just beyond the Dorset border in Somerset is Hamdon Hill, where a Liassic limestone was long quarried to lend a lovely mellow golden aspect to so many villages in the area, including Montacute, where the National Trust's beautiful Montacute House is perhaps the greatest tribute to the qualities of this exceptionally attractive stone. Alas, it is not as hard-wearing as the stuff of Portland and Purbeck, and the remaining structures of Ham stone will be among the first casualties of our incomparable heritage of stone buildings.

To the north east, in Wiltshire, Chilmark has supplied a notable limestone of creamy-

Left: West India Docks, London. Part of the great dock system of the Thames, the West India Docks were opened in 1802, and later extended by Millwall Dock.

white colour which sometimes weathers to a greenish tinge. Salisbury Cathedral and Wilton House were built of it. The quarry was closed before the Second World War, however, and is now a deserted and over-grown relic of medieval industry.

The future of quarrying

Quarrying is arguably, along with agriculture, the most ancient and continuous of all British industries, but it seems now to have at least one foot in the grave. Stone has become a very expensive building material in comparison with brick, concrete and other man-made substitutes. Many of the once-famous quarries all over the country have closed down, and some of those that remain open are occupied only in producing roadstone or crushed material for other industrial uses. Deserted quarries are among the most melancholy industrial sites, attracting folklore and becoming scenes of accident, suicide and murder, but many of these great holes in the ground could still provide valuable and lasting homes and factories if a revival of interest in stone building, much

Above: The modern Portland masonry works, with sawing machinery. Different types of saw are used for special purposes in stone-cutting. Primary sawing can be done with circular saws which may be over eleven feet in diameter, and have blades impregnated with diamond segments; or with frame saws with up to twenty-five blades. Wire saws are also used. After cutting the rough-hewn blocks to a more or less regular shape (foreground), secondary sawing to accurate sizes takes place, and machinery is also used to dress the stone to required shapes, with curves, grooves and so on.

talked about and hoped for in some quarters, should ever come to pass. (See also the sections on Granite in South West England, and Slate in East Midlands, Wales and North West England.)

Where to go

Portland is reached by road from Weymouth via Chesil Bank. The harbour and break-water are on the north side of the peninsula.

On the east coast near Easton is Durdle Pier, the only remaining 18th century quay, from which much stone was shipped.

The Purbeck quarries, some of which are still in use, are generally south of A351 between Corfe and Swanage.

Hamdon Hill is near A3088 west of Yeovil, and Chilmark on B3089 west of Salisbury. Working quarries should never be entered without the owner's permission. Apart from the illegality of trespassing, they can be dangerous places.

Ship and boat building

Hampshire and the Isle of Wight have a long association with the sea which is still in powerful evidence today, and in remarkable variety, too. From the world-famous annual Cowes Regatta to the illustrious ocean liners sailing up and down Southampton Water, these most central of England's south coast counties hold a large share of interest in the busy activity of the English Channel.

Bucklers Hard

The New Forest, which *was* new when William the Conqueror hunted in it, had become a major source of timber for the Royal Navy by Charles II's reign, and a shipbuilding centre was founded at Bucklers Hard in the following century by the Duke of Montagu, who planned to make the place into a trading port.

When the Napoleonic Wars came, this tiny village built forty of the men o'war which sailed in the British fleet, including HMS *Agamemnon*, Lord Nelson's favourite ship. The wide main street of Bucklers Hard was filled with weathering timber ready for the four thousand men who worked in the shipyards, and the house of one of the builders, Henry Adams, is now the Master Builder's House Hotel. There is a Maritime Museum here, too, which has a model of *Agamemnon* as well as guns, charts and other

exhibits. In addition, several cottages have been restored, with interiors as they would have been in the 1890s.

Cowes

Cowes is known everywhere as the yachting capital of Britain, but it has considerable industrial and military importance, too. During the Second World War, Cowes

Left: HMS *Victory* at her permanent berth in Portsmouth. Lord Nelson's famous flagship, built at Chatham, led the British fleet at the Battle of Trafalgar and convinced Napoleon that he could not beat Britain at sea. The ship now forms part of the Royal Naval Museum.

Right: Fitting out a Hovercraft in the Vosper Hovermarine workshops at Woolston, Southampton. This craft is a 500 series 27 metre personnel carrier.

Left: One of the men o'war built of New Forest oak. HMS *Illustrious* was a 74-gun ship of the line, launched in 1789. She served against the French under Vice-Admiral Hotham, in an action in the Mediterranean which was criticized by Nelson, then serving under Hotham. The ship was wrecked in a gale off the Italian coast in 1795.

Castle was the operational headquarters for the Normandy landings. In more recent times, it has been the birthplace and head-quarters of the British Hovercraft industry.

A great deal of damage was done to Cowes' wharves and warehouses by enemy action during the war, so it is nearly all modern today, but one old stone-built ware-house survives in Medina Road.

The headquarters of the Royal Yacht Squadron is on Victoria Parade below the castle, where guns are fired to start the races.

Portsmouth

The naval dockyards at Portsmouth are on the north east side of the city, and are not open to the public except for access to Nelson's flagship HMS *Victory* and its Royal Naval Museum, but the long maritime his-tory of Portsmouth and its naval traditions are evident in almost every street and corner.

Richard the Lionheart built the first dock here in the twelfth century, and Henry VII built the world's first dry dock, where *Victory* is now permanently moored. The dockyards cover a large area, with building slips, dry docks, a school of naval architec-ture and a navigation school. The harbour has been Britain's chief naval arsenal since 1545, when the English fleet assembled here for the engagement with the French off Spithead. Also housed here are the Royal Navy's gunnery school, torpedo headquar-ters and a submarine base.

Southampton

Southampton, too, has a long history of seafaring. Crusaders, Puritans and tourists have sailed from this port over the centuries, and it is now Britain's chief passenger port, although it is a great trading port as well. Southampton Water still carries huge oil tankers and container vessels as well as the world's finest cruise ships. The port benefits from four high tides a day in the Solent, due to the Isle of Wight acting as a 'buffer'.

Southampton's superb natural harbour was always an open invitation to develop a worthy dock system, and land reclamation was carried out earlier in this century to enable extensive dock and railway construc-tion to take place. The new quay wall could accommodate eight of the world's biggest liners at the same time.

The city's Maritime Museum is in Bugle Street, in a fourteenth century building known as the Wool House. It accommo-dated Spanish prisoners of war in the eight-eenth century.

Where to go

Bucklers Hard is on Beaulieu River, on minor road south of Beaulieu village, reached from Southampton (A326) or Bournemouth (A337), in both cases turning off on B3054. This road leaves A337 at Lymington.

Cowes is the northernmost town on the Isle of Wight, reached by ferry or Hovercraft from mainland ports. The town lies astride the Medina estuary, and the main boatyards are at East Cowes.

Canals

The great canal age in Britain, which dawned in the middle of the eighteenth century, was very largely a monopoly of the industrial Midlands and north (see north west England), but the south had its moments in the story of canal building, too. The landscape of central southern England was altered significantly, if not as dramatically as some other parts of the country, by the relatively short-lived need for more inland waterways than the existing rivers provided.

The Oxford Canal

Quite early in the canal-building era, engineers, coal magnates and other businessmen had realized the enormous potential of a canal to link the Trent with the Thames, giving the products of northern industry a more direct route to Oxford and the capital than the land and sea transport used hitherto.

The first positive step in this direction was taken in 1769, when an Act was passed for a canal to link the Coventry Canal with Oxford, where it would join the Thames, or Isis, as the upper river was called. The Dukes of Marlborough and Buccleuch were among the supporters of the scheme, as well as the Vice-Chancellor and several dons of the university, and James Brindley was appointed Engineer and Surveyor. Those who feared for the future of Newcastle's coal-shipping business managed to get a clause in the Act forbidding the transportation of coal down-river past Oxford.

Progress was very slow because of argu-

Above: Part of the flight of seventeen locks at Caen Hill, Devizes, on the Kennet and Avon Canal. Seen here in 1969, when they were derelict, the locks are now in course of restoration.

Left: The Dundas Aqueduct, on the Kennet and Avon Canal, was designed by John Rennie and built in 1800 to carry the canal across the Avon.

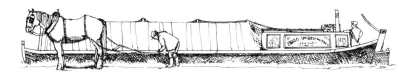

ments about junctions and tolls, the threatened resignation of Brindley, and the cost which exceeded all expectations, and by 1778 the canal had only reached Banbury. Peals of bells and a brass band heralded its opening, for it brought Warwickshire coal to the town at less than a pound a ton. There, however, the work stopped. Brindley had died in the meantime and Samuel Simcock took his place.

It was eight years before work got under way again, after arguments about the pros and cons of continuing the canal to Oxford or making the River Cherwell navigable from Banbury. The canal was finally opened on New Year's Day, 1790, using parts of the natural bed of the Cherwell and coming from Banbury via eighteen locks. The total length of the Oxford Canal was ninety-one miles. Soon one-hundred-pound shares had almost doubled in value.

When the Grand Junction Canal opened in 1800, it took some trade away from the Oxford Canal, which was no longer the shortest route between London and the Midlands. A decision was then made to cut a more direct course for the Oxford using tunnels and aqueducts, which had been avoided before by following a winding course round the natural contours. The new route was opened in 1834, reducing the length of the canal to 77½ miles. By this time, however, the London and Birmingham Railway was looming on the horizon.

The Oxford Canal was designated as a 'recreational and amenity waterway' in 1968, and the British Waterways Board and private companies charter boats for canal cruises at Oxford and Banbury. Nuffield College stands on the site of the former wharf at Oxford.

Other canals of the region

The Oxford Canal was a major north-south waterway, but others improved east-west communications between the Thames and

Top: A narrow boat on the Oxford Canal. Horse power soon gave way to steam power, but the unchanging aspect of canal transport was the traditional decoration of their boats by bargemen. Castles and roses were among the most common motifs.

Above: The Crofton Pumping Station. Two Cornish beam engines pumped water to the summit level of the Kennet and Avon Canal from Wilton Water, forty feet lower.

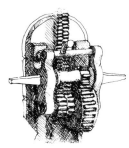

Above: Winding gear on lock gates. A boat enclosed in a lock is raised or lowered by opening the gates at one end.

the Severn. Early in the nineteenth century, the wide Kennet and Avon Canal was opened for barges and the narrower Wilts and Berks Canal for narrow boats, and these routes gave the Oxford Canal some competition.

The Kennet and Avon linked the much earlier River Kennet Navigation with the Avon at Bath, and brought Somerset coal as far east as Reading. At its peak, the canal carried around 350,000 tons of traffic a year, but the railways reduced its tonnage by more than half in a relatively short period.

The Wilts and Berks Canal connected the western end of the Kennet and Avon with the Thames at Abingdon, and this in turn was linked to the Thames and Severn Canal by the short North Wilts Canal.

The Kennet and Avon and the Wilts and Berks continued in commercial use until the early years of this century. The Wilts and Berks was then neglected and formally abandoned. The Kennet and Avon, owned by the Great Western Railway by that time, had also become unnavigable, but there is hope that this canal may be fully restored.

Where to go

Several fine bridges of brick, cast iron or timber exist over the Oxford Canal in Oxford itself. Folly Bridge on A4144 is a three-arch stone bridge over the Isis.

The Dundas Aqueduct is at Limpley Stoke (off A36 between Bath and Bradford-on-Avon).

At Devizes, a mile from the town centre, an impressive series of twenty-nine locks raises boats nearly 250 feet between the town and Semington. Seventeen locks are closely grouped at Caen Hill.

Crofton Pumping Station is at Great Bedwyn, Wiltshire (unclassified road south of A4 between Marlborough and Hungerford).

At Theale, Berkshire (south of junction 12 on M4 and A4 west of Reading) a flight of twenty-one locks on the old Kennet Navigation raised boats 134 feet. Sheffield Lock is unusual in having sides of timber and turf. Later ones were built with brick and timber.

Railways

This part of England features in the story of railways largely because the construction of the Great Western Railway turned Swindon from a small and insignificant market town into one of the great railway capitals of Britain.

Cobbett called Swindon 'a plain country town' in 1821. It was, he said, in 'the real fat of the land'. Thirty years later, it was in the forefront of the great railway revolution, with huge engineering workshops as well as housing for the workers.

Brunel's achievement

The Great Western Railway was conceived and built by that giant among engineers, Isambard Kingdom Brunel, to link London with Bristol. He did not simply jump on the railway bandwagon which had been set rolling in the north and Midlands, but re-thought the whole business from scratch. In purely engineering terms, he was far in advance of his contemporaries. He ignored the now 'standard' gauge (4 ft 8½ ins) in favour of a 7 ft 'broad' gauge. He saw that this would facilitate greater freight capacity, increased passenger comfort and higher speeds, and he went to immense lengths to achieve as level and straight a line as possible throughout its course. 110 of the total 118 route miles were built to a gradient of less than 1:750.

The hilly country at the southern extremity of the Cotswolds presented the biggest problems. Between Wootton Bassett and Bath, the gradient reached 1:100 for one section of three miles which included the *tour de force* of Brunel's line, the two-mile-long Box Tunnel. The success of the whole enterprise was dependent upon solving what was then the greatest tunnelling problem ever attempted.

The tunnel was begun in 1836 under the stage-management of the 30-year-old Brunel. It was to go 3212 yards through the limestone hills with sufficient width for two tracks of the GWR's 7 ft gauge. Four thousand men and three hundred horses were employed in its construction at one stage. Brunel's detractors called the enterprise dangerous and impracticable and, indeed, a hundred men lost their lives on the job, but Box Tunnel was completed in 1841 with a

typical Brunel flourish at its western end, a portal surmounted by a balustrade of classical design. The whole line had cost about five million pounds.

The GWR chose a site near Swindon as a suitable point for a locomotive works, with sound reasoning. It would be a convenient place to change to locomotives which could tackle the steeper gradients at the western end of the line. It would also be a suitable point for a junction with the proposed Gloucester and Cheltenham branch line. The original engine workshops were built with stone excavated from Box Tunnel, and the men who came here for jobs watched Swindon grow into a railway metropolis.

The 'Sleeping Giant'

The advantages of the GWR's broad gauge were obvious to everyone by this time, but it had come too late. The Great Western became isolated from the rest of the system. The minority has to toe the line, even when it is right and the majority wrong, and it was obvious for a long time that the GWR would

scape of the former Great Western Railway. Box Tunnel remains one of the monuments of railway engineering. The viaduct at Chippenham and the bridge crossing the Thames at Maidenhead are further examples of Brunel's genius. The latter has two of the largest and flattest arches ever built of brick. Its critics predicted that it would collapse as soon as the first train crossed it. The bridge was opened in 1838 and is still in use.

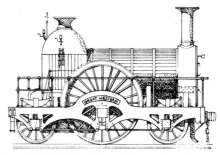

Below: GWR 4-6-0 Castle Class *Kenilworth Castle*, built at Swindon in the 1930's.

Above: *Great Western*, the first of the broad-gauge locomotives built for GWR at Swindon.

Above: Interior of the engine shop of GWR works at Swindon in 1932. A King Class 4-6-0 locomotive is seen being overhauled. The works were built at the instigation of Daniel Gooch, the company's noted locomotive builder, and were constructed with stone excavated from Box Tunnel.

Left: No. 6000 *King George V* emerging from Box Tunnel, with Westinghouse Air Brake fitted (on left of boiler) for the locomotive's prestige visit to the U.S.A. in 1929. The locomotive is preserved at Bulmer's cider factory, Hereford. The two-mile-long tunnel was built by Brunel.

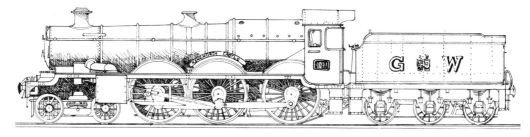

eventually have to change. The last broad-gauge locomotive, 'Tornado', emerged from the Swindon workshops in 1888. Three years later, the Company decided on complete conversion to standard gauge, and work commenced in 1892.

Thousands of extra men were taken on to carry out the conversion of more than four hundred miles of track, since lines now went to the West Country too. Vast sidings at Swindon became packed with broad-gauge rolling stock as local station masters cleared their sidings. In one weekend, the job was virtually done. The sidings at Swindon remained to be changed when the rolling stock had been cleared.

Brunel's touch is still visible in the land-

Where to go

A journey by rail from Paddington to Bristol is one way of seeing the landscape of this particular industrial revolution.

A small museum of the Great Western Railway is maintained at Swindon in Faringdon Road, and some historic locomotives are preserved there, as well as a replica of the broad-gauge 2-2-2 loco *North Star* built in 1837.

The Great Western Society preserves an impressive number of GWR steam locomotives at its Didcot Railway Centre, adjacent to the British Rail station (A4130 south of Oxford).

Carpet manufacture

The chief areas of modern British carpet production are Kidderminster, Yorkshire and Scotland, but it is appropriate to include the industry in this section, for the finest types of wool carpet were introduced here and take their names from their places of origin – Wilton and Axminster.

Carpet making spread from the East to western Europe in the Middle Ages, and after the revocation of the Edict of Nantes many Protestant weavers came to England from France and the Netherlands. Under the patronage of Henry Herbert, the ninth Earl of Pembroke, a carpet factory was set up in 1745 at Wilton, where for some time carpets had been woven by French Huguenots. William III had in fact granted Wilton a Royal Charter for the monopoly of carpet weaving in the area, and it is said that two master weavers who wished to come here from France had to be smuggled out of the country in wine casks.

Meanwhile, at Axminster, a cloth weaver by the name of Thomas Whitty, who had attempted to copy on his own looms a Turkish carpet he had seen, began weaving hand-knotted carpets to which he gave the name 'Axminster'.

It was from these important beginnings that knowledge of carpet weaving spread to the north of Britain.

Methods of manufacture

The difference between a Wilton and an Axminster carpet is simply in the type of weave. The names are not trade marks, and around fifty companies in Britain make them today. Nor are they necessarily made entirely of wool. A proportion of nylon gives added

Above: The original home of Axminster carpets. This stone-built factory in Silver Street, near the church at Axminster, Devon, is where Thomas Whitty wove and hand-knotted the first Axminster carpets from 1755 onwards. Carpets are still made, nowadays entirely by machinery, in a more recent factory in the town.

wearing qualities to a wool carpet, and rayon and acrylic fibres are among other materials used.

Wilton carpets, which can be plain or figured, have pile yarns which are warp threads woven into the carpet. Loops are woven over sharp wires which cut the loops when they are lifted out, leaving a velvety pile which is finished by a shearing machine like an outsize lawnmower. Axminsters have their tufts inserted separately and tied under the warp.

Before the introduction of mechanical looms, the hand-weaving of carpets was a slow process in which weavers sat side-by-side threading, knotting and cutting the tufts. Nowadays, fast modern machines perform the complicated processes of weaving, backing and finishing to the high standards which are the hallmarks of carpets bearing the name of Wilton or Axminster.

Left: The 'shed' on a Wilton wire loom. The projecting wires (left) carry small blades, and are withdrawn sideways to cut the loops of yarn, leaving U-shaped tufts held firmly in place by the weft. The section in the foreground has already been cut to give the carpet its familiar velvety pile.

Where to go

Wilton lies on A30 three miles west of Salisbury. The Royal Wilton factory can be visited at certain times.

Axminster is in Devon, at the junction of A35 and A358 north west of Lyme Regis. Thomas Whitty's original factory was near the church. The new factory, which can be visited by appointment, is near the railway station.

Blanket making

The weaving tradition of Witney, in Oxfordshire, goes back a very long way. The town lies on the fringe of the Cotswold sheep-rearing country, and Domesday Book records two mills here. A fulling mill existed at Witney in 1223, powered by the River Windrush, and the town had a well-established commitment to the weaving of broadcloth by the Tudor period, when mills were spread out along the river on the town's west side. Witney had the advantage of readily available wool and water-power, and an easy trade route to London via Oxford. A Staple Hall had been built early in the fourteenth century.

Growth of the blanket trade

White blankets had become the principal product of Witney by the seventeenth century, when more than three thousand local people worked at carding and spinning, fulling and weaving the coarse wool of the local breed of sheep. Thomas Early, a Quaker, began making blankets in 1669, and the Early family is still in business. An important trade was developed by the Witney manufacturers with North America, where the native Indians are said to have bought Witney blankets, which are still exported to Canada and the United States.

The Company of Blanket Weavers built Witney's Blanket Hall in 1721 for the weighing and measuring of blankets, and it stands there still, in High Street, with its clock telling passers-by the approximate time of

Above: Richard Early demonstrating the operation of an eighteenth-century hand loom, which incorporates Kay's fly shuttle. Eight generations of the Early family have made blankets at Witney.

Below: Early's surviving eighteenth-century blanket mill. The first power looms reached Witney in 1860.

day, single-handed, as it were.

When hand-powered and water-powered looms began to be replaced by steam-power, and Yorkshire took most of the wool business away from the Cotswolds, the concentration of blanket-making in the hands of families such as the Earlys, Marriotts and Colliers, who entered into informal co-operation to modernize the industry, enabled Witney to survive unscathed.

John Early had installed spinning machines at New Mill in 1818 which spun yarn for other manufacturers as well as for his own purposes, and in the latter half of the nineteenth century, Charles Early installed steam power at Witney Mill.

The modern blanket factories dominate the town's outskirts today, mainly stone-built ranges of the last century, in which the three-centuries' tradition of blanket-making still flourishes.

Where to go

Witney is on the River Windrush at junctions of A40, A415 and A4095, twelve miles west of Oxford. Early's blanket mills are in Mill Street and Smith's mills in Bridge Street. Part of the Early mill by the river is on the site of a fulling mill which stood there in 1277. Two breastshot water wheels once powered the New Mill.

Greater London and Northern Home Counties

Bedford

BEDFORDSHIRE

Stewartby

Buckingham

A6

BUCKINGHAMSHIRE

Luton

Stevenage

HERTFORDSHIRE

A1

A10

Aylesbury

A41

Hertford

Chiltern Hills

St. Albans

Watford

High Wycombe

A40

GREATER LONDON

Clerkenwell

Bermondsey

The industries of England's capital in many cases developed from the people who came to live in it, while the industries that grew up beyond the city were more the result of evolutionary factors. The industries chosen to represent London in this volume are typical of the wide-ranging activities of the metropolis – from small local crafts to printing.

miles 0   10   20

Printing

The printing industry is so widespread and so immensely varied in its techniques and applications, that the whole of this book would be needed to do it any kind of justice, but it is far too important to be left out of any account of our industrial heritage.

London's entitlement to be regarded as the printing capital of Britain is beyond question, despite the importance of the industry to Watford and several other large towns and cities. William Caxton had set up his printing press at Westminster by 1476, having learned the art of printing from movable types on the Continent. His was an extremely primitive and laborious method of printing compared with today's highly mechanized processes, but it was instrumental in establishing the basis of the modern English language, and Caxton's books included Chaucer's *The Canterbury Tales* and Malory's *Le Morte d'Arthur*.

Caxton was succeeded by Wynkin de Worde, who lived in Fleet Street and set up a press 'at the signe of the Swane'. He cut many new type-faces and his books were notable for their elegance. Since that time, Fleet Street has become world-famous as the 'street of ink', and most of our national newspapers are printed in or around it.

Modern printing methods

In Caxton's day and for long afterwards, every letter was a single piece of metal cast in a mould, and each line of printing had first to be set up from these individual letters, then spaced out and locked in a 'chase', together with the woodcuts from which illustrations were printed. The chase was put on the press and inked, and each sheet of paper was placed in position and pressed down on the type to produce an impression. When the required number of pages had been printed, the type was 'distributed' again before the next page could be set up.

In the late nineteenth century, faster methods of type-setting were invented, in which complete lines of type could be set and cast, and the metal afterwards melted and used again. Nowadays, fast computer typesetting is done by compositors sitting at keyboards; and electronic scanners reproduce colour photographs by breaking them down into the dots you can see if you

Top: An old photograph showing a composing room, lit by gas. The cases of type contain many different type-faces in varying sizes measured in 'points'. (This book is printed in 10 pt.)

examine printed pictures with a magnifying glass.

The printing presses themselves, meanwhile, have evolved into high-speed machines which either lift one sheet of paper at a time automatically from a stack, or print on a continuous roll, or 'web', delivering printed sheets cut to size at the other end.

Above: Compositor setting up type in 1912.

Where to go
A tablet on the wall of Westminster Abbey commemorates Caxton, whose first English press was in a nearby alley.

Fleet Street stretches from the Strand to Ludgate Circus. Some national papers (e.g. Daily Express, Daily Mail) give guided tours by prior arrangement.

Between Fleet Street and Farringdon Road, many process engravers make plates for printing illustrations.

Shipping

The Thames estuary has been vitally important through two thousand years of English history. The Romans, realizing its potential as a port opposite the mouths of the Rhine and Maas which reached right into Europe, built the first quays on it. By the time of the Norman Conquest, London was well established as a major trading centre, and William the Conqueror built the Tower for the defence of the river approach to the city.

During ensuing centuries, the port expanded steadily, with the building of new wharves and warehouses, and the first Customs House in 1382, where the poet Chaucer was for a short period Comptroller of Petty Customs. Wool was the chief export, whilst merchandise of every kind was landed from France and Russia, Genoa and Venice, Arabia and the Orient.

Growth and long shadows

By the Elizabethan age, the busy river had become a symbol of Britain's trading prosperity and maritime confidence, and the port continued to grow through the Stuart period, when Samuel Pepys saw the first wet dock at Blackwall. (Another soon followed at Bermondsey so that London could cope with the largest merchant vessels then afloat.) At this period more than eighty per cent of Britain's imports passed through London.

There was another side to this story of unbounded success, of course. Shipping movements on the river were dictated by tides and by the old London Bridge, the only bridge across the river in London at that time, under which only the smallest vessels could pass. The congested Pool of London harboured waterfront crime and low life of every kind, from prostitution and drug addiction to smuggling and murder, and areas such as Limehouse and down-river Deptford – where a naval dockyard had existed since 1485 – won a measure of notoriety.

A wet dock was built at Rotherhithe, the East India Company expanded the docks at Blackwall, and those at Bermondsey became the Greenland Dock from which whaling ships operated.

Right: *Cutty Sark* in her permanent mooring at Greenwich. The last surviving tea-clipper, this famous ship was engaged in the China tea trade during the nineteenth century, and was then preserved for many years at Falmouth before coming to London.

Below: A view of the Royal Docks. Consisting of the Royal Victoria (foreground), Royal Albert (upper left) and King George V Docks (upper right) this great system – the largest impounded docks in the world – is entered from the stretch of the Thames known as Galleons Reach.

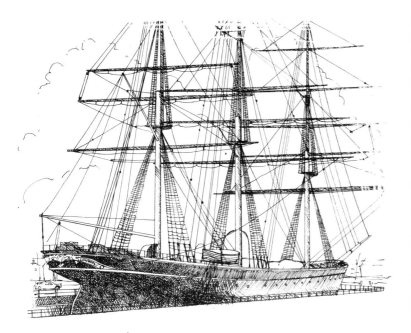

By the early nineteenth century, three large enclosed docks had been built, and these were instrumental in organization of shipping on the river, reducing congestion and increasing security. The West India and London Docks were up-to-date docks for large ships, and were followed by Victoria Dock, opened in 1855, and the Royal Albert Dock a quarter of a century later. The Royal Albert was the largest dock in the world at the time, and the latest Thames developments, with their huge warehouses, hydraulic cranes, and projecting jetties instead of quay walls, were soon attracting immense tonnages.

The Port of London Authority was set up in 1908, with statutory powers to control all aspects of the port's business, but despite extensive rebuilding and the laying of miles of railways to increase efficiency in the movement of merchandise in and out of the docks, the companies had over-reached themselves, and some major rethinking was necessary to keep London in competition with other rapidly expanding ports such as Liverpool and Glasgow.

Modernization

Two world wars delayed the much-needed modernization of the docks for thirty years, by which time Rotterdam had overtaken London in the annual tonnage that passed through it. Both ports had had millions of pounds worth of damage done to them by German bombing.

A massive reconstruction programme got under way, however, and soon London's tonnage exceeded all previous records. The docks began to face the new challenges of modern merchant shipping presented by colossal super-tankers and container handling, which was developed 20 miles down river at Tilbury, initially in a highly-charged atmosphere of resentment by dockers.

St Katharine's Dock had suffered such severe damage during the war that it was considered beyond repair and was closed in 1968. It has since been redeveloped very imaginatively as a yacht marina; its warehouses, partly designed by Telford, converted into shops and trading floors for the World Trade Centre.

Below: London Docks in about 1920. This area was known as the 'wine gauging ground'; here wine was tested for alcoholic strength, so that the amount of duty could be assessed.

Where to go
The Royal Naval College at Greenwich stands between the river and the National Maritime Museum. The Museum's exhibits include marine paintings, ship models and naval relics.

The permanent berth of the *Cutty Sark* is near Greenwich Pier.

Leather goods

We shall never know who discovered the means of tanning animal hides to make leather. It was a thriving business practised by the British tribes when the Romans arrived, and the imperial army increased the demand by using leather for its footwear, parts of uniforms and equipment, harness, tents and vessels for carrying water and wine. As well as cattle hides, the skins of horses, goats, pigs, deer and seals have been used for making leather, which was one of the most indispensible of raw materials before plastic started to take over.

London's medieval leather trade grew up in Bermondsey, which has remained the centre of leathercraft in the capital ever since. You have only to cross Tower Bridge to the south side of the river to come to streets with such names as Leathermarket, Tanner Street and Morocco Street. The Leathersellers, incorporated in the fifteenth century, are among the wealthiest of the City livery companies, and the great market for leather goods was Leadenhall, where, as Defoe says: 'Every Wednesday is kept a market for raw hides, tanned leather, and shoemakers' tools . . . .' The various craftsmen in leather each had their important trade guilds – the

Below: Photograph showing leather being cleaned and pared at the Neckinger Leather Mills, Bermondsey, in 1862. These necessary processes precede tanning, and involve the removal of fat, hair and blood. The man who thus prepares skins for dressing is called a 'fellmonger', 'fell' being another word for skin.

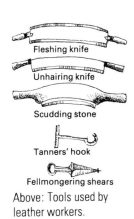

Fleshing knife

Unhairing knife

Scudding stone

Tanners' hook

Fellmongering shears

Above: Tools used by leather workers.

shoemakers, the glovemakers, the saddlers, and so on.

Tanning and dressing

Tanning is the process by which skins are converted into the imputrescible substance which is known to all Teutonic languages by the same word – leather, leder, läder, etc.

In medieval times, vats were used to prepare skins for tanning, but from the seventeenth century stone-lined pits or 'puddles' became common in large tannery yards. In these the skins were soaked in milk of lime, which aided cleaning and the removal of flesh, blood and hair. The longer this soaking was given, the softer would be the resulting leather. It was then washed to remove the lime and scraped to remove the residue of fat, which went to the tallow chandlers.

One of the oldest tanning materials was oak bark, but other vegetable tanning agents have also been used, as well as chemical agents such as aluminium salts and animal or fish oils (with which chamois leather is prepared). The older methods of vegetable tanning could take up to two years.

When it has been tanned and dried, the rough hide goes to the currier for dressing. After further cleaning, it is soaked and shaved to reduce it to even thickness, and dyed. The special tool or knife used for paring thin leather is called a skiver. Heavy rolling and brushing is all that is required for finishing sole leather, but other leathers might be glazed, pigmented, grained or

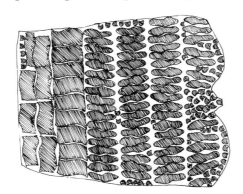

Above; Drawing showing how a tanned hide is cut up for boot-making. No part of the hide is wasted. Parts left between the shaped pieces are used to build up the heels.

varnished, according to their requirements for furnishing, gloves, handbags, straps, bookbinding, patent leather shoes and so on.

Growth of the leather trade

By the end of the eighteenth century, when all but the very poor were wearing leather shoes, the demand for leather throughout the country was enormous, and it has been estimated that next to wool and iron, leather was Britain's most important manufacturing industry at that time.

The area south of the Thames around Bermondsey had the country's biggest concentration of tan-yards. Bermondsey supplied an eighth of the nation's leather, and a reputation for suppleness in the English product brought it an export trade, too.

The tanning business, with its accompanying stench of putrefying flesh, did not make the area attractive to residential development, and with the Rotherhithe dockland flanking it on one side, Bermondsey became one of the worst slum areas in London, described by Dickens in *Oliver Twist* as having roofless and empty warehouses, crumbling walls and houses 'so filthy, so confined, that the air would seem too tainted even for the dirt and squalor which they shelter . . . dirt-besmeared walls and decaying foundations; every repulsive lineament of poverty, every loathsome indication of filth, rot and garbage . . . .'

Much rebuilding took place in Bermondsey after that. The tenement blocks which replaced the slums were not much better, but they lasted until the extensive clearance and redevelopment of the present century.

Where to go

Leathersellers' Hall is in St Helen's Place, Bishopsgate. It was rebuilt in 1960 after wartime bomb damage.

Leadenhall Market is on the site of a basilica at the centre of Roman Londinium, not far from the Bank of England.

Bermondsey's own Leather Market is a dignified building in Weston St.

Articles of fine leatherware from all periods can be seen in the Museum of London.

Furniture manufacture

Right: Chiltern beech woods, Buckinghamshire. The Chilterns are covered with carefully tended woods and coppices of beech still used in furniture making.

The great furniture industry, which now occupies so much factory space and so large a proportion of the labour force at High Wycombe in Buckinghamshire, began as a woodland craft in the beechwoods of the Chiltern Hills, where independent wood-workers called 'chair-bodgers' worked in primitive huts making chair legs, spars and stretchers and various other items on their pole-lathes. Town wits called them 'chairopodists', but they were highly skilled craftsmen, to whom the modern mechanized industry will always remain indebted.

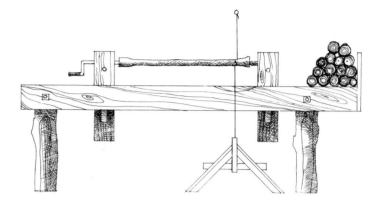

The bodgers' methods

The 'bodgers' spent most of their working lives in the woods, moving about like nomads to set up their shacks for a season where the beech plantation was ready for thinning out. The men were totally dependent on the trees for their livelihood, and they treated the woods with rare respect. Selecting beeches from the closely-grown straight trees, they felled only enough to encourage the upright growth of saplings by providing light and space, so that fresh timber was always replacing that taken away.

One man would work with saws, axes, chisels and the vital pole-lathe to produce as many as eight hundred chair legs a week, which then went to the craftsmen in small factories who made up and finished the complete chairs.

Above: Diagram showing the mechanics of a pole-lathe.

Below: A typical Chiltern timber yard with sawn planks seasoning 'in stick'.

Left: Oast houses at Tonbridge, Kent. A fine example of a traditional hop-drying kiln in the 'Garden of England', where most British hops are grown.

Chiltern craftsmen created the famous Windsor Chair, allegedly so named because George III had one and called it by that name, but it is actually much older than Farmer George's reign. Its legs and back were of beech, and its seat of elm.

Felled trees were cut into lengths of about two feet, which were then split into quarters and roughly shaped ready for turning on the pole-lathe. This was undoubtedly the earliest device invented for wood-turning. It consisted of a long pole, usually of larch, which turned the work alternately backwards and forwards by means of a treadle. This exploited the natural springiness of the pole with a hemp rope attached to the pole's loose end and wound round the wood to be turned, before being attached to the treadle. As the treadle was depressed, the tightened rope turned the wood one way, and as it was released, the spring in the pole turned the wood the other way.

As well as parts for chairs, the bodgers made spokes for wagon wheels, tent pegs and stools.

Growth of the factory industry

Gradually, as wood-turning machinery became available, and a more affluent society increased demand for well-made furniture, it was inevitable that the whole production of chairs should move from the woodlands to factory floors, along with other furniture manufacturing. In the early part of the nineteenth century, High Wycombe possessed only two furniture factories, turning out chairs and other pieces with legs supplied by the woodland craftsmen. In the second half of the century, the factories multiplied to fifty, and then to a hundred, and the manufacturers boasted that they could turn out more than a million chairs a year. One of the earliest factory owners was James Gomme, who founded what is today probably the biggest and best-known company in High Wycombe.

The bodgers slowly disappeared from the beechwoods, which could no longer supply the massive quantities of timber required, so that foreign timber began to be imported on a large scale. Much local timber is still used, however, and the furniture industry's influence on the landscape is still seen in the carefully tended coppice woodlands of the Chilterns, and in the busy timber yards scattered around the area.

The timber yards season and prepare the wood and cut it down to size so that the factory buyers can select their requirements. Then the machinists can get to work on shaping, veneering, polishing and upholstering finished articles. These can be produced by fast and efficient means that the bodgers never dreamed of, but which rarely have the style, and never the individuality, of the old hand craftsmen's furniture made with a lifetime's skill, experience and love of timber.

Above: Interior of Thomas Glenister's chair factory at High Wycombe about 1890, showing the driving belts to the lathes, on which legs and other parts of the chairs were being turned by this time.

Above: A Windsor chair. Before machine manufacture, the legs would be made in the woods by a 'bodger'. Legs and back were of local beech.

Where to go
The museum at Castle Hill, High Wycombe (A40 or M40 between London and Oxford) has fine examples of local craftsmanship, with chairs from a long period of woodland industry.

Chiltern timber yards can be seen piled high with teak from Guyana, walnut from Africa, mahogany from South America, and other foreign timbers.

Straw plaiting

The plaiting of straw was a cottage industry in the Chiltern Hills, where women and children learned the craft in order to supplement the pittances earned by their menfolk on the land. The Chilterns were a poor area. They never enjoyed, even temporarily, the huge prosperity which the Cotswolds had with the wool trade. Sparsely populated, their inhabitants survived in the main on arable farming and woodland crafts, and wages were always lower than in the Midlands and the north.

Straw plaiting was established in England, it seems, by James I, who brought French families from Scotland (where they had been taken by his mother, Mary Queen of Scots) and settled them under the Napier family at Luton Hoo. From here the craft spread into the northern Chilterns and became a very important local trade, Luton itself becoming the chief centre of the straw hat industry, employing the women to do most of the work in their homes.

Hard-earned bread

Girls were taught to plait straw at a very early age, and they and their mothers worked long hours to earn a guinea a week. A typical farm labourer in the early nineteenth century might earn no more than twelve shillings a week, out of which he had to pay perhaps two shillings rent for his cottage and keep his family, with bread at eight pence a quartern loaf. So the extra money was desperately needed, and young girls sometimes sat up all night in freezing winter to produce sufficient work by candlelight to earn their wages. They had to deliver it to Luton, usually on foot and often from many miles away, two or three times a week.

The straw used by plaiters was wheat straw, winter-sewn wheat being best because it was tough and pliable. The top length of straw only was used, from the ear to the first joint, and it was damped first to make it workable. The plaiters obtained their straw in bundles from the local markets, supplied by farmers who cut it by hand for the purpose, because machinery broke the stems.

The people prized their independence of spirit, and caused much concern to Christian

Above: A straw plaiter at work around the turn of the century. This highly respectable-looking lady, sitting in a comfortable home with latticed windows, is clearly enjoying the creative pastime and is not desperate for the money, as were most of those engaged in the cottage industry which was dying out by this time. Note the straight and even straws in the jug. Farmers often cut straw by hand for the purpose.

moralists who were shocked by their 'lamentable ignorance', and by the rate of illegitimate births among them.

Straw plaiting never became a factory industry. Changes in fashion and materials led to this cottage craft becoming virtually extinct, and it has left scarcely a sign on the landscape that it ever existed, but to the women of the Chiltern Hills, the plaiting of straw was a way of life for two or three centuries and has a right to a place in the story of Britain's industry.

Where to go
Tools and products of straw plaiters and hat makers can be seen in the museums at Hitchin, Hertfordshire (A505 north east of Luton) and at Wardown Park, Luton (A6 north of town centre).

Clock making

The craft of horology might not, at first sight, seem to justify description as an 'industry', but as with many other trades in London, the concentration of clock and watch makers in Clerkenwell undoubtedly helped to mould the character of the district.

Significant movements
The 'sweet and wholesome ayre' referred to by Stow in 1598 made the growing village of Clerkenwell a fashionable residential area, but during the Great Fire, many refugees fled to it, and merchants and tradesmen began to settle and carry on their businesses there, in what was then still a salubrious contrast to the overcrowded City they had left.

Clock makers were among those who came to the area in small numbers towards the end of the seventeenth century. The Clockmakers' Company was incorporated in the City in 1631. Its members drew other craftsmen with them, for the watchmaker, as Campbell wrote in 1747, 'scarce makes anything belonging to a Watch; he only employs the different Tradesmen among whom the Art is divided, and puts the several Pieces of the Movement together . . . .'

Above: A four-sided astronomical clock made in 1768 by Christopher Pinchbeck. The dials show the time of day, tides at 43 points, signs of the zodiac and sidereal time (measured by the motions of the stars). This clock is in the Royal Collection.

Below: A Clerkenwell clockmakers' workshop in 1851.

By the end of the eighteenth century, some eight thousand workers in Clerkenwell were engaged in the clock and watch business, many of them working in their homes, making cases, painting dials and so on. But from a few small workshops, factories evolved, very often specializing in some particular aspect of horology.

Winding down
The trade suffered severe setbacks around this time, however. The import of Swiss watches was bad enough, but when Pitt imposed a tax on the ownership of clocks and watches, the effect was such that many Clerkenwell craftsmen were put out of work. In due course, the tax was repealed, but the damage had already been done, and it was to be repeated in 1861 when Gladstone removed tariffs on foreign clocks and watches which had given the local workers some protection.

The clock makers who were left in business worked in cramped workshops with insufficient lighting and old-fashioned methods, in a densely overcrowded district which had become notorious as a centre of radical reform. (Lenin printed a newspaper at Clerkenwell Green for smuggling into Imperial Russia.)

The trade has never disappeared entirely from Clerkenwell, and some revival is hoped for to reinforce the jewellers and precision-instrument makers who carry on the traditions of skilled craftsmanship there. Nevertheless, the district has continued to decline as a centre of clock making during this century, but Clerkenwell Road still remains, behind the roar of heavy traffic, as a source of income and interest to those interested in the horological sciences.

Where to go
Fine collections of clocks can be seen at the Science Museum and Victoria and Albert Museum. The National Maritime Museum at Greenwich has a fine collection of chronometers.

The Crown public house on Clerkenwell Green has local clocks telling the time in all parts of the world.

Brick making

From the Stuart period onwards, brick and stone slowly began to replace timber, cob and wattle-and-daub for vernacular building, except in certain areas such as Devon and the Welsh border counties where the traditional materials continued to be used. The Great Fire of London and the absence of any local building stone gave a great impetus to building in brick in the London area north of the Thames.

Many large and important buildings had gone up in brick much earlier – Eton College and Hatfield House are among the finest examples in this region – but until the seventeenth century bricks were too expensive for the houses and cottages of ordinary folk.

Early brick making

Before the Industrial Revolution and mass-production of bricks for the accommodation of vast population movements from the country into the towns, bricks were made in local kilns, or 'clamps' and from widely varying local materials. Itinerant brick makers worked on or near the sites of building projects until they had produced sufficient bricks for the job, before moving on elsewhere.

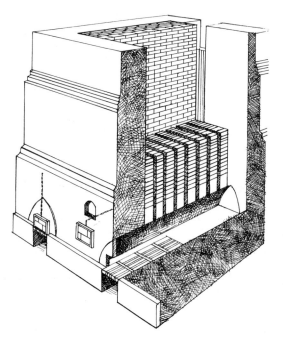

Left: Diagram of a coal-fired brick kiln. Various types of kiln have been used in brick making. The Romans used small rectangular kilns with one fire tunnel, which evolved into the Suffolk type shown here. This had two or three fire tunnels below the stacked bricks. The open tops were sealed with old bricks during the three days of firing.

According to the kind of clay or brick-earth available on the spot, and the maker's skill in moulding and firing, bricks could have a great range of colours, sizes and textures. The clay – sometimes two types of clay blended together to give the best results – was squeezed in a 'pug-mill', powered by a horse or donkey, to eliminate impurities and reduce the clay to workable consistency. It was then pressed firmly into wooden moulds and left to dry for two or three weeks before being fired. The bricks were called 'green' before firing. The 'clamp' method of firing involved stacking the dried moulds with layers of 'breeze' (or coal slack) between and above them, and burning them for several days. This method resulted in uneven firing and many 'wasters'.

Left: A forklift truck unloading burnt bricks from a modern tunnel kiln. Bricks are stacked in the chambers in such a way that hot air circulates all round the bricks. The brick chamber arches have holes which release hot air. The hollow in the top of the bricks is called a 'frog'. Fletton bricks are light pink or creamy, with 'kiss marks' of darker colour where they were in contact with others in the kiln.

Above: The London Brick Company's works at Ridgmont, Bedfordshire. These huge works grew up to exploit the clay called Oxford Clay by geologists. Formed during the Jurassic period, it has a high carbon content and so saves fuel in firing. Until mechanical moulding was introduced, bricks were made by hand. Modern factories, such as this one, manufacture vast numbers of bricks.

Mass production of bricks

As the demand for bricks increased, so mechanical methods of making them were invented. Friedrich Hoffman introduced a kiln in 1858, with a series of chambers radiating from a tall central chimney, which enabled a continuous process of charging, firing and unloading to take place. Meanwhile, machinery had been developed to replace the old pug-mills for compacting the clay and forcing it through rollers which pressed it into metal moulds.

The small widely-scattered clay-pits gave way to vast quarries in which mechanical excavators and draglines extract the raw material, and independent brick makers disappeared in favour of large plants relying on rail transport to convey the product to customers.

London and the Home Counties, having no building stone, were in the forefront of brick building on a large scale, and extensive brickworks grew up in Bedfordshire and Huntingdonshire, where huge deposits of the so-called Oxford Clay were ideally situated for supplying the capital and the south and east Midlands with the immense quantities of bricks they needed.

The famous brickworks at Fletton, near Peterborough, were already producing over 150,000 bricks a day by the end of the nineteenth century. Aesthetically, mass-production was disastrous. Millions upon millions of bricks, standardized in size and colour, turned the towns and cities of Victorian England into places of dreary uniformity. But economically, the brick industry went hand in hand with Welsh slate. Both supported the Industrial Revolution by housing an exploding urban population.

Modern brick making

In 1926, Sir Malcolm Stewart, who had taken over a small brickworks near Ampthill in Bedfordshire, began to build a model village which he called Stewartby, to house the workers at his rapidly expanding factory. The modern town is the home of the London Brick Company, which also owns the Fletton works, and is believed to be the largest brickworks in the world today, producing in the region of seventeen million bricks a week.

Where to go

Stewartby is off A418 five miles south of Bedford. Old Fletton is due south of Peterborough on A605.

Sulphur pollution from the forests of tall brick chimneys is responsible for many dead trees to be seen nearby.

An unusual conical brick kiln is preserved at Nettlebed, Oxfordshire (A423 between Wallingford and Henley-on-Thames), where a local brick industry began in the 15th century.

South East England

The south east is often thought of as the least industrialized corner of England, with the possible exception of East Anglia. But the thick forests which covered the region for thousands of years formed a coalfield which extends beneath the sea-bed, and there were large deposits of iron ore in the rock. The exploitation of nature's provisions accounts to a large extent for the clearance of the forests, without which Kent could hardly have become the 'garden of England'.

Surrey is still one of the most heavily wooded of English counties, but the industries which required so much timber have passed to other regions, and as a result we have inherited much beautiful countryside, with such industry as is left being confined to agricultural concerns.

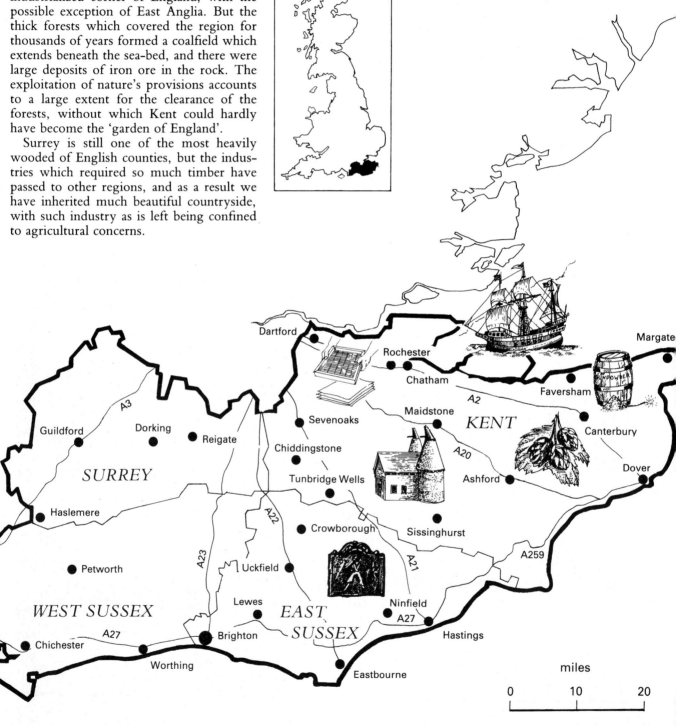

Brewing industries

It is only since the sixteenth century that British ale has benefited from the addition of hops, which give it its bitter flavour. Hops are thought to have been introduced into Kent from the Netherlands, and have remained one of the county's chief crops ever since, the deep well-drained loam of the Garden of England being ideal for hop-growing. Kent grows well over half of all the hops used by British breweries, the other most important growing area being Hereford and Worcester.

Growing and harvesting

One male hop plant is used to fertilize about every hundred females, and it is the fruit of the female plants – which look like pale green cones – which is used in the brewing process.

Until recent years, the standard practice was to train the vines up poles, usually cut from ash or chestnut and up to sixteen feet in height, linked together with coir yarn. Here at once we have two of the subsidiary requirements so closely associated with Britain's oldest traditional beverage. The huge need for poles meant that coppice woodlands of ash and chestnut were as evident in the Kentish landscape in the past as the hop fields and orchards. About four thousand poles were generally set up to every acre of ground, with a renewal rate of about ten per cent a year, so a lot of timber was needed.

Coir yarn is made from the fibres of coconut shells. The fibres are stripped off and soaked until soft enough to be beaten and spun into ropes of considerable strength. Nowadays, hops are grown on permanent frameworks of posts and galvanized wire, so the demand for both poles and yarn has been much reduced.

Harvesting begins at the end of August, and until the advent of elaborate machinery, the hop-picking season was one of the great annual events of south east England. A large casual labour force was needed, and thousands of Londoners took their annual holidays at this time so that whole families

Below: Hop pickers at work in Kent. The harvesting of hops in late summer and early autumn, before the days of mechanization, used to create a huge need for casual labour, and Londoners came to the country in thousands to join the locals in gathering the fruit. The conditions they lived in were often deplorable, but not worse than the slums many of them had temporarily escaped from, and at least they had fresh air and a sense of freedom which was notably absent from their working days in the city.

Above: Fruit of the female hop plant (*Humulus lupulus*).

Below: Cut-away of oast house, showing drying floor, air control vents at top of kiln, cooling floor and press, which packs hops into canvas sacks.

could spend idyllic fortnights in the country, paid for by what they earned picking hops.

Oast houses

The kilns or oast houses in which the harvested hops are dried are among the most familiar scenes in calendars and colour books of rural Britain, but the round buildings with conical roofs and white-painted cowls turning in the wind are out of date now. Modern kilns, if less picturesque, are more efficient.

The oast houses with circular kilns date mostly from the mid-nineteenth century, and were designed in this way in order to retain heat. Hops were spread on a drying floor about half-way up the kiln and hot air was blown up through them and out at the top, the air being carefully controlled by trapdoors beneath the cowls, for if hops are over-heated, the oils essential to the brewing process evaporate. When the hops have been dried, they are cooled and packed into canvas bags for delivery to the breweries.

Using the hops

The breweries add the hops to the liquid called 'wort', which has been obtained by steeping malt in hot water, thus causing the starch in it to be converted to sugar and dextrin. Boiling the wort together with the hops precedes the fermenting process which turns the sugar to alcohol. The hops not only counteract the sickly taste of malt by giving beer its distinctive bitterness, but also act as a preservative.

The best areas for seeing the hop-fields of Kent are in the valley of the River Medway and its tributaries to the east of Tonbridge; and on the other side of the North Downs between Faversham and Canterbury.

Thousands of old-style oast houses can still be seen, though many have been converted into houses. One fine group is at Sissinghurst Castle (National Trust) where a tea-room is incorporated into the buildings. Others are at Chiddingstone, Pembury and Boughton.

At Lewes, East Sussex, two breweries built mainly in the nineteenth century survive near the town centre. One has a malt house nearby, and is used now as a bottling plant and store. The other, Harveys, is still in operation as a brewery. Both preserve single cylinder steam engines, one horizontal, the other vertical.

Where to go

In addition to the sites mentioned above, the processes of brewing, kegging and bottling can be seen at the brewery of Shepherd Neame, Court Street, Faversham, where guided tours are arranged on working days throughout the year. Applications should be made in writing at least one month in advance.

Sissinghurst Castle is on A262 north east of Cranbrook.

Naval dockyards

The River Medway, though insignificant on the map compared with its neighbour the Thames, has seen many of the most important comings and goings in the history of England, and towns such as Sheerness, Chatham and Rochester have long held a high place in the story of our naval and merchant shipping.

The Romans had a base at Rochester, and William the Conqueror built the castle there to guard the river crossing. The Vikings had sailed up the Medway in the tenth century, and in 1667, during the second Anglo-Dutch war, Admiral de Ruyter sailed his Dutch fleet up the Medway in one of the most daring raids in naval history, sinking four British ships and bringing the war to a speedy end with the Treaty of Breda.

Early dockyards

Henry VIII had established the Royal Dockyard at Chatham in 1546, and the town and docks expanded during Elizabeth's reign. Charles II developed the docks at Sheerness, on the Isle of Sheppey, when Samuel Pepys, his Clerk to the Acts of the Navy, who pressed several urgently needed naval reforms on Charles and James II, helped the king to lay out the ground for a 'yard to lay provisions for cleaning and repairing of ships'. Sheerness had the disadvantage, however, when compared with Chatham, of an exposed site liable to bad weather and flooding, so Chatham always had pride of place as the Royal Navy's main dockyard. Sheerness continued to be developed, nevertheless, and Sir John Rennie built a new dockyard there at the end of the Napoleonic Wars.

Nelson's flagship *Victory* was built at Chatham and launched in 1765, perhaps the most famous of all the notable ships built here, and by that time many of the present dockyard and naval buildings were in existence. The docks are nearly two miles long, with several building slips and wet docks.

The dockyards today

Entrance to Chatham Dockyard can only be obtained by special permission, but the gates alone are worth seeing, with the royal coat of arms above them. Old ships' figureheads are displayed at the dockyard, where the

Above: A ship's figurehead at Chatham Dockyard. Such ornamental devices were attached to the prows of ships, under the bowsprit, in the days of sail.

Below: An engraving of 1755 by Canot, showing the Medway scene and layout of 'His Majesty's Dock Yard at Chatham'.

Navy still has a refitting base, sometimes occupied by nuclear submarines, and warehouses, tarring house, hemp store and saw mill, bell mast and workshops keep company with eighteenth-century administrative and residential buildings.

Sheerness outlived its usefulness as a naval dockyard, and the navy ceased to use it in 1960. The boatstore there, a modern-looking multi-storey building of iron frame construction, was actually built in 1860 – one of the earliest buildings of its type.

Rochester's commercial docks are of great interest, and a good deal of the shipping activity at the mouth of the Medway today is concerned with oil – there are large refineries on the Isle of Grain opposite Sheerness.

Where to go

Chatham and Rochester are best reached via A2 from London, and A249 off this road to the north, seven miles beyond Chatham, leads to Sheerness. The Archway Block and Boatstore there are both interesting examples of 19th century architecture. Chatham Town Hall has a scale model of 'Victory' in its council chamber. The real ship is at Portsmouth.

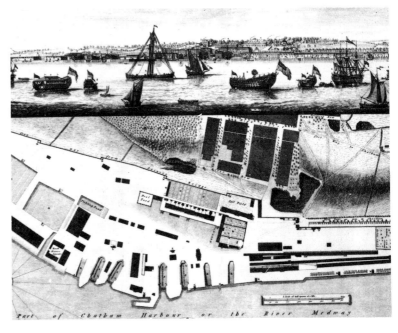

Part of Chatham Harbour or the River Medway

Gunpowder

The origin of gunpowder is very obscure, credit having been given for its discovery, or invention, in the past to the German Berthold Schwartz and the English friar Roger Bacon, between whom the title of being first in the field has been much disputed. In fact it is now certain that the Chinese used gunpowder long before either of these venerable Europeans, and the best that can be said for 'Doctor Admirabilis' as Bacon was nicknamed, is that he was perhaps first to use it in England. By the sixteenth century, at any rate, gunpowder had become a substance of both war and peace and was to have enormous influence on the future of mankind.

Gunpowder, as every schoolboy knows, is made from sulphur, potassium nitrate (saltpetre) and charcoal, and its earliest peaceful uses were in quarrying and mining. The tin mines of Cornwall were using gunpowder before the end of the seventeenth century. Ash was found to be best for making the charcoal required, so coppice woodlands were planted to ensure continuing supplies.

Early factories

One of the major centres of gunpowder manufacture in Britain was at Faversham in Kent, where production started in the mid-sixteenth century and continued for three hundred years. The gunpowder factories were water-powered, and there were at least half a dozen of them around the town. One of them exploded in the seventeenth century, and a contemporary report states that 'the blast was not only frightful, but it shattered the whole town, broke the windows, blew down chimneys, and gable-ends not a few; also several people were killed at the powderhouse it self, though not any, as I remember, in the town.' Because of the danger of such accidents, the gunpowder mills were generally sited near woods, where the growing timber was used to screen houses from blasts.

Royal Powder Mill

The oldest of the Faversham factories was the Home Works, and this became the Royal Powder Mill in the eighteenth century. During the following century, however, more sophisticated explosives such as dynamite and gelignite began to replace gunpowder for blasting purposes, and the factories eventually had to close down.

Two pairs of mills within the Home Works complex, known as Chart Mills, had been rebuilt around 1815 and were in operation until 1934, and these have been preserved by local enthusiasts, who managed to save Chart Mills from demolition during clearance of the whole area to make way for a new housing estate.

Where to go

Faversham lies on A2 London-Canterbury road. The gunpowder mills are on the west bank of the river, half a mile from the town centre.

The restored Chart Mills were powered by one large water-wheel between each pair of mills.

Below: The Oare Gunpowder Works at Faversham, Kent, around 1925. The young employees in this photograph are making canisters to contain the gunpowder. The handling and storage of gunpowder, as well as its testing, were matters requiring great security, and strong-walled powder houses were built. Testing was often done with small howitzers and mortars which fired shells at high angles and low velocity.

Iron working

One does not readily associate the south east corner of England with extractive industry, but in medieval times, before the rise of the Midlands and the north of England's industrial strongholds, the Weald of Kent and Sussex was the principal centre of iron working in Britain. The Weald is an area between the north and south downs where rocks older than the chalk occur, and which once yielded iron ore. An early archaeological study of Wealden iron-working identified well over two hundred sites where iron was worked until the industry more or less petered out in the eighteenth century.

Early iron working

The Romans are known to have worked iron in the south around Hastings and Battle, probably on sites already operated by Britons, and a pot vessel from the Roman period in Hastings Museum shows an iron-smith at work. By the time of the Plantagenet kings, vast quantities of horse-shoes and nails were being supplied, and difficult as it is to imagine, the Weald must have resounded with the noise of forges and hammers turning out tongs and cauldrons, hinges and firebacks, guns and cannons. Skilled workers came from the Continent and improved local techniques.

Smelting was done with charcoal, and thus the iron industry here aided the deforestation of the landscape from which shipbuilders and gunpowder manufacturers also demanded timber. The shortage of timber helped the spread of the iron workers further inland towards East Grinstead.

Decline

The same timber shortage is one of the reasons advanced for the gradual disappearance of the iron works. Ashdown Forest had already become open heathland by the Tudor period, when there were fifty-one furnaces in operation in Sussex, succeeding the workings in Kent which had already been reduced to negligible proportions. A century later, the number was down to about twenty. Imports of cheaper and better-quality iron contributed to the decline, too, and the water-power upon which the works depended was dried up by serious droughts in the eighteenth century.

Above: A nineteenth century gunmaker in Rochester made this extraordinary fire-arm, called a 'Duck's Foot'. All four barrels were fired at once, the weapon being intended for use in riot control!

Below: An iron fireback made in Sussex in 1636. The design shows an iron worker with his forge and tools and some of his products, and might be a self-portrait of the maker, one Lennard.

The last iron furnace to work in the south east was at Ninfield, East Sussex. It ceased operations around 1820, having supplied iron to the government during the Napoleonic Wars. By this time, the iron industry had been established on a large scale elsewhere, and the technological revolution had left the Weald far behind. Visible remains of working sites consist largely of pools, dams and small slag heaps.

Where to go
The museums at Lewes, Battle and Hastings all have exhibits on the iron industry, and the Weald and Downland Open Air Museum at West Dean, West Sussex (A286, five miles north of Chichester) is worth visiting.

At Ashburnham (4 miles west of Battle) is the last smelting furnace in Sussex.

'Hammer ponds' whose water supplied power to forges, can still be found, especially in St Leonard's Forest, between Horsham and Crawley.

In the inner bailey of Pevensey Castle (A259 near Eastbourne) is a gun made at Robertsbridge.

In the churchyard at Wadhurst (B2099 south east of Tunbridge Wells) are a number of locally-made cast iron tombstones.

Paper making

The earliest record of paper making in Britain is a reference in Wynkin de Worde's *De Proprietatibus Rerum* to John Tate's paper mill at Stevenage in Hertfordshire. De Worde's work was printed on Caxton's press at Westminster, using Tate's paper. In 1588 Queen Elizabeth granted a licence to the German Spielman to make paper at Dartford, Kent, and since that time the county has held first place in the art, and later the industry, of making paper.

The enormous variety of paper made by machinery for specific uses today may be said to owe its origins to the ancient Egyptians, who made papyrus from reeds, and we should give thanks to those ingenious ancients for so much that we take for granted today – newsprint, brown wrapping paper, fine writing and printing papers, stamps and banknotes, cardboard cartons, wallpaper, greaseproof paper and so on. The name of James Whatman, who started making high quality cartridge paper at Maidstone in 1760, is still a household word among watercolour artists.

Methods and materials

Until the end of the eighteenth century, all paper was made by hand, using mainly rags as the raw material. The rags were first cleaned and boiled and then beaten into pulp. When the pulping process was mechanized, it was done by hammers driven by water-

Above: Paper making by hand. The operator is lifting the 'deckle' from the liquid.

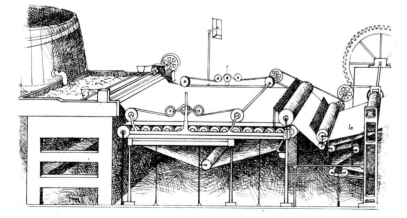

Above: An early paper-making machine. The liquid pulp flows on to a moving web (centre) and is drawn off right as a continuous sheet to be dried on rollers.

wheels. The pulp was then loaded into a vat and mixed with water and sometimes china clay, to a creamy consistency. The operator (who was called a 'vat man' long before the government gave a new meaning to the phrase) then dipped into the mixture a frame called a 'deckle' with a fine wire mesh in the bottom. The water was drained off and the pulp fibres left behind, these being turned on to a bed of felt by the next operator, called the 'couch man', and subjected to great pressure. The resulting sheet was then dried and pressed, and given a coat of size and behold, after drying and pressing once more, you had one sheet of paper!

Modern paper making

Basically, paper is still made in the same way today, but with the spread of printing, the demand for paper grew so fast that mechanization of these slow processes became an urgent necessity. It was not until 1803, however, that the real answer came in the form of a machine built by the Fourdrinier brothers at Frogmore End in Hertfordshire. Based on a French invention, it fed pulp on to a moving wire mesh and produced paper on a continuous roll, or web, which could then be cut to required lengths. Modern paper-making machines can be several hundred feet long.

The huge increase in types of paper, with different colours, thicknesses and textures, and coated and uncoated surfaces, only began in the latter half of the nineteenth century, and led to a need for raw materials to replace – or at least supplement – the old rags, worn-out ships' sails and even old rope that paper makers had used for centuries.

Demand for pulp

Esparto grass from North Africa and the Iberian peninsula was among the more successful materials used, but the huge demand of developed countries for newsprint led to the use of wood-pulp, which has given some guarantee of a well-maintained forest landscape in an island which, before the Industrial Revolution, was rapidly using up every scrap of wood it had left. Britain today does not have either the timber or the capacity for making all the paper it needs, and large quantities of paper are imported, chiefly from Canada and Scandinavia.

China clay is used mainly in the production of the shiny 'art' papers upon which most high quality colour printing has been done in the past, although modern printing techniques permit such printing on 'calendered' papers, given a smooth but not shiny surface by rolling under pressure between metal cylinders, and this paper is of more lasting quality, though it is inevitably more expensive.

Wookey Hole

The paper-making industry is not one which has left a great deal in visible remains of its past, since it is a vital continuing process whose premises expand and prosper, and huge firms like Reed, Wiggins Teape, and Dickinsons have rationalized the former widely scattered small mills. But one interesting survival is at the famous Wookey Hole in Somerset, where the Hodgkinson family made fine paper in a mill dating back to early in the seventeenth century. Madame

Above: The Hayle Paper Mill at Maidstone, Kent – the modern extensions of a mill originally run on water power. Turkey Mill and Springfield Mill are among other local factories with nineteenth-century survivals in an area which has made paper since Tudor times. At Dartford, another important centre of the industry, the Eynsford Mill continued to produce hand-made paper until the early 1950's.

Tussauds are the unlikely owners of this mill today, along with the adjacent caves, and demonstrations of paper-making by hand are given there.

Where to go

The British Paper and Board Makers' Association developed an excellent museum of paper making at St Mary Cray, Kent, but this has since been transferred to the North Western Museum of Science and Technology at Manchester.

The Hayle paper mill at Maidstone (off B2010 south of town centre) is a little-altered building with millpond and water-wheel.

At New Hythe (unclassified road from A20 north west of Maidstone) the Reed company began on a modest scale in the 1920's, to become the huge Reed Paper Group.

London's Science Museum also has an important section on the paper industry.

Eastern England

To East Anglia (usually defined as Suffolk, Norfolk and Cambridgeshire) I have added Essex, which belongs to it in spirit if not in title. True, the southern part of that county includes outlying areas of Greater London, but the industries that give Essex its special character derive directly from the land.

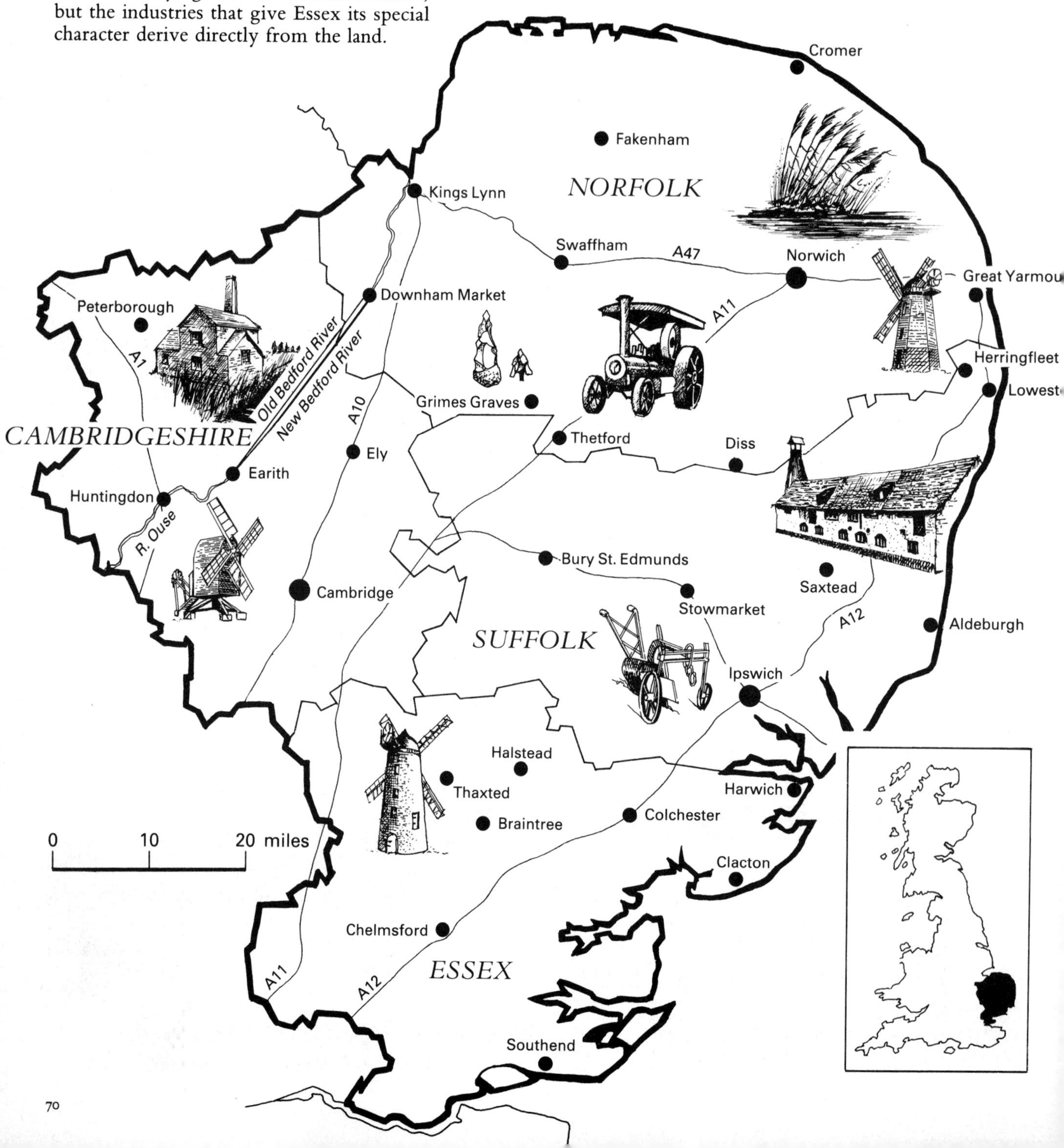

Cromer

Fakenham

NORFOLK

Kings Lynn

Swaffham   A47   Norwich   Great Yarmou

Downham Market

Peterborough

A1   Old Bedford River   New Bedford River

A10

Grimes Graves

A11

Herringfleet

Lowest

CAMBRIDGESHIRE

Ely

Earith

Thetford   Diss

Huntingdon

R. Ouse

Cambridge

Bury St. Edmunds

Stowmarket

Saxtead

A12

Aldeburgh

SUFFOLK

Ipswich

Halstead

Thaxted

Braintree

Harwich

Colchester

Clacton

0   10   20 miles

Chelmsford

A11   A12   *ESSEX*

Southend

Thatching

It is a frequent and much-mistaken assumption among townsfolk that thatching is an almost extinct country craft like chair-bodging or hand lace-making. In fact, there is still a very considerable business in thatching, for houses with thatched roofs survive in large numbers throughout the country, though mainly south of the Mersey–Humber line. One recent estimate put the number at about fifty thousand thatched buildings in England.

Until cheaper roofing materials such as Welsh slate became universally available, most vernacular buildings in England were roofed with thatch. This material was relatively cheap and usually available from within the locality. It was also light in weight and so did not require heavy roof timbers to support it. Houses that were once thatched but have been re-roofed with slates or tiles can usually be recognized by the roof's steep pitch, which helped rainwater to run quickly off the top surface.

Methods and materials

The materials used for thatching over the centuries have included straw, flax, heather, broom, sedge and reeds. The straw used was mostly wheat or 'long-straw' – although the straw of rye, oats and barley has also been used. In the days when reaping of corn was done by men with sickles, they cut off only the ears of the wheat, and the brittle straws were gathered later and stored for thatching. Nowadays, the combine-harvester crushes and breaks the straw, rendering it quite useless for this purpose, but occasionally a farmer will satisfy a demand for long-straw by harvesting his wheat by old methods.

Long-straw is laid on the roof in 'yealms' – flat bundles which have been damped – in overlapping courses or 'lanes'. Starting from the eaves upwards, and from right to left, the thatcher works along a roof using his individual method of fixing and progress. Some thatchers sew the thatch in position using tarred twine and an iron needle.

Below: Putting a new roof on an inn in Norfolk. The thatcher is seen working upwards from eaves to ridge, and from right to left. The rough edges of the thatch will be trimmed afterwards, to give the neat appearance seen on the completed extension, right. The whole job will take several days. Loose and rotten material is combed out of the old thatch first, and there will be a lot of sweeping up to be done afterwards.

Others use hazel runners and pegs driven in with a mallet. A considerable overhang at the eaves ensures that dripping rainwater is thrown clear of the walls. Straw is carried up the ladder to the roof on a 'jack' – a pronged fork usually made of hazel – that is the equivalent of the bricklayer's hod.

One drawback of straw roofs is that they are liable to attack by mice and sparrows, and this is why they are nearly always seen with coverings of fine wire mesh. A good wheat straw roof will last for up to thirty years.

Norfolk reeds

The tallest of our native grasses, *Phragmites communis*, commonly called in East Anglia the Norfolk reed or Norfolk spear, has long been recognized as the best material for thatching. In Norfolk and Suffolk there is consequently more surviving thatch than in other parts of the country, and even thatched church roofs can still be found.

The reeds grow in the broads and marshes of the area, and are more expensive than other materials, because they are more difficult to cut and more difficult to use, but a well-thatched roof of Norfolk reeds may last sixty or eighty years and does not require protection from birds.

Reed thatching has a closer texture than straw, and the thatcher uses a tool called a 'leggat' to push the dry reeds into position, for they do not need damping. This tool is somewhat akin to a carpet-layer's stretcher, and is a square board with studs and a handle.

Some thatchers trim and finish each stretch of thatch before they move their ladders along. Others thatch the whole side of the roof first and trim it all afterwards. There are many variations in decorative techniques on ridges, eaves and gables, and sometimes even the surface areas are laid in attractive-looking tiers. Each thatcher has his own style, and one thatcher can recognize another's work by the way it is done. Sometimes in East Anglia, when roofs were to be tiled, a layer of Norfolk reeds was laid beneath them as a form of insulation.

Wind and rain are the thatcher's enemies, but when his work is done, fire is the chief hazard to thatched buildings. If a roof caught

fire in medieval times, the only way to save the building was to pull off the burning thatch with a long fire-hook. Some of these tools survive, often being kept in village churches. There has been much banning of thatch in towns over the centuries, but with modern fire-proofing, the danger of fire often comes from defective chimneys rather than from the inflammability of the thatch itself.

Right: The tools of the Norfolk reed thatcher, showing shears, mallet, leggat, side rake, knives and yoke or 'jack', and iron thatch hook, spar and needle. When an iron needle is used to sew thatch, the twine is tarred to make it weatherproof. The thatch hook is used to fix hazel runners which hold the thatch in position. The spar is an iron staple for fixing straw rope.

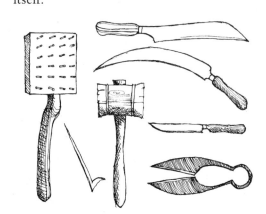

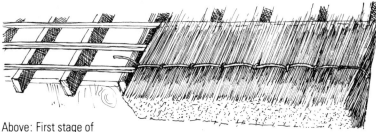

Above: First stage of thatching a roof. Working right to left, straw or reeds are laid from the eaves upwards in overlapping layers.

Above: Method of finishing ridge. Straw or sedge is fixed across rolls laid lengthways, and trimmed to decorative shapes.

Where to go

East Anglia is the best place to see roofs of Norfolk reed. The centre of the Norfolk thatching industry is on the north side of the Broads around North Walsham (A149 south of Cromer).

Horsey (B1159 north of Great Yarmouth) is one of the main reed-growing centres.

Some cottages thatched with sedge can still be seen in the area of Cambridgeshire between Ely and Newmarket. Sometimes sedge was – and still is – used in conjunction with other materials, sedge being especially good for forming a ridge of thatch.

Windmills

The harnessing of the wind as a free source of power is an idea whose origin is lost in antiquity, but it is known that windmills were used in Persia in the tenth century. No nation turned this ingenious medieval device to more profitable use than the Dutch, who used it to grind their corn and hull their rice and barley, drain their land, pulp their rags for paper-making, and who in 1592 designed the first wind-driven saw-mill. It was probably from the Netherlands that the windmill first came to Britain.

The first references to British windmills occur late in the twelfth century, when only the lord of the manor could afford to build one, but over the next two or three hundred years they became widespread in the more windswept eastern parts of Britain. It is estimated that there may have been ten thousand windmills in England at one time.

Types of mill

Windmills are of three types – post mills, tower mills, and smock mills. The oldest is the post mill which consists basically of a housing for the machinery pivoted on a central vertical post. The whole mill could thus be turned to bring its sails into the wind, this being done by means of a long tail pole stretching out from the mill with a small wheel at its end to facilitate movement along the ground.

The sails turn a windshaft carrying a gear-wheel which drives the horizontal mill-stones. The underframe of two timber cross-trees and supporting quarter bars stands on piers of brick or stone, and the whole is usually enclosed by a circular building which also serves as a store-house.

Surviving post mills

There is no greater demonstration of the craft and ingenuity of the medieval carpenter than the surviving interior of an old post mill with all its working parts made of wood. Among the best-known post mills are Pit-stone Mill, Buckinghamshire, owned by the National Trust and restored to working order, which has the date 1627 carved on one of its timbers; and Bourn Mill, Cambridge-shire, of similar date, restored in 1931 and also open to the public. The post mill on Saxtead Green, Suffolk, is in the care of the

Above: Windmill at Saxtead Green, Suffolk. This is a post mill of the late eighteenth century which has been restored to full working order and which can be visited. The building is 46 feet high and the sails have a span of nearly 155 feet.

Department of the Environment, and this is of late eighteenth-century construction.

Tower mills

Tower mills were a later development. These are solid, fixed structures of brick or stone, usually circular, in which only the cap, which carries the sails, turns in the wind. Tail poles for turning the sails did not work well in tower mills, and other methods were invented. The best of these was the addition of a fantail by a miller called Edmund Lee in 1746. This consists of a wheel of vanes at the back of the cap, set at right angles to the sails. When the wind is not striking the sails, it strikes the fantail, and this automatically turns the sails into the wind again. A brick-built tower mill at Ixworth, Suffolk, is one of the few mills of this kind still in commercial operation. It was built in 1821. Norfolk Windmills Trust has restored a tower mill of 1860 at Billingford. In Essex a fine restored tower mill can be seen at Thaxted.

Smock mills
The third type of windmill, called a smock mill, is basically the same thing as a tower mill in its operation, but has an octagonal tower of weatherboarded walls, usually painted white. It is called a 'spinnekop' in the Netherlands. There is a good example at Herringfleet, Suffolk, built in 1823 and maintained by the county council now.

Perhaps the finest smock mill in England is the Union mill at Cranbrook, Kent. This was built in 1814 and is also in the care of the county council. It is sometimes said to be the tallest mill in the country, but that distinction properly belongs to a tower mill at Sutton, Norfolk, which has a total height of almost eighty feet. It was erected in 1789, but was burnt down and rebuilt in the following century.

Technical improvements
With the coming of the Industrial Revolution, the surprisingly complicated all-timber machinery gave way to iron gears and windshafts. Finally, the windmill succumbed altogether to steam power, but not before many improvements had been made in the efficiency of working mills. Sails, in particular, got a lot of attention in attempts to harness maximum wind-power. Most mills had four sails, but some had five, six or even eight. The only remaining eight-sail mill is at Heckington, Lincolnshire, and that county also possesses the surviving five-sail mills and one with six sails.

The sails of the early windmills were wooden frameworks to which canvas was attached, fixed to tapering beams called stocks. Because the angles were fixed, the miller could only slow down the sails in high wind by stopping the mill and adjusting the sails one by one – a lengthy job. An eighteenth-century Scottish millwright solved this problem with sails which could be

The smock mill at Great Thurlow, Suffolk. The working principle is the same as in a tower mill, only the architecture being different in any essential respect.

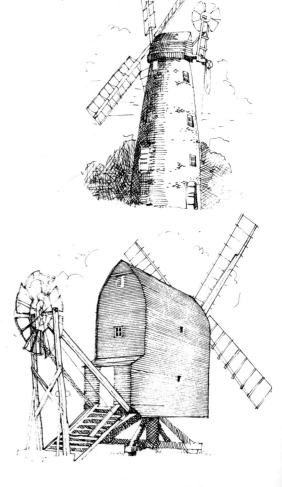

Billingford Mill, Norfolk. A fine example of a tower mill, built in 1860. In this type, only the cap turns on top of the solid structure.

The post mill at Great Chisill, Cambridgeshire. The whole building revolves on the central oak post; the fantail ensuring that the sails are always turning into the wind.

either of the Carboniferous sandstone called Millstone Grit, from Derbyshire, or of French burr stone.

Windmills used for drainage were designed under Dutch influence, naturally enough, and so are usually of the smock type. The windshaft drove a large scoop wheel which raised water to a higher level for carrying to drainage channels. Examples of drainage mills can be seen at Wicken Fen, Cambridgeshire, owned by the National Trust; and at Reedham, Norfolk, where the Berney Arms Mill is preserved by the Department of the Environment.

Above: Diagram of a typical post mill, showing how the sails turn gear wheels which drive two sets of millstones. The speed is controlled by changing the angle of the wooden slats.

operated like the shutters of a Venetian blind according to the wind force, and further refinements of this idea were made early in the nineteenth century.

In corn mills, grain was fed to the mill-stones by gravity through a chute which trickled it into the eye of the revolving upper stone. The meal was then fed to the rim of the lower stationary stone by radial grooves. Next, it fell into a meal spout and thence to a bin on the floor.

The mill-stones – now seen so often as garden ornaments or as signs at the entrances to villages and National Parks – were made

Where to go

Many windmills survive in addition to those mentioned, the greatest concentrations being in Lincolnshire and the south east, apart from East Anglia, but some are delapidated and others have been converted for residential use.

Mills mentioned in the text:–
Pitstone: B488 from Linslade or Tring. ¼ mile south of Ivinghoe.
Bourn: A45 from St Neots towards Cambridge, approaching A14 crossroads.
Saxtead Green: A1120 east from Stowmarket.
Ixworth: A143 north east of Bury St Edmunds.
Billingford: B1118 eastwards from Diss, then minor road left to Brockdish.
Thaxted: A130 south east of Saffron Walden.
Herringfleet: B1074 north west of Lowestoft.
Cranbrook: In town, A229 between Maidstone and Hastings.
Sutton: A149 from North Walsham or Great Yarmouth, then minor road east of Sutton village.
Heckington: A17 east from Sleaford.
Wicken Fen: Off A1123 south of Ely, west of Wicken village.
Reedham: One mile west of Great Yarmouth. The mill is not accessible by road. Can be reached across the marshes by boat or from Berney Arms Railway Station.

Malting

Because the eastern and south-eastern counties of England are where most of the barley is grown, it is here that we find the biggest concentration of malt-houses, or 'maltings'. They are especially common in Suffolk, Essex and the eastern fringe of Hertfordshire, often distinguished by their long rows of windows along two-storey buildings and by the cowled tops of their kilns.

Malting is the process by which barley is converted into malt for the brewing of ale. In the old-fashioned method, the barley grain, after being cleaned and soaked in water for two or three days, became swollen with its increased moisture content. It was then spread out on the floors of the maltings and exposed to air at a constant temperature. This process caused germination to take place and proceed to the right stage, which generally took between two and three weeks. Then the grain was roasted in kilns to produce malt, and after cooling and removal of the rootlets, it was delivered to the breweries.

Control of the drying process produced variations in the colour and flavour of the malt, according to its requirement for pale ale, brown ale or stout.

The modern method of malting is essentially the same, but it has been speeded up and streamlined by 'drum' malting instead of spreading the barley out on floors, and by air conditioning and electrical heating in the modern buildings of a more centralized industry.

Surviving maltings

Many old-style maltings can still be seen, although – as with the Kentish oast-houses and the windmills – they have often been taken over for other uses nowadays. Some of the best surviving buildings are at Diss, Norfolk, where one range dates from 1788; Ipswich, Suffolk (Dock Street); Stowmarket, Suffolk (Station Road); Mistley, Essex, where one range was built in 1807; and at Bishops Stortford and Ware.

Perhaps the most famous maltings, however, are those at Snape in Suffolk. Some of these nineteenth-century buildings are still used commercially, but part of the complex has been converted into a fine modern concert hall.

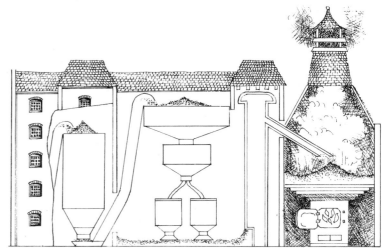

Top: The maltings in Station Road, Stowmarket, showing characteristic kilns of the old type.

Above: Diagram of a typical malt-house showing the progress of barley grain through soaking and drying, to the roasting process in kiln at right.

Where to go

Diss is on A1066 between Thetford and Lowestoft. Stowmarket is beside A45 between Ipswich and Bury St Edmunds. Mistley is on the estuary of the River Stour near Manningtree (B1352). Bishops Stortford is on A11 north of Harlow, and Ware on A10 near Hertford. The Snape Maltings are on the south bank of the River Alde, south of the village, which is best reached by A12 from Ipswich or by A146, A145 and A12 from Norwich, turning east on A1094 south of Saxmundham.

Agricultural implements

East Anglia's interest in tools for agriculture, as we have seen, goes back a long way, but it is a surprising fact that the development of sophisticated and efficient tools and machinery was very slow in these parts. Right into the eighteenth century, farmers were using crude tools of wood and wrought iron which were technically not much in advance of the flint tools of their prehistoric ancestors. This slowness was due in part to the cheapness of labour and a consequent lack of incentive on the part of the farmers to look for economies.

The influence of the men who were slowly turning agriculture into a science, however – men such as Robert Bakewell, Jethro Tull and Charles 'Turnip' Townshend – had widespread effects. By the middle of the eighteenth century, the huge improvements demonstrated in agricultural production by more efficient farming methods had put the invention and manufacture of implements and machinery on a commercial footing.

Mechanical progress

The biggest improvements in the earlier stages were to ploughs. The arable farmers of East Anglia were working out more efficient methods of ploughing their soil with the aid of local blacksmiths and carpenters who made tools to individual requirements, resulting in an immense variety of shapes and sizes. John Brand, an Essex blacksmith, invented the swing plough, drawn by two horses, and what is more, made it of iron.

Others had worked out the optimum curve for the mould-board, which turns over the furrow cut by the plough-share, and in the 1780's Robert Ransome of Ipswich introduced self-sharpening ploughshares of cast iron. By the mid-nineteenth century, Ransomes were making over eighty different types of plough with replaceable cast iron parts, and machinery on the land was reducing the need for casual labour, so that children were able to stay longer at school.

Machines were made for clearing the ground of weeds, for raking corn stubble, for reaping and threshing; but these advances were not always greeted with delight by those who did the back-breaking work they

Top: Ransome's improved Kentish turn-wrest plough. The special purpose of the turn-wrest device was in ploughing on hillsides. It was driven horizontally along the sloping ground and the mould-board turned the furrows all in one direction.

Above: A nineteenth-century steam traction engine being used to drive farm machinery. Steam power was at its height towards the end of the century, before the internal combustion engine began to make its impact on agriculture.

were designed to prevent. As the Luddite riots against textile machinery were taking place in the towns, workers in the country were smashing threshing machines, and magistrates appealed to farmers to dismantle their machinery.

Steam power had a relatively short-lived success in agriculture, for ploughing, threshing, haulage and other uses. The Ransome company was again in the forefront of development, building small stationary engines that could be taken from farm to farm, and later introducing an engine that conveniently burnt straw for fuel instead of coal.

Burrells of Thetford, Norfolk, were among those whose traction engines included some for use on the land, and these were the first moves towards the large tractor-drawn machines and combine-harvesters of today's farming landscape.

Where to go
Local museums include the Bridewell Museum at Norwich and the Farmland Museum at Haddenham, Cambridge (A1123 five miles south west of Ely).

The Bressingham Steam Museum at Diss, Norfolk (A1006 east of Thetford) has an outstanding collection of steam engines, some of them agricultural. Daniel Albone's Ivel tractor of 1902 (Science Museum) brought the internal combustion engine into agricultural use.

Flint working

It was in 1870 that a piece of excavation in Norfolk, carried out by Canon Greenwell, had such sensational results that it could really be labelled 'industrial archaeology' without any dispute over the use of words.

A large number of depressions in the ground near Thetford had long been known as Grime's Graves. There were literally hundreds of them. The name came from 'Grim', a popular alternative name for the Norse god Odin, or Woden, identified by Christians with the Devil. But these curious craters in fact had nothing to do with death or burial.

Prehistoric tool factory

Excavation revealed a shaft and narrow radiating tunnels dug into the chalk more than twenty feet below the ground, and it soon became clear that the area was a Neolithic mining district. Perhaps as long as four thousand years ago, men of the late Stone Age worked here to extract flint for their tools and weapons.

As research proceeded, the scale of the prehistoric operations became clear. Picks made from red-deer antlers were found, as well as the shoulder blades of large animals, possibly used as shovels, together with carvings and ceremonial objects, in a great complex of shafts and tunnels over an area of thirty-four acres. Some shafts went down forty feet to cramped passages where miners worked by the light of tallow lamps which left their sooty marks on the roofs.

The flint brought up from the mines was fashioned into axes, knives, arrow-heads and other implements by what we now call 'knapping'. Flint is a very hard material which chips when struck with another stone, and by this means can be shaped to give a point or a sharp cutting edge and then polished. The mining and knapping of flint has been called the first industry of Western Europe, and it is evident that the Norfolk workers had a lively export trade as well as a home demand from the population centres in southern England.

Best-quality flint is hard and black, and the flint mined from Grime's Graves was of a particularly durable kind now known as 'floorstone'. Recent experiments have shown that tools made from this kind of flint were remarkably efficient.

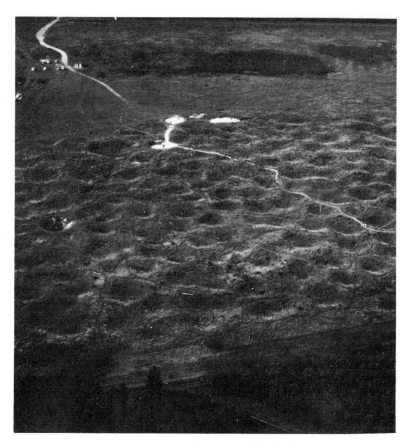

Top: Aerial view of Grime's Graves. This landscape of craters and spoil heaps was made by man in what was obviously a boom industry of prehistoric Britain.

Above: A flint dagger and a pick made from the antlers of a deer. These tools were found in Grime's Graves.

Flint working today

Flint has been an important material ever since those times. Many houses and most churches on the chalk belt of southern and eastern England are built of it, and flint is still knapped in Norfolk for purposes such as building repair work, and even for making flint-lock guns for export. One of the local public houses is called the 'Flintknappers Arms'.

The Department of the Environment has made two of the pits accessible to the public. One descends the shafts on iron ladders, and it is advisable to wear old clothes.

Where to go

Grime's Graves lie north of Santon Downham, surrounded by pine forest. Use A134 from Thetford, turning left on the road to Santon Downham, then right along a track to the clearing.

Land reclamation

The 'fen' lands of the east of England extending through Norfolk, Suffolk, Cambridgeshire, Bedfordshire and Lincolnshire, represent a triumph of agricultural engineering. Roughly two thousand square miles of flat marshland, once under shallow sea-water, were drained during the course of two centuries and are now fertile arable fields, divided not by the walls or hedges found in most other parts of the country, but by dykes and ditches. The digging of channels to drain flood-waters has gone on in this part of England for many centuries, having been begun on a small scale by the Romans, but it was not until the seventeenth century that the huge work of permanent drainage to reclaim land from the sea, and make it habitable as well as fertile, was begun in earnest.

The Dutch mastermind

The largest landowners in this flat and flooded eastern expanse were the Earls of Bedford, and one of them, serving Queen Elizabeth in the Netherlands, had been impressed by the recovery of land by the Dutch, who were such past masters at driving back the sea that they had a proud saying: 'God created the world, but the Dutch made Holland.' In 1630, the fourth Earl promoted a scheme to copy the Dutch example, in which thirteen 'co-adventurers' joined him, and they employed a Dutch engineer to supervise the works.

Cornelius Vermuyden had already carried out other drainage works in England, including the Royal Park at Windsor, and had begun the drainage of Hatfield Chase in Yorkshire under commission from Charles I. But none of this work, nor the smaller undertakings here of other Dutchmen, was on the ambitious scale of the Fens scheme. Nothing approaching it had been attempted in Britain before. The Earl of Bedford sank over a hundred thousand pounds into the project, and Vermuyden, who was eventually knighted by the king, gave the greater part of his life to it.

The first move was to dig a canal, twenty-one miles long, from Earith in Cambridge-

Below: Workmen clearing the bed of the so-called Bedford River towards the end of the nineteenth century. Two of these long straight drainage canals were constructed in the seventeenth century by the Dutch engineer Cornelius Vermuyden. This is the Old Bedford River. The New Bedford River, made parallel to the first about twenty years afterwards, has a wider channel.

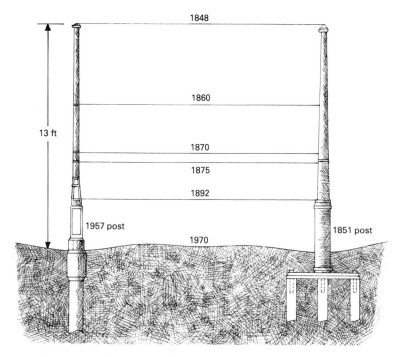

1848

1860

13 ft

1870

1875

1892

1957 post

1970

1851 post

Left: The Holme Fen Post near Peterborough. In 1851, a cast iron pillar from the Great Exhibition was driven 22 feet through the peat, replacing the original 1848 wooden post, to prove the theory that the fens were sinking. This theory was indeed correct, as the diagram shows.

Right: In 1957, the 1851 pillar was replaced by a new post, which shows ground levels in previous years.

shire to the Ouse near Downham Market in Norfolk, to drain the so-called Bedford Level. (Some years afterwards a parallel canal was dug to assist drainage further, and these two long straight cuts are called the Old and New Bedford Rivers.) When the job was done, water which had for centuries spread over the land ran out to the sea, and animals could be grazed and crops grown where only fish had swum before.

Problems and setbacks

Dutch immigrant farmers grew crops of cole-seed and rape on the new fields and incurred the scorn of Englishmen who regarded such stuff as 'trash and trumpery', but the long-experienced Dutchmen knew exactly what they were doing. Their crops helped to remove excess salt from soil which had only recently been beneath the sea.

Local hostility to the Dutch was not just an argument about crops, however. Fenmen had earned a living from the shallow waters as fishermen. They had cut reeds for thatching, and caught waterfowl for the markets. Outsiders called them 'fen-slodgers'. Now their livelihood had been literally drained away, and they began a campaign to impede reclamation, going about in gangs at night,

cutting the newly-built dykes and attacking Vermuyden's labourers. By 1642 much of the Fens had been laid waste again. It was seven years before the work was re-started, but within a decade the job was done and the Earl of Bedford had paid off all the mortgages he had incurred in order to finance the great work.

The problems were not over yet, though. Gradually the estuaries of the rivers Ouse and Nene, carrying all the waters away from the freshly won land, began to silt up, and the black peaty earth shrank when it dried up and began to sink, so that the canals were soon above the level of the surrounding land. This was an overwhelming factor that Vermuyden and his employers had failed to anticipate. Moreover, labour was scarce for manning the new farmland, which had been uninhabitable before. Workers had to be brought from distant villages, at high cost to the landowners.

What began as an unforeseen problem soon escalated into a crisis. Frequent complaints of flooding came from the farmers and it seemed, paradoxically, that the more water was pumped out, the worse the problem became, because the soil continued to sink as it became progressively drier.

The Fenlands today

One of the most dramatic possibilities for the future is the draining of the Wash. This has been much talked about, but we English have been too timid, so far, to launch a project similar to the Dutch reclamation of the Zuyder Zee which has been done with spectacular success in the present century. A few thousand acres have been reclaimed from the Wash since the Second World War, but the drainage of the whole inlet would give another three hundred square miles to our farmers and possibly provide a fresh-water reservoir for eastern England.

The Fenlands need no museums to record their past, for the landscape is itself a museum without walls of the long but profitable work of drainage. Vermuyden's Old Bedford River can still be seen, straight as an arrow, in a geometric landscape very like that of Holland, which Aldous Huxley likened to 'a tour through the first books of Euclid.' Many Dutch immigrants settled in these parts to exploit the land their engineers were creating, and their influence is evident in the bulb fields of Lincolnshire and the elaborately gabled buildings of the region. (An area to the west of Boston is still called Holland Fen.) Driving along the roads one finds oneself above the level of the fields on either side, since many roads were made along the tops of dykes.

A partial solution lay in windmills. Hundreds of them were built to pump water in the eighteenth century. They were succeeded by steam-driven pumps, which were more efficient, and which have since been replaced in their turn by pumps driven by electricity.

More land to be won

Meanwhile, recovery of land to the north of the Bedford Level was proceeding. Many thousands of acres of fen and marsh in Lincolnshire had been drained and cultivated, and by the early years of the nineteenth century, huge areas in Cambridgeshire, Suffolk and what used to be Huntingdonshire had been turned from seascape to landscape.

The digging of new canals to speed the flow of water from the lowlands to the sea assisted the newly installed steam pumps in keeping the pastures and arable fields free of water. By 1850, much of the Fenland was 'traversed by excellent roads and railways' and was mostly 'freed from the overflow of floods'. The most fertile soil in Britain was by now legendary, and those who had opposed its recovery were reaping rich harvests of corn instead of filling baskets with eels.

Above: Cut-away drawing of the pumping station at Stretham, Cambridgeshire, where a beam engine was used to scoop water to a drainage channel at a rate of over a hundred tons per minute. The engine was built in 1831, and the large waterwheel, erected in 1896, replaced an earlier and smaller one. It has a diameter of 37 feet 2 inches.

Where to go

At Stretham, Cambridgeshire (A10 four miles south of Ely) a steam engine built for drainage in 1831 is preserved *in situ* and may be seen by visitors. Ironically, this process reversed the whole point of previous water-wheels. The water-wheel was used to drive beam engines for various purposes in mills, but here the beam engine was used to drive the water-wheel, which raised water into a dyke.

Wicken Fen, a nature reserve owned by the National Trust, to the east of Stretham, is an area of undrained peat-land which gives a good idea of what the Fens were like once.

Early pumping machinery for drainage is discussed under Windmills.

West Midlands

The west midlands is one of the most heavily concentrated industrial areas of Britain, and its industries were presented to it on a plate, as it were, by nature. Thus most of them have very ancient origins. The underlying rock held the mineral deposits which resulted in the region's concentration of miners, engineers and mechanics, whilst the soil above ensured the continuation of a long agricultural tradition away from the urban centres of heavy industry.

Two new towns were designated in this area in the sixties, to absorb some of the increasing industrial population, and the largest of them, Telford, was named after the great Scottish civil engineer who did so much important work in this area when the Industrial Revolution, which began here on the banks of the Severn, had got under way. Abraham Darby, too, is one of the key figures in modern British industry (see Iron working). He and his descendants played a vital role in setting the Industrial Revolution in motion.

I have included the Cotswolds in this section because, although they stretch south as far as Wiltshire their main communications and most popular areas with visitors unquestionably belong to the west midlands.

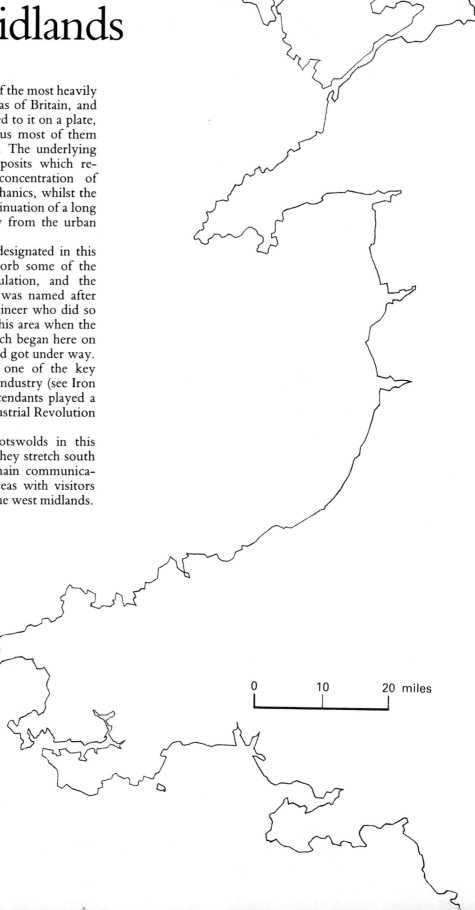

0   10   20 miles

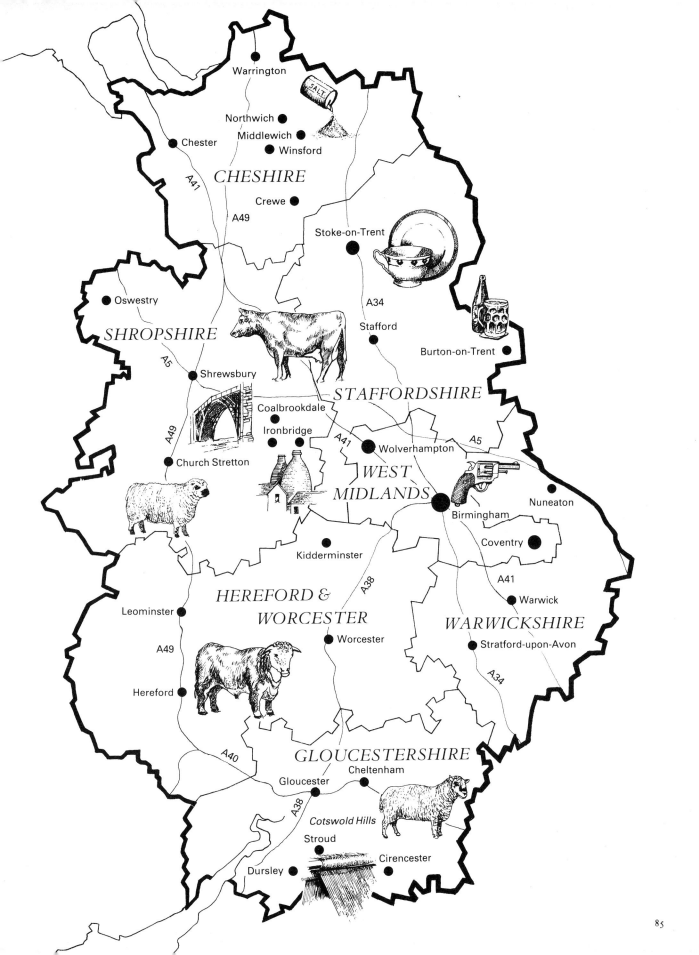

Warrington

Northwich
Middlewich
Winsford

Chester

CHESHIRE

A41

A49

Crewe

Stoke-on-Trent

A34

Stafford

Burton-on-Trent

Oswestry

SHROPSHIRE

A5

Shrewsbury

STAFFORDSHIRE

Coalbrookdale

Ironbridge

A49

A41

Wolverhampton

A5

Church Stretton

WEST MIDLANDS

Birmingham

Nuneaton

Kidderminster

Coventry

A41

HEREFORD &

WORCESTER

A38

Leominster

Worcester

WARWICKSHIRE

A49

Warwick

Stratford-upon-Avon

Hereford

A34

GLOUCESTERSHIRE

A40

Cheltenham

Gloucester

Cotswold Hills

A38

Stroud

Cirencester

Dursley

Salt mining

The Keuper Sandstone which forms the Cheshire Plain covers the source of that county's most important industry since at least as long ago as Roman times, for beneath it lie extensive salt beds. Men of the Bronze Age are known to have extracted salt in some other parts of Britain, but from the Saxon period onward, Cheshire has been the nation's most important source of salt. Several ancient routes are known as 'salt ways', by which merchants carried the valuable stuff to all parts of the country on trains of pack-horses.

Salt was obtained at various places in earlier times by evaporation from sea-water and tidal rivers, before the discovery of inland brine springs at Droitwich and in Cheshire. The 'wich' name ending is a good clue to the existence of salt workings at some time in the past.

Middlewich supplied salt to the Roman army, and was then called Salinae. Northwich and Nantwich were also well established as salt-producing towns by the time of the Norman Conquest.

The discovery of rock salt in the seventeenth century replaced the evaporation process by chemical extraction from salt brought up from mines. The Marston Mine at Northwich was one of the largest workings. Later still, bore holes were sunk into the deposits and water circulated in them so that salt could be pumped up in solution and evaporated. It was also discovered that brine salt could be pumped up in solution from old mines where flooding had occurred. The increasing scale of salt working led to the River Weaver being made navigable to provide better transport facilities.

The chief effect of the modern salt industry on the landscape has been the formation of large pools or 'flashes' owing to the ground sinking above old salt workings. They are particularly evident around Northwich, where the walls of houses, too, have shown the alarming effects of subsidence. The dramatic collapse of a mine in 1838 was traced to a forgotten working of a hundred years before. Some of the pools have now become nature reserves. The Trent and Mersey Canal passes through this landscape at a higher level than the land surface around it, which has sunk since the canal was built.

Top: An old Cheshire salt mine. Men are seen digging the raw salt, which was loaded into horse-drawn trains of barrel-shaped wagons.

Above: Part of the Newbridge Salt Works at Winsford, around 1920. A barge is seen in foreground on the River Weaver. Derelict drying sheds remain at the site.

Fortunes of common salt

Salt is used in many chemical processes as well as for human consumption, and one of the most important is the production of soda, for soap making among other things. In 1873, a scientist, Ludwig Mond, and a businessman, John Brunner, went into partnership at Winnington to make soda by an ammonia process which did not produce the atmospheric devastation of the old sulphur process. Brunner, Mond & Co. Ltd amalgamated in 1926 with three other large chemical manufacturers, and became Imperial Chemical Industries.

Where to go

There is a Salt Museum at Weaver Hall, London Road, Northwich (A559 between Chester and Manchester).

The Lion Salt Works, on Northwich's north east side, still pumps brine and extracts salt by evaporation. The works can be visited on summer afternoons.

At Winsford (A54 south of Northwich), timber drying sheds can be seen. Underground workings are still in operation, producing mainly raw salt for icy roads.

Small arms

It was the local iron deposits which ensured that the Midlands became a major industrial centre. At the time of the Domesday Book, Birmingham was a poor country hamlet: as it grew into a market town, manufacturers began to converge on it and aid its growth. In time, Birmingham moved towards specialized manufacturing of highly finished metal goods, leaving the heavy industry to the neighbouring Black Country.

By the end of the seventeenth century, gunsmiths were well established in the town, making flintlock muskets, and pistols. During the Napoleonic Wars, the British Army got two-thirds of all its firearms from Birmingham manufacturers contracted by the government.

Mills grew up which specialized in the grinding and boring of gun barrels, the making of cartridges and other aspects of firearm use and manufacture. A special Act of Parliament in 1813 gave Birmingham the right to its own proofing authority, and the town built its Gun Barrel Proof House, where barrels are still tested today. No gun can be released for sale – at home or abroad –

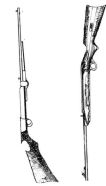

Top: A pre-1914 BSA sports gun and, right, a modern .22 calibre BSA air rifle.

Below: A gunmaker at work in Birmingham's 'Gun Quarter'. Visitors to the town remarked on the 'noise of anvils'.

until its barrel has been definitively proved and stamped accordingly.

The famous Birmingham Small Arms factory – latterly more famous for BSA bicycles – was built at Small Heath in the nineteenth century, when a number of local gunsmiths formed a group to manufacture arms on a large scale. At one time the gunsmiths had their own area of the town, the so-called Gun Quarter, where lock, stock and barrel were made.

Where to go

Birmingham's Museum of Science and Industry, in Newhall Street, has a collection of locally made small arms.

The Proof House stands in Banbury Street, with a large plaster insignia above the columns of its doorway.

Gunmakers' workshops of the early 19th century survive in Loveday Street and Bath Street – among the few remains of the old Gun Quarter, where one of the local pubs is called 'The Gunmakers' Arms.'

Iron working

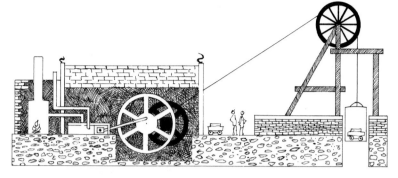

As the River Severn flows down from the Welsh mountains, circling Shrewsbury and continuing eastwards, it enters an attractive and heavily wooded gorge, described by Arthur Young as 'a winding glen between two immense hills which break into various forms, and all thickly covered with wood, forming the most beautiful sheets of hanging wood.' The valley was created, geologists believe, by ice-bound water gradually wearing away the carboniferous rock base and making a new course for the river. It is known today as the Ironbridge Gorge, and it is one of the world's power points – a place where events have thrust the process of civilization forward in a great surge. For it is arguable that what we call the Industrial Revolution was born right here.

The primeval forests had formed coal measures in the area, and at the beginning of the eighteenth century, the centre of the valley's vitality was the mining community whose village had been given one of those hideous names so beloved of Victorian capitalists – Coalbrookdale.

Crisis in timber supply

At this period, the most important raw material to the English economy was wood.

It was used not only for fuel and for building houses, ships, windmills, wagons, furniture, knitting frames and so on, but also provided charcoal for smelting ore and making gunpowder, as well as the raw material for paper making. The demand for timber was thus colossal, and as it began to outstrip supply the need for new materials became an urgent one – something like the crisis the world now faces in the imminent drying up of oil supplies.

From the sixteenth century onwards, the increasing use of coal as a domestic fuel and a source of industrial power provided some slight easing of the problem, but the great need was to find a technique for the mass-production of iron. Because of the shortage and slow process of using timber for smelting, one ironmaster reported that, early in the eighteenth century, more than two-

Above: Diagram of the steam-powered winding engine at Blists Hill mine. It is preserved by the Ironbridge Gorge Museum Trust.

Below: Detail of the ironworks engine house at Blists Hill.

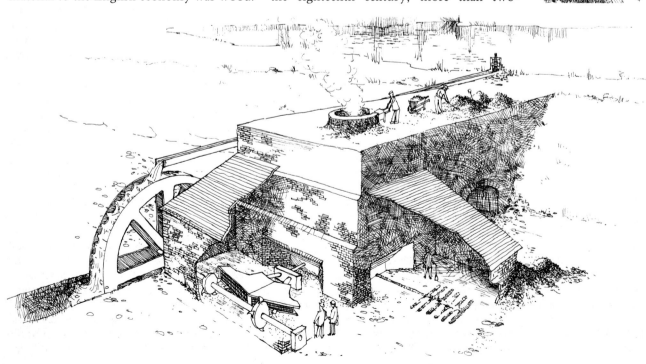

Above: 'An Iron Work, for Casting of Cannon'. This engraving of 1788, by Wilson Lowry after George Robertson, shows the Calcutts ironworks at Jackfield, on the south bank of the Severn. Alexander Brodie had purchased the works two years earlier.

Left: Artist's reconstruction of the Old Furnace at Coalbrookdale. Water channelled from the pool drives the overshot waterwheel which powers the bellows. Iron ore, coke and limestone are fed in at top, and molten iron flows into sand pig beds below.

thirds of Britain's iron was being imported.

Some of the earliest charcoal blast furnaces in England had been built on the edge of the Shropshire coalfield, where the underlying rock provided ironstone and limestone as well as the coal seams. A great programme of tree-planting had taken place here, to replace the felled woodlands and produce more timber for use by the iron industry.

Abraham Darby's breakthrough

Ironmasters had half realized the solution to their problems for a century before the new process came into regular use, but the technical means had not been discovered. Instead of smelting the ore with charcoal in slow processes aided by water-wheels, they needed to do it with cheap coke produced by the rapidly-expanding coal mining industry. The method was first used successfully at Coalbrookdale in 1709, by a Quaker iron-master named Abraham Darby. He was the son of a Dudley locksmith, and had progres-sed to iron working through a period of

brass-founding in Bristol. His success was due in no small part to the peculiar proper-ties of the local coal, called 'clod', which produced a coke resembling charcoal more closely than other coals.

Despite the fact that it was forty years before the new process was widely practised, in the course of the following century the output of pig-iron in Britain was increased by nearly three thousand per cent, and the western world was experiencing a revolu-tion such as mankind had not seen since the invention of printing. The availability of ideal coal, so close to good deposits of ironstone, gave Shropshire a head start over those other parts of the country where ironworking became an important industry.

Darby's descendants and other masters forged ahead with new developments, in-cluding transportation by rail and the use of steam power. Improvements to James Watt's steam engines were made and utilized here, and a steam blowing engine installed by Watt at John Wilkinson's blast-furnace at

Right: Gladstone Pottery, Staffordshire.

Overleaf: The Iron Bridge, Shropshire. This famous bridge was erected in 1779.

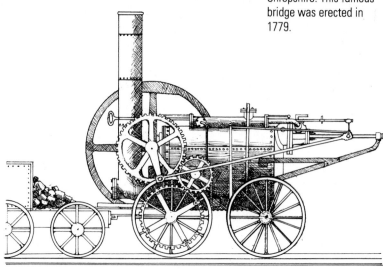

Willey effectively freed the ironmasters from their dependence on water power. Richard Trevithick came to Coalbrookdale for assistance with the construction of his pioneering railway locomotive. The first iron rails and wheels were cast in the valley; the first iron boat was built at Willey Wharf; and a new process for boring cannon was invented.

The plates for Brunel's *Great Britain* were rolled here, too. Cylinders for Newcomen steam engines were cast in iron to replace brass. The towns and villages of the Shropshire coalfield doubled their populations in little more than fifty years, and Ironbridge grew up to accommodate the overspill of workers from Coalbrookdale.

Artists came to the valley to paint the 'satanic mills' whose roaring blast-furnaces threw flames into the sky and seemed like an appalling vision of hell. Turner, John Martin, De Loutherbourg and John Sell Cotman were among those who came to record their impressions of this apocalyptic gorge.

The consequences for this small area of east Shropshire – a country which was, on the whole, little known except as a sheep and dairy-farming area – were enormous. Manufacturing industry brought huge changes in its wake which are still evident. Not least among them, a county which has always been (as it still remains) a stronghold of the Church of England, suddenly sprouted a luxuriant local crop of Nonconformist chapels.

The men who worked in the iron industry were not subject to the physical dangers that constantly accompanied the coal miners, but they worked in twelve-hour shifts through day and night in the continous smelting process, including Sundays, until the nineteenth century. Women and children were employed to a limited extent. Some women seem to have worked underground in the iron ore mines, and they also worked at the surface, picking out ore. Boys were given work in the blast furnaces from the age of seven upwards.

Collapse

In the second half of the nineteenth century, the Shropshire iron industry suffered a dramatic collapse. There are several reasons to account for the remarkable disappearance of an industry which had set the wheels of the Industrial Revolution in motion. Partly, the absence of a long industrial tradition meant that its foundations were not solid enough to bear the pressures of competition by constant adaptation and modernization. Mineral resources were being run down, too, and the area was less well placed than other industrial centres for communications and transport.

Furnaces were blown out and forges and rolling mills closed down. Unemployment and soup kitchens loomed large, and workers who had come here in the boom years moved on, leaving the fiery scenes of the Ironbridge Gorge almost like ghost towns.

Enduring fame

Since 1959 a great deal of work has been done to recover the paraphernalia of this great industrial centre. The Old Furnace, built by Sir Basil Brooke in 1638, and used by Abraham Darby in his successful experiment, was excavated from beneath fourteen thousand tons of slag. Thousands of visitors come to gaze reverently at this unimposing old brick furnace as if it were the most sacred of religious relics, for it is now one of the centrepieces of the Ironbridge Gorge Museum – an open-air museum of industry which has won Europe's 'Museum of the Year' Award. Its finest exhibit, however, is the iron bridge itself from which the gorge takes its modern name.

Much of the early Coalbrookdale production had been carried south across the Severn by ferry, a means of transport that

Above: A drawing of Trevithick's Coalbrookdale locomotive. The Cornish inventor built the first railway locomotive at Darby's Coalbrookdale iron works in 1802.

Above: One of the new uses found for local cast iron was in tombs and monuments. Broseley and Madeley churchyards have examples, including this fine one to William Baldwin. John Wilkinson, the Broseley ironmaster nicknamed 'Iron-mad Wilkinson', had himself buried in a cast iron coffin.

Left: Ironbridge Gorge
Museum, Shropshire.
Remains of the Coalport
China works form part of
this museum, developed
around the cradle of the
Industrial Revolution.

soon became quite unequal to the task. It was Abraham Darby II who decided to build a bridge across the river to facilitate transport by road, and it was he who decided to build it of iron. It was actually his son, Abraham III, who completed the project. A Shrewsbury architect, Thomas Farnolls Pritchard, drew up the original design for a hundred-foot single-span bridge to be supported by masonry abutments on both banks. Darby cast the iron and built the bridge to a modified design. The building was completed in three months without any obstruction to river traffic. It was opened in 1781 and quickly became one of the wonders of the modern world.

Many other fascinating remains of the Severn valley iron works are open to view in this most remarkable of industrial landscapes. They are far too numerous to be listed here, but worthy of special mention are the Hay Inclined Plane and the blowing engines known as David and Sampson (sic).

Above: The former Great Warehouse of the Coalbrookdale Company is now a Museum of Iron. It tells the history of Coalbrookdale as well as the story of iron making.

Above: The Severn Wharf and Warehouse at Ironbridge. Built in neo-Gothic style, it is now a visitor centre for the Ironbridge Gorge Museum.

Where to go
The towns and villages of the Shropshire coalfield are being enveloped by the new town of Telford, between Shrewsbury and Wolverhampton. The Development Corporation has places of industrial fame well sign-posted. Guides to various sites and monuments are published by the Ironbridge Gorge Museum.

Ironbridge and neighbouring sites are best reached via M6, leaving at junction 12 and following A5 to Telford. Nearest railway station is Shifnal (4 miles). David and Sampson are double-beam blast furnace blowing engines, preserved at Blists Hill Open Air Museum, Madeley. The Museum also includes the Hay Incline, which was built to raise tub boats two hundred feet from one water level to another on the canal system devised to overcome transport problems.

The Potteries

It was no mere accident that brought the modern pottery industry to north Staffordshire, where in Arnold Bennett's day the familiar landmarks of the district's brick 'bottle ovens' were always seen through an atmosphere of thick smoke. The area had the essential supplies of clay at hand, as well as coal and water. Pottery had been made here at least as far back as 2000 B.C, and finds of Roman and Saxon pottery have been made in the district from time to time. It was not until the Industrial Revolution, however, that the area around Stoke-on-Trent mushroomed into the great metropolis of British pottery manufacturing that it still is today.

Early techniques

There are several different types of pottery, including earthenware, stoneware, porcelain and bone china. Each one has its own distinctive characteristics based on the ingredients and the manner of firing and decoration, but the aristocrat of them all is porcelain, which was in the main responsible for the growth of the modern industry.

Until the seventeenth century, the secret of making fine white porcelain, for a long time a Chinese speciality, was unknown in Europe. Increasing imports of Chinese work, mainly through the Dutch East India Company, led European potters to try all sorts of experiments in imitation of this fine oriental ware. The discovery of the secret of making true hard porcelain is usually credited to Friedrich Bottger of the Meissen factory in Germany. Sèvres were also soon making porcelain in France, and in England a Plymouth chemist, William Cookworthy, discovered the art, which consists in simple terms of fusing kaolin with alabaster at extremely high temperatures.

English manufacturers soon modified this process by using the ash of burned animal bones as their calcareous flux. The resulting ware was called 'bone China', which has been universally adopted in Britain and has remained virtually exclusive to this country.

Wedgwood and his followers

The early English factories were widely distributed – at Bow and Chelsea, Bristol and Derby, Worcester and Coalport, among

Above: Edward Davis's statue of Josiah Wedgwood outside the railway station at Stoke-on-Trent. It was unveiled in 1863. A bronze copy stands outside the modern Wedgwood factory at Barlaston.

other places. Although pottery making had been a continuous tradition in Staffordshire, it was not until Josiah Wedgwood set up his business at Burslem in 1759 that the area began its rise to fame and fortune. Josiah was by no means the first Wedgwood to make pottery here. His family had been potters for many years, but it was he who gave a new impetus to the industry.

Ironically enough, porcelain was not then and has never been since, high on the list of Wedgwood's products, but his business skills and influence played an important part in the growth of the Potteries. The demand for his popular cream-coloured earthenware, boosted by royal patronage and then shrewdly renamed 'Queen's Ware', led to expansion and mechanization under steam power, and laid the foundations of pottery making on an industrial scale.

Other ambitious potters established factories in the 'five towns' of Tunstall, Burslem, Hanley, Fenton and Longton, which eventually combined to become the modern city of Stoke-on-Trent. Josiah Spode, Thomas Minton, William Copeland and Job Ridgeway were among the more successful and enduring names of potters who were in business in the district in the late eighteenth and early nineteenth centuries. Well over a hundred factories were in operation in the early part of the nineteenth century, and by its end, the number had doubled.

A good many unscrupulous business methods were adopted in the rivalry to produce quality china to satisfy the great demand from all classes of society since tea had become a fashionable beverage. Designs were unrepentantly copied from Meissen and oriental patterns, and small firms cashed in on more famous names by using their trade marks without scruple. Meissen's crossed swords were much copied. One local firm marked its earthenware 'Vedgewood', and another called itself the 'Dresden Porcelain Company.'

Those companies that flourished and prospered were generally the ones that were constantly vigilant in the search for improved techniques, and employed the best modellers and painters. The original design for Wedgwood's famous 'jasperware', with

Left: Thomas Lovatt, one-time chief ornamenter at Wedgwood's Etruria works, shown ornamenting a Portland vase around 1898. This style of vase is named after the Greek two-handled vase discovered in the seventeenth century and owned by the Duke of Portland before its sale to the British Museum in 1946.

Right: Trimming dishes, and placing tea-cups in 'saggars'. Clay wares may be trimmed or 'fettled' before firing. Wares were placed in saggars, made of refractory clay, for the firing process, the saggars being stacked high in the ovens.

Above: Fine specimens of vessels by Wedgwood (top), Minton (centre) and Spode (bottom). The Wedgwood vase is of jasperware, and features the Nine Muses in white relief. The Minton china bowl and cover was part of a service made for the Emperor of Austria. The Spode ice pail is in blue and gold with hand-painted landscapes.

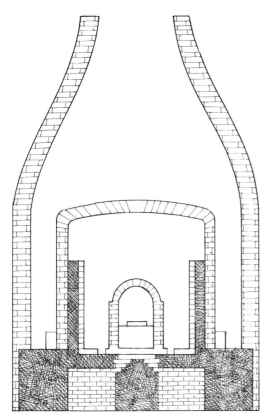

Above: Diagram of bottle kiln. The outer shell was called the 'hovel'. The inner part was the oven, in which pottery was fired by heat distributed evenly from four fire-mouths.

Above: A marl hole or quarry with the potteries of Longton, in 1905. Marl is soil formed of clay and limestone, and the presence of suitable clay for earthenware accounts for the concentration of the industry in the area.

Right: Pottery stacked in a muffle kiln, used for firing ware decorated after normal glazing. Muffle ovens were smaller than other types and firing was done at lower temperatures.

its white classical relief on blue or green backgrounds, was made by the sculptor John Flaxman. Mintons employed several well-known French artists. Thomas Minton himself, who was trained as an engraver, is believed to have originated the famous 'Willow Pattern' for Spode before setting up his own company.

Not all the Potteries' activity was devoted to fine ornaments and tableware, of course. At Hanley the Twyford factory became famous for its sanitary ware, and other products were no less important. Mintons became well known for their ceramic tiles. Perhaps because the potters were aware that the new streamlined mass-production of their goods tended to damage the image of artist and craftsman creating fine pieces, individually modelled and painted, they came to dislike the word 'factory' and called their establishments 'pot banks'.

Technical developments

The basic process of making pottery consists of compressing the clay to remove air bubbles, then moulding it to the required form either by 'throwing' on a potter's wheel, or by shaping it in a mould. It is then fired in a kiln at various temperatures according to the type of pottery being made, to produce a hard and relatively impermeable article.

Glazing is applied for decorative purposes and to increase impermeability. Earthenware was glazed at one time by throwing salt into the kiln where it formed a vitrified surface on the pottery being fired. China and porce-

The Potteries scene today

Stoke-on-Trent has a kind of self-congratulatory air about its prosperous past which is as impressive in its own peculiar red-brick fashion as the architectural pride of the Cotswold wool towns.

The Wedgwood Memorial Institute stands on the site of Josiah Wedgwood's first factory, and there is a statue of the great man above the porch. Another statue of him greets the visitor emerging from the railway station.

Several local buildings were erected at the expense of the town's wealthy potters, such as Hartshill's Holy Trinity Church, built by Herbert Minton, son of the famous firm's founder. Herbert became a local M.P, and a statue of him stands outside the Minton factory. The church of St Peter-ad-Vincula contains memorials to some of the town's most distinguished potters – Wedgwood, Spode, Copeland, William Adams, etc.

Stoke-on-Trent is a much cleaner place today than it used to be, and it has an encouraging look of continuing activity about it. Many of the old buildings still stand, however, and there is an increasing awareness of the heritage, and concern to preserve what remains of this great and famous industry's fascinating past.

lain were originally glazed with a lead glaze which caused a disease commonly known as 'potter's rot'. The Coalport factory in Shropshire introduced a less hazardous feldspathic glaze for which it was awarded the Royal Society of Arts Gold Medal in 1820.

Modern methods have made the old bottle kilns redundant, and most of them have disappeared, along with the permanent haze. Pottery is now fired in automatic tunnel kilns run on electricity, pottery for firing being passed through them on small trucks, and although many of the smoke-blackened terraced house remain, Stoke-on-Trent is a smokeless zone today. Much amalgamation has taken place in recent years, combining smaller companies under the umbrellas of giant industrial groups.

Where to go

Gladstone Pottery at Longton was named after the statesman, who laid the foundation stone of the Wedgwood Institute in 1863. It is now a museum of the industry, where processes of pottery making can be seen in genuine working conditions.

The Minton works has a fine museum exhibiting products of their famous name from its earliest days to the present.

Also worthy of mention here is the Coalport Museum in Shropshire, where remaining parts of the old works are preserved as a working museum by the Ironbridge Gorge Museum Trust. Coalport production was transferred to Staffordshire after the First World War, but the firm began production on the banks of the Severn in the 1790s.

Agriculture

Parts of the West Midlands are among the richest agricultural land in Britain, and the landscape reflects the early and successful preoccupation in this region with the provision of food, but the variety of the local scene is remarkable. Any journey to west or south from Birmingham soon leaves behind the smoking factory chimneys and carries the traveller through hills and valleys, fields and meadows where man worked at growing crops and raising animals long before anyone thought of words like 'industry' and 'mass production'.

Patterns of farming

Across much of Staffordshire and the northern half of Shropshire, the red soils of the Midland Plain are largely used for dairy farming. Herds of Friesian cattle in traditionally small flat fields are still a familiar sight, and Milk Marketing Board lorries are familiar sights on the country roads.

In the South Shropshire Hills, thousands of sheep graze the slopes, whilst in Hereford & Worcester the lush pasture land supports the famous Hereford beef cattle, and rich soils produce every kind of crop from corn and hops to plums and cider apples. The Vale of Evesham is particularly famous for its vast orchards and market gardening land.

Above: An end-over-end butter churn of the late nineteenth century.

Below: The Working Farm Museum at Acton Scott, Shropshire, where nineteenth-century arable farming techniques are demonstrated with steam-powered machinery. Here, threshing is seen in progress.

Farther south, in the Cotswold Hills, sheep farming is a centuries-old occupation which has contributed much to the appearance of towns and villages as well as to the open country. In this great centre of the wool trade in Elizabethan times, rich merchants built the fine churches of Cotswold stone, and the Enclosure Acts brought the building of dry-stone walls round fields and meadows which are such a distinctive feature of this delightful area.

Changing farming practice

Arable farming is bringing the most far-reaching changes to the landscape today. As machinery replaces manpower on the land, hedges and trees are being uprooted to create fields and make more economical use of giant agricultural machines. The modernization of farms and their buildings goes on apace, and picturesque old barns and farmyards are being replaced by concreted yards and milking sheds and tall metal silos. None of these changes can be said to improve the landscape, but efficient food production in an over-populated country must take precedence over purely aesthetic considerations.

Where to go

18th century hop kilns can be seen around Bishops Frome, Hereford & Worcester (B4214 south of Bromyard).

The famous mill at Bibury, Gloucestershire, is maintained as a museum of cornmilling. It is on A433 between Burford and Cirencester (where the Royal Agricultural College has its headquarters).

At Bemborough, Gloucestershire, is the Cotswold Farm Park, run by Joe Henson, who has succeeded in breeding farm animals similar to various historical varieties, and who preserves rare breeds in danger of extinction. The farm is near Temple Guiting, off B4077 between Broadway and Stow-on-the-Wold.

The Acton Scott Working Farm Museum in Shropshire (off A49 Ludlow–Shrewsbury road) preserves and exhibits animals and equipment used on a typical farm of a century ago.

Brewing

The brewing of beer is an ancient and very widespread practice, but one of its chief centres today is Burton-on-Trent in Staffordshire, where at one time ninety per cent of the working population was employed in the breweries.

The ancient Egyptians are known to have made beer from barley, so the beverage had venerable origins long before the British became addicted to it. Ale-houses made their own beer, in cellars or outhouses, for centuries before brewing became a large-scale commercial enterprise, but Burton-on-Trent's pre-eminence in the industry originates from the discovery, attributed to a thirteenth-century monk, that water pumped from the local sandstone after seeping through gypsum deposits gave beer an excellent flavour.

Above: The ale bank – casks of ale available for delivery – at the Bass Shobnall Maltings, Burton-on-Trent. These buildings are now part of Allied Breweries.

Modern brewing

William Worthington and William Bass were among the first industrialists to capitalize on this fact in the mid-eighteenth century, when the Trent had been made navigable and an export market was opened to them in Russia, India and elsewhere. It is said that Catherine the Great of Russia was 'immoderately fond' of ale from Burton, while the term 'I.P.A' (India Pale Ale) was originally used for beer brewed specially for the Indian market. The familiar red Bass triangle was the first trade mark to be registered under the 1875 Trade Marks Act.

Brewing in the simplest terms consists of three stages once the barley has been converted to malt. The liquid produced by steeping malt in hot water is first boiled with hops. Then it is put in large vessels where yeast is added, the resulting fermentation converting sugar to alcohol. It is then cleaned and stored in casks for a time which varies according to the requirements of the final product. Pale and bitter ales require longer storage than mild ales.

Burton-on-Trent had about forty breweries towards the end of the nineteenth century, and their transport requirements produced a conglomeration of railway lines crossing the town's streets in every direction. The growing impatience of motorists held up at level crossings was not relieved until 1960 when the A38 by-pass opened.

Above: The final outcome of hop- and barley-growing, malting, brewing, coopering, glass-making and bottling.

In recent years, much amalgamation has taken place to form giant industrial groups from many of the smaller companies, and the modest beginnings of Bass and Worthington have grown to the sizeable concern of the Bass Charrington Group, but the imposing town houses of their founders can still be seen in High Street.

A craft closely associated with breweries in the past was that of the cooper. Sometimes in the old days itinerant coopers went from brewery to brewery, but later they were employed by the breweries to make casks of oak, which were always considered best for storing beer until metal casks came into common use, partly as a result of the high price of imported timber.

Where to go

A 19th century building of the Bass company at Burton-on-Trent has been converted into a museum of the brewing industry. The history of the industry is shown, and exhibits include a model brewery. Many of the town's old maltings can be seen in the museum, together with their unmistakable kilns.

The Ansells Brewery of Allied Breweries, at Aston Cross, Birmingham, arranges guided tours on some working afternoons by arrangement.

Woollen cloth

Next to the limestone of which their towns and villages are built, nothing has shaped the modern appearance of the Cotswolds more than the woollen industry. A trade agreement on cloth exports was made by King Offa of Mercia with Charlemagne in the eighth century, and various royal and monastic sheep farms existed in medieval times. Villages would be demolished by wealthy monasteries in order to create new pasture land, and great markets grew up for wool trading. Cotswold sheep were famous for their large size and thick white fleeces, and foreign buyers placed their orders for wool even before the sheep were shorn.

The shearing was the great annual event. For most of the year, the labour force required for running a sheep farm was small – the shepherds were the important people. But when shearing time came, every able-bodied person was brought in to help, and itinerant workers found employment for the short season. The completion of shearing was followed by village feasts and much rustic merry-making.

Above: Sheep shearing with the sprung-handle shears which were in use for centuries before the advent of electrical shearing machinery.

Below: The fulling stocks at Cam Mills, near Dursley. The mill was rebuilt in 1815 and these stocks, powered by a beam engine, were built at that time. The fulling stocks have since been dismantled.

Growing importance of the cloth trade

Before the discovery of the 'fulling' process, by which the weaver's open mesh is shrunk and thickened into cloth, the finishing method was a laborious process of treading the cloth for hours in an alkaline solution. Those who did it were called 'walkers' or 'tuckers'. Fulling mills are first recorded in the late twelfth century. They were dependent upon water power, by which hammers were driven to pound the fabric in water and the clay substance which became known as 'fuller's earth'. Many mills were built beside Cotswold streams from that time onward. They helped to enable English clothiers to beat foreign competition in both price and quality, and by Elizabethan times the European market was dominated by English cloth rather than the formerly predominant Flemish product.

The manufacturing system was that capitalist clothiers bought the wool, passed it out to spinners and weavers who worked in their homes, and then the clothiers carried out the fulling in their own mills.

Plain white broadcloth was the stuff with which so many fortunes were made by clothiers and merchants, and their fine houses of Cotswold stone still stand as monuments to their new self-regard, whilst the churches they built – often said to have been 'built on the backs of sheep' – contain equally impressive memorials to their good works.

Working conditions

As usual, however, the people who did all the hard work – the cottagers who wove millions of fleeces into the cloth that made their masters rich men – did not always benefit from the wealth they created. Over the centuries various causes of depression in this huge domestic industry brought hardships – the imposition of the Wool Tax; increased mechanization; experiments in methods and marketing. Women and children had to carry out carding and spinning to supplement meagre family incomes from weaving, and children became deformed and diseased by long working hours in unhealthy conditions.

Eventually, exploitation led to the inevitable results – strikes, riots and the stealing of bread. The grave of one alleged rioter against power looms can still be seen in the churchyard at Trowbridge, Wiltshire. Thomas Helliker was nineteen years old when he was hanged at Salisbury in 1803.

The demands of a rapidly increasing national population for meat led to changes in the physical nature of Cotswold sheep. These in turn affected the cloth industry. Cross-breeding and richer pastures produced the well-known 'Cotswold Lion', which produced a lot of meat but a coarser wool, much of it suitable only for worsted articles.

By the advent of the nineteenth century, Yorkshire was taking precedence in cloth manufacture. The local markets declined, and many people in the Cotswolds, put out of work by the closure of local mills, migrated to the north of England. The Cotswold streams were not big or powerful enough to cope with the demands of mass-production machinery, and by the time steam power came, Yorkshire had taken the bulk of the cloth industry away from the Cotswolds.

Above: Detail of fulling stocks in a water-powered mill. The mechanization of the fulling process took place as long ago as the late twelfth century.

Above: A typical eighteenth-century weaver's cottage of Cotswold limestone at South Woodchester, near Stroud.

Where to go

Weavers' cottages, fulling mills and clothiers' mills can still be seen throughout the Cotswold area. Trowbridge and Bradford-on-Avon in Wiltshire, Uley and Nailsworth in Gloucestershire, are among rewarding places. Sheppard's Mill at Uley (B4066 near Dursley) where the famous Uley Blue cloth was made, was owned by Edward Sheppard, who built Gatcombe Park, now Princess Anne's home. Cloth is still manufactured in this area. Scarlet tunics for the Guards, green cloth for billiard tables, and white cassocks for the Pope are among the region's products.

Painswick and Chipping Campden are among well known Cotswold places where the prosperity of clothiers and merchants is evident in the stylish architecture of their town houses.

East Midlands

Apart from Derbyshire's Peak District, the area included in this section is one of the least visited parts of Britain, and so much of its industry is unfamiliar to many people. Its natural raw materials, such as lead in Derbyshire, iron in Northamptonshire, coal in Warwickshire and Nottinghamshire, and stone in Leicestershire, have provided some employment for centuries, but manufacturing industry was created in the region to occupy vast numbers of employees, both male and female, in the red-brick factory environment that is so familiar to east Midlanders. Hosiery, lace, boots and shoes have brought long prosperity to local workers in modern times, whilst the area has several smaller and more localized industries which are of unusual interest though very little known. One of the scenic features of the rolling Midland landscape is the ever-present church spire, and church bells can be heard ringing across wolds and meadows. Many of these bells were cast and tuned by Taylors of Loughborough, and I remember the late Mr Paul Taylor, some years ago, tapping out his pipe in a miniature inverted bell on his desk and telling me that some people who claim to make bells only make gongs. He was an accomplished musician, as well as an engineer, and his company's musical instruments are no insignificant part of Britain's industrial heritage, though hardly ever mentioned in books about the nation's products.

Louth

A46

A16

Lincoln

Horncastle

Skegness

ark

LINCOLNSHIRE

A17

Boston

Grantham

A1

Spalding

A16

Oakham

Stamford

Corby

Kettering

Vellingborough

0   10   20   miles

Hosiery

The growth of the hosiery trade since the seventeenth century has been the dominating influence on the red brick towns and villages of the western half of Leicestershire. Although responsible for a rather dreary landscape, it has until recent years been a highly successful industry, largely accounting for Leicester itself being named by the League of Nations in the 1930's as 'Europe's most prosperous city'. But it came to that exalted position through much suffering and injustice.

A Nottinghamshire curate is usually credited with the invention that created the hosiery industry. The Rev. William Lee of Calverton is said to have been provoked – by watching his wife knitting stockings by hand – into working out a means of making the job quicker and easier. He invented the stocking frame in 1589, with a separate needle for each loop, so as to make a whole row of stitches at one operation, instead of casting all the loops on to one needle. The knitting was still a laborious business, as thread had to be placed over each needle by hand, and it took two centuries to mechanize this operation successfully. Nevertheless, William Lee and his wife can be said to have given birth to one of Britain's great industries.

The Framework Knitters

Nottinghamshire was the first county to build and exploit the wooden stocking frame, but Leicestershire soon overtook it. The demand for stockings was from both sexes then, of course, and the clatter of stocking frames could be heard in more than a hundred Leicestershire towns and villages, bringing the poor from the country areas to work in what was at that time still a cottage industry. The knitters valued their independence and many were Nonconformists. Leicester was to become known as the 'Metropolis of Heresy', and chapels of the Baptist, Methodist, Unitarian and other persuasions sprang up everywhere.

Technical improvements came fast. In 1758 Jedediah Strutt developed the mechanization of rib-knitting, and continuous ingenuity in the trade led to greater versatility of the machinery. Warp knitting came in 1775, using a separate thread for each needle

instead of the same thread for the whole row as in weft knitting. This produced a fabric which could be cut up into pieces like cloth and sewn together to make garments.

Clouds of discontent began to loom on the horizon, however, as opportunities for frame-owners and their agents grew. The stocking frames were hired out by their owners to 'masters' or middlemen, and it was they who employed the workers to operate the machines in their homes, to earn increasingly scanty wages at piece-work rates. The knitters themselves had to pay a weekly rent for the machines out of their earning, as well as paying a woman to seam the stockings, and if the machines broke down, they had to be their own mechanics, with the consequent loss of income in time spent on repairs. Added to that, iniquitous practices by the masters led to dire hardships among the knitters, who sat at their frames for thirteen or fourteen hours a day to scrape together perhaps four shillings a week.

The Luddite Rebellion

Several circumstances eventually combined to bring the Midlands framework knitters to

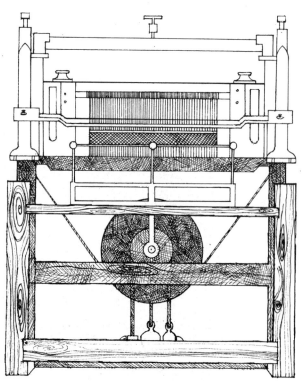

the brink of starvation. The advent of trousers for men reduced the demand for stockings. Disastrous harvests put the price of bread beyond the knitters' means. Increasing mechanization took work away from them. The Napoleonic Wars put an end to exports. 'Cut-ups', as the warp-knitted garments were called, were the last straw for the hard-pressed hosiery workers.

The first signs of revolt came in 1773, when a mob in Leicester destroyed a newly-invented machine which they saw as a threat to their livelihood. The so-called Luddite Rebellion, which spread over Leicestershire, Derbyshire, Nottinghamshire and Yorkshire, is commonly supposed to have taken its name from a half-witted youth at Anstey, Leicestershire, named Ned Ludd, who smashed a stocking frame in retaliation for a punishment he had received. In two years, Luddite mobs wrecked a thousand machines. A mob in Leicester stoned the Mayor, who died from his injuries. At Loughborough, a factory watchman was shot and wounded during a riot in which fifty-three machines were wrecked.

The government, with its mind full of the

Above: A framework knitter at work. Taken at Kegworth, north Leicestershire, in 1950, the photograph shows Mr Pymm, the last man to operate a hand stocking frame in the county.

Left: Diagram showing the structure of an early stocking frame. Lee's original invention produced fabric with a selvedge on both sides, which had to be sewn, but he developed a fashioning method by transferring loops at the edges.

Right: A framework knitters' shop at Wigston, Leicestershire.

consequences of revolution in France, talked of sedition and political insurrection, and made machine breaking a capital offence. Byron's maiden speech in the House of Lords was in protest against this move. He eloquently defended knitters such as he had seen in Nottinghamshire, 'meagre with famine, sullen with despair, careless of a life which your Lordships are perhaps about to value at something less than the price of a stocking frame. ...' Their Lordships were no more impressed, however, than the Commons, where Sir Francis Burdett and Samuel Whitbread made similar protests.

Growth of factory industry

Violence on a large scale subsided towards the middle of the nineteenth century. By this time, many thousands of stocking frames were in operation in Leicestershire alone, and the frame owners were increasingly inclined to build 'shops' where knitters worked on the premises and the masters were eliminated. Some of the early factories can still be found in the region, as well as the old knitters' cottages, with high windows running along the buildings below the eaves

Right: An interior of a Leicestershire hosiery factory in the 1930's, with bobbins of yarn on the floor. A degree of specialization grew up with the factory industry, Derbyshire being noted for silk stockings, Nottinghamshire for cotton, and Leicestershire for worsted.

Below: Diagram of a circular knitting machine. The first such machine, called a 'tricoteur', was invented in 1816 by Sir Marc Brunel. However, only after improvements by the Belgian Peter Claussen and the invention of the latch needle by Townsend did the machine come into widespread use.

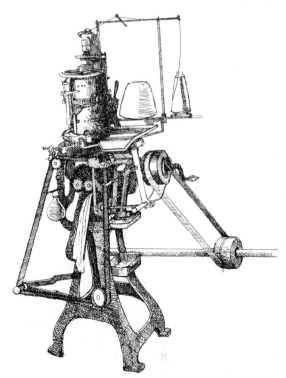

to get maximum light.

Soon power-operated frames began to appear, frame-renting was abolished, and child labour – illegal after 1870 – was replaced by women employees. Gradually the last surviving hand frames found their way into local museums.

A circular machine called a 'tricoteur' invented by Brunel way back in 1816 to produce seamless knitted tubes, only came into general use thirty years later when improvements had been made to it, but then the invention of the latch needle by M. Townsend of Nottingham gave further impetus to circular knitting development.

Soon the knitting process was not merely making seamless or fully-fashioned hosiery, but was capable of producing every kind of garment which had previously been made

sand people, mainly women and girls, and produced three hundred million pairs of stockings a year.

Modern fashions – particularly the mini-skirt – created a demand for tights instead of stockings, and the hosiery industry continued to progress, but despite a machine which can produce a pair of tights in three minutes, and which has been called 'the ultimate in producing a complete garment from a knitting machine', the industry has lately had a hard time against foreign competition.

The visitor may still see multi-coloured bobbins of synthetic yarn in circular motion about their vertical axes through Leicestershire factory windows, but the industry's greatest days are past, and if Leicestershire's hosiery factories are not yet subjects for the archaeologist, at least the landscape of four hundred years of stocking making is a distinctive part of our heritage, for it has shaped the lives of the people as well as the look of the places. Every village which has been busy in the hosiery trade would qualify as a town in many other parts of Britain, and the dull but clean rows of red brick housing and factories are characteristic of one of the least visited industrial areas of Britain.

only by weaving.

In 1857 Luke Barton invented the machine known as the straight bar rotary frame which had a self-acting mechanism for fashioning. By the 1930's Leicestershire hosiery manufacturers employed nearly fifty thou-

Above: The arms of the Framework Knitters, one of the early unions of workers, founded for mutual protection and benefit.

Where to go

The hosiery manufacturing area of west Leicestershire can be reached easily by public or private transport from any part of the country. The Newarke Houses Museum, in The Newarke, Leicester, has knitting machines and other displays of knitting technology.

Framework knitters' cottages survive at Calverton, Nottinghamshire and Hinckley, Leicestershire, while early workshops can still be found at places such as Leicester, Loughborough and Wigston.

At Ruddington, Nottinghamshire (A60 south of Nottingham) a Framework Knitters Museum has been set up in Chapel Street, with old cottages and workshops as well as machinery.

Eighteenth and nineteenth century factories can be seen in Leicester at Bath Lane and Frog Island.

Swithland slate

Right: Sheep farming, Warwickshire.

Overleaf: Magpie Mine, Sheldon, Derbyshire. A bleak reminder of the lead mining industry.

Slate being such an important product of Cornwall and Cumbria, reference to the slate-working industry of Leicestershire is rarely found except in purely local literature, yet it has influenced the Midland scene for centuries, and Swithland slate has a fascination all its own.

Swithland Wood, north west of Leicester on the fringes of Charnwood Forest, is well known in the area as a beauty spot in springtime, when it is carpeted with bluebells. It also contains rain-filled quarry pits which were first worked by the Romans and produced a great deal of slate from the twelfth century until they were finally abandoned in the nineteenth century because of competition from the cheaper (and duller) Welsh product. The slate was also quarried later at Groby and other nearby sites, but it all went under the name of Swithland, though it was often coarser in grain than the original.

Swithland slates were being used for roofing town houses in the locality as early as the fourteenth century, when country cottages were still thatched, but by the eighteenth century nearly all local housing was roofed with the rough-hewn slates of variable colour which can still be seen in forest villages, gleaming beautifully after a shower. Slates were laid so that their size increased downwards, the largest slates being at the eaves, and as they weathered, they attracted lichens to add to their colourful appearance. The slates were mostly of a blue-grey colour, with greenish tints, but occasionally purple, too. A group of cottages at Woodhouse Eaves is built entirely of slate-stone from the Swithland quarries, and is most attractive.

At the beginning of the nineteenth century the quarrymen were paid half-a-crown a day to drill and blast great blocks of slate that might weigh well over a ton, then raise them to the surface by tackle and horse wheel. There the sawyers would reduce them to manageable proportions.

Headstone art

Slate was also used for kitchen sinks, mantelpieces, millstones and cheese presses, but perhaps most noteworthy was the widespread use of Swithland slate for tombstones, which has given many Leicestershire churchyards a particular distinction. This hard laminated slate was found to be an eminently suitable material for intricate engraving, lasting much longer than slabs of limestone or sandstone which weathered badly and became illegible in a short time. As it was also lighter in weight, it was cheaper and easier to transport than other stone, so it was favoured all over Leicestershire and in adjoining counties. The slabs were about six feet in length, as a rule, with about five feet showing above ground. They were polished on the face only at first, but later slabs were given smooth surfaces on both front and back. In the eighteenth and nineteenth centuries, particularly, the engraving of Swithland slate headstones became an important local art form which can still be studied without difficulty.

Swithland's church of St Leonard has one of the oldest surviving slate monuments in

Above: Sarcophagus to Sir Joseph Danvers in Swithland churchyard. The stone wall encloses consecrated ground. Sir Joseph's dog is on the outside of the wall, but in the same tomb!

Left: These cottages in Maplewell Road, Woodhouse Eaves, are built of rubble from the Swithland quarries, as well as having roofs of Swithland slate, and show the high aesthetic qualities of the local material when compared with the uniform grey of Welsh slate.

Left: Bell casting, Leicestershire. The foundry of John Taylor & Co. at Loughborough has been making finely tuned bells here since 1840 for all parts of the world.

Above: One of the overgrown and rain-filled quarry pits in Swithland Wood, where slate was quarried in Roman times, and again for six hundred years from the thirteenth to nineteenth centuries. The last quarry stopped working in 1887. In the Stuart period, a Swithland slate roof was a must for a large house: by Georgian times, even cottages were roofed in rough-cast slates from these pits.

Left: The wall monument to five children of Sir Joseph Danvers, in Swithland church, was made of Swithland slate in mid-eighteenth century. The central shield with inscription is of brass.

its graveyard (1673), and one of the most spectacular inside – a hanging wall-monument to the children of Sir John Danvers, which Sir Nikolaus Pevsner has called 'a tour de force of the slate workers'. Sir Joseph Danvers is buried half inside and half outside the church. He refused to be buried on consecrated ground if his favourite dog could not share his grave, so an eccentric compromise was reached! His sarcophagus of 1745 is a much-decorated piece of work by John Hind.

The Local Craftsmen

The local men who made these monuments were sometimes schoolmasters who taught writing in village schools, or sign-painters and other craftsmen who engraved headstones in their spare time. Henry Castledine of Syston was a schoolmaster; Robert Waddington of Clipston was the parish clerk. The work of many others is known, such as that of William Charles of Wymeswold, Jonathan Buckerfield of Leicester, and William Bonser of Burton Overy. The Hind family produced a long line of slate engravers whose work appears in several Leicestershire villages. Robert Hind of Swithland had a part-ownership of the quarries at the beginning of the nineteenth century.

In most cases, the calligraphic inscriptions and assorted motifs on the slates were incised, but occasionally they are found in relief, the surface of the slabs reduced by ambitious craftsmen to highlight their designs. These monuments to the slate industry can be found scattered from one end of the county to the other.

Where to go

The churchyards of St Margaret and St Mary de Castro in Leicester are rich in Swithland slate headstones, as are those at Loughborough and Narborough, whilst many other churchyards throughout the county have smaller numbers.

Swithland slate roofs can also be seen, particularly in Charnwood Forest villages such as Woodhouse Eaves and Newtown Linford. Swithland Wood stretches north from B5330 towards Woodhouse Eaves.

Lead mining

Lead deposits have been mined in several parts of Great Britain over the centuries since the Roman occupation, and have left their marks on the landscape of the Mendips (Somerset) and the Stiperstones (Shropshire) among other places. But nowhere is the story of lead mining more dramatic than in the Peak District of Derbyshire, where great grassy scars run across country for miles. These mounds are the waste-heaps resulting from exploitation of the long vertical walls of mineral deposits, called 'rakes'. Each one is identified by name – Tideslow Rake, Deep Rake, Watersaw Rake, etc. A small rake is called a 'scrin'.

There is little definite evidence that the Romans worked the lead deposits in Derbyshire extensively, but it is almost inconceivable that they did *not* do so. Silver was the chief currency of their world, and it was obtained from lead, the latter forming an important by-product for use in water-pipes, coffins and so on. The yield of silver in Derbyshire was low, but lead mining continued into the present century.

Above: The top of a disused mine shaft, of which thousands remain in the Peak District.

Below: The nineteenth-century engine house and chimney of Magpie Mine, at Sheldon, are among the buildings preserved by the Peak District Mines Historical Society.

Medieval development

In the Middle Ages Derbyshire lead was supplied for the roof of Canterbury Cathedral, and probably for Ely Cathedral too. The lead mining region was divided up into 'liberties', in which miners could explore and extract lead under strictly controlled conditions. Techniques of mining and separating the ore were gradually improved, particularly by German engineers who came in the sixteenth century, and Wirksworth became the centre for marketing the lead. When Defoe visited the town, he noticed that there was little trade in it except 'what relates to the lead works', and this provided one of the most graphic descriptions of his whole travels, with observations about men clad entirely in leather working sixty fathoms deep for five pence a day.

The local mining and trading laws were administered by Great Barmote courts, with the King's Barmaster presiding over twenty-four jurors. The independence of these courts was jealously guarded for centuries, and they had power to settle all disputes

arising in the industry, which was no small task, for the miners were 'of a strange, turbulent, quarrelsome temper...'

Techniques and decline

The extracted ore, before being carried by pack-horse to the smelting mills, had to be crushed and separated from the rock in which it was found. This was done at the surface by women and boys using flat hammers called 'buckers', until power-driven 'stamps' were introduced. Then the ore was transferred to 'buddles'. These processed the crushed material under running water so that the heavy ore remained and the residue was washed away.

Methods of smelting the ore varied according to time and place, but in the Peak District the early charcoal-fired 'boles' eventually gave way to shaft furnaces and then coal-fired reverberatory 'cupold' furnaces. The smelting industry migrated to the area east of the Derwent to use the more abundant timber for firing the hearths. The new sites were closer to trade routes and the ports from which one of Britain's most valuable exports was at that time shipped.

As the uses of lead increased – for plumbing and roofing, underground gas and water pipes, the manufacture of paint and sulphuric acid – so the industry expanded, and by the middle of the eighteenth century there were probably five thousand men working deep in the earth to dig out the lead ore of the Peak. It has been estimated that five or six thousand tons of lead were being extracted per year around 1789. Much of the experience gained by lead miners over centuries of operations proved invaluable to the newer coal-mining industry.

Water was clearly of the utmost importance to the lead miners, and if natural streams were not conveniently flowing nearby, artificial channels would be cut, from bogs or ponds, to provide running water. Ironically, however, water was to bring about the downfall of Peak District lead mining through flooding. Although elaborate drainage systems and pumping engines were employed in the mines, the high cost of keeping the workings dry became uneconomical when foreign competition forced lead prices down.

Dangers and remains

Lead mining was hard and dangerous work for the men who toiled in the bowels of the earth all their working lives, often for small rewards, but they at least knew what they were doing. There are great dangers today for those who explore the remains of this industry in Derbyshire and elsewhere. Thousands of mine shafts pepper the Peak lead-mining region, and most of them are uncovered and unprotected. Some old mines can be entered and explored, but this should never be done without guidance.

The Peak District today

Above ground, the evidence of lead mining is easily seen. The spoil-heaps are but one aspect of a desolate landscape where man has exploited the earth's riches for nearly two thousand years. Engine houses, furnaces, winding gear, and the roofless 'coes' – huts where miners kept their equipment – are among the industrial relics of the Derbyshire Dome where, according to some experts, there is still as much lead ore remaining to be extracted as has been mined in the last thousand years.

Top: Ruined engine house at Old End Mine, Crich.

Below: Manual winding gear, called a 'stowse', above a shaft at Magpie Mine, Sheldon.

Above: A typical 'rake' in the lead mining district of Derbyshire. These long fissures, where miners extracted lead ore from veins below the surface, sometimes stretch for several miles across the landscape of the Carboniferous limestone where lead occurs.

Where to go

The Peak District Mines Historical Society (headquarters at Bakewell, Derbyshire) is responsible for care of monuments of the industry. Many sites are open to visitors, the best known of which is Magpie Mine at Sheldon, where buildings, engines and mine shafts are preserved.

At Lathkilldale, Over Haddon, an engine house and other mine workings can be seen as well as Mandale Sough, a drainage channel one mile long which took twenty-three years to dig. (By the time it was finished, the mine workings had gone lower than the levels it was designed to drain.)

Sheldon lies 3½ miles west of Bakewell on unclassified road from Ashford on A6. Over Haddon is 2 miles south west of Bakewell, on an unclassified road off B5055.

The Peak District Mines Museum is at Matlock Bath.

Bell-casting

The making of bells is not a trade which has had much effect on the visible landscape, but the result contributes a great deal to the character of British towns and countryside, where church bells ring out across streets and meadows to call the faithful to worship.

Bell-founding was an English craft that developed locally in the Middle Ages. Most of the bell-makers were itinerant artisans, who cast their bells on site, near the church for which the bells had been commissioned. Fields near churches and cathedrals can still be found with names like Bell Field, Bell Pit, and so on.

John Taylor and Company

One such craftsman was John Taylor, who came from Oxford in 1839 to recast the church bells at Loughborough. He liked the place, and decided to set up permanent premises there. Nearly a century and a half later, John Taylor and Company are still casting bells in one of the only two foundries left in Britain; the other is in London.

How bells are cast

In early times, bells (which were nearly always small hand-bells) were made of thin plates of iron shaped and riveted together. Various other metals and alloys were used subsequently, including silver, antimony and brass, but modern bell-metal, proved by long experience to be most satisfactory in tone, is an alloy of copper and tin, in a proportion of about 4:1. Any other mixture might look like a bell, but it won't ring.

Modern bell-casting is only marginally different from the perfected method which has been in use for four hundred years. A clay mould of the inside of the bell was made first – around a brick foundation if the bell to be made was a large one. Then a layer of beeswax was built up around this to the shape and thickness of the finished bell. After that, a further mould of clay was packed round it, and the whole thing was baked. The result of this was that the clay hardened and the beeswax melted, leaving a space between the inner core or 'crook' and

Right: The first illustration shows molten bell-metal being poured into the modern type of mould at a temperature of 1100°C. The second illustration (far right) shows bells ready for tuning, which is done by removing metal from the inside rim to give rich musical tones.

Left: A large bell in course of completion at Taylors' foundry. It was made for the National Cathedral, Washington DC.

the outer shell or 'cope' of clay, into which the bell-metal was then poured and allowed to set. This process was called by the French *cire perdue* 'lost wax'. When the clay was broken away, the bell was ready for tuning and polishing. Tuning was done extremely accurately by chipping the inside rim.

Taylor's bells

Bells made by Taylors grace many British cathedrals and churches. The most famous of Taylor's bells, however, is perhaps 'Great Paul', made for St Paul's Cathedral in 1881. It was the largest bell in the British Commonwealth, measuring nine and a half feet across its mouth and weighing 17 tons. It took ten days to transport the bell to London by road, with the director of the transport contractors leading the way on a tricycle.

The war memorial in Loughborough's Queen's Park is a unique brick-built campanile, erected in 1923, housing 47 perfectly-tuned bells cast by Taylors. They vary in size from seven inches to six feet four inches (four tons, four hundredweight) and Sir Edward Elgar composed a Memorial Chime for the first recital, which was given by the carillonneur of Bruges, M. Anton Brees.

Bells from the Loughborough foundry can be heard throughout the world, in Florida and Texas, Bombay and Singapore, New Zealand and Australia; not only in churches, but in town halls, universities and other secular buildings.

Above: 'Great Paul' on its journey to London in May 1882. The transport contractor led the very important passenger on its ten-day journey from Loughborough to London.

Where to go

Loughborough is on A6, eleven miles north of Leicester. Bells have been transported by canal, road and rail from John Taylor & Company's premises here (which are not normally open to the public) to all parts of Britain. Among English cathedrals with bells from Loughborough are Chester, Lichfield, Lincoln, and Winchester.

Great Paul is in the south west tower of St Paul's Cathedral, and is rung for five minutes every day at one o'clock by an automatic timing device.

Lace making

Nottingham's modern lace industry arose out of attempts to bring to hand lace making the kind of mechanization which the Midland manufacturers had brought to the hosiery trade. In the second half of the eighteenth century, the stocking frame was used to make a net which could be used as the background for pillow lace, but this was not a success, and it was left for John Heathcoat to invent the bobbin net machine in 1808, which was the foundation for all lace manufacture by mechanical means. Nottingham soon became its undisputed capital, with the trade heavily concentrated in the ancient part of the borough.

Further boosts were given to the local industry by an advanced machine invented by John Leavers, and by the application to this of the Jacquard pattern apparatus in 1834, which enabled intricate designs to be made. Steam-powered factories began to appear some years afterwards, and by 1885 Nottingham alone had 2,250 lace-making machines at work. A great programme of house-building led to a nation-wide fashion for lace curtains, and expansion of the trade continued with the demand for lace bridal veils, dress fabrics, table covers and all sorts of lace trimmings. By the second half of the nineteenth century, ten per cent of Nottinghamshire's working population was engaged in the lace trade.

The other side of the coin

The rapid growth of the lace and other industries was not entirely beneficial to Nottingham, however. The town had been regarded as one of the finest in England before the Industrial Revolution. One traveller described it as 'Paradise Restored' in the seventeenth century, and Celia Fiennes regarded it as the neatest town she had ever seen. But by 1845, it was one of the most squalid manufacturing towns in the country.

The Luddite riots already described on page 106–108, had affected the lace trade as well as the hosiery trade, and were indeed much more serious in Nottinghamshire than in Leicestershire. The gangs of men purported to receive their instructions from a 'General Ludd' who (like an earlier local bandit of more widespread fame) supposedly had his hide-out in Sherwood Forest.

As the textile industries expanded, and

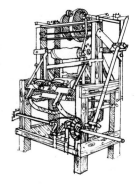

Above: An early example of lace-making machinery. The breakthrough in mechanical lace-making was made by Heathcoat's 'bobbinet', which could imitate hand-made pillow lace.

Below: The finishing room of a Nottinghamshire lace factory between the wars—not a man in sight!

people moved from the rural areas into the town to get employment, every conceivable bit of space had to be used to build houses to accommodate them. Nottingham was unable to expand outwards, because it was almost surrounded by open fields which remained unenclosed in spite of the urgent need for land. So the pressure on space increased, and Nottingham's workers soon found themselves living in appalling and overcrowded slums. The mayor called enclosure an 'unsightly monster', but it was nothing to the unsightly monster that Nottingham became in so short a time, and although the corporation finally achieved enclosure of the common fields in 1845, it was much too late. Not until after the First World War did Nottingham's slums begin to be cleared to make way for the modern city we see today.

Prosperity

One of the results of such frightful congestion in Nottingham itself was a partial dispersal of the lace trade to other towns within easy reach of the main centre, and Beeston, in particular, benefited from this. Trade

Above: The Anglo Scotia lace factory, Beeston, built in Gothic style around 1870.

Below: The Nottingham Lace Market was built in the nineteenth century.

union activity which achieved higher wages for Nottingham workers also contributed to the limited spread of the trade to outlying areas.

Oddly enough, Nottingham's famous bicycle industry also owed something to the lace trade, since engineering firms which made the machinery for lace-making were able to produce cycles quite easily. Many local cycle firms actually evolved from the lace industry, and diversity brought about Nottingham's modern growth and prosperity.

Where to go
In Nottingham itself, the finest monument to the lace trade is the Lace Market not far from the centre of the modern city. It is an ornate commercial precinct built at the height of the industry's 19th century expansion. Nottingham's Industrial Museum, at Wollaton Hall, exhibits lace making machinery and examples of its products, whilst the Museum of Costume and Textiles in Castlegate traces the development of lace making by hand and machine.

A fine lace factory can be seen at Beeston, south of the city, whilst Stapleford has an interesting group of lace makers' cottages in Nottingham Road.

Iron and steel

The presence of iron in the rock in parts of the East Midlands is indicated by the stone-built villages of northern Northamptonshire and eastern Leicestershire. In villages such as Rockingham and Great Easton, and many of those in what used to be Rutland, the stone – which is actually limestone very similar to that of the Cotswold villages – has been turned into rich brown and rust colours by the presence of iron oxide. Corby, the local centre of iron and steel processing, was itself a little village of stone cottages hardly more than a hundred years ago.

Extracting the iron

Deposits of iron in the Jurassic limestone are at relatively shallow levels, and open-cast mining has been used to extract the ore. Around the turn of the century, steam shovels were used to shift the overburden, to be succeeded by electrically-driven excavators and then the enormous walking draglines which cut great scars across the landscape at Weldon, a little to the east of Corby.

At one time, the extracted ironstone was 'calcined' over burning coal on the quarrying site, to remove volatiles from the ore before it was taken to the blast furnaces around Wellingborough and Kettering. The local capacity for smelting was limited at first, and a large proportion of the ore went to Derbyshire. It was of poor quality, and could only be used for basic purposes.

It was the construction of local railway lines in 1879 that revealed the presence of iron deposits near Corby, and production of wrought or 'puddled' iron began on a large scale. The Gilchrist-Thomas process enabled phosphoric ore to be used for steel-making by removing impurities from iron which had previously been considered unsuitable, but although this method was perfected in 1880, the Northamptonshire iron producers were slow to take advantage of it. It worked by an adaptation of the original Bessemer process (see under Wales) adding lime which removed the phosphorous by a chemical reaction, forming calcium phosphate.

Growth of the steel industry

In the 1920's, however, Corby's steel works exploded the stone-built country village into a red brick town of terraced houses and belching chimneys. In 1939, with the threat of war heralding rearmament, Corby pro-

Above: An early steam shovel loading ore into railway wagons for transport from the quarry to blast furnaces for smelting.

Below: Aerial view of the British Steel works at Corby, the main centre of modern iron and steel working in the East Midlands. A new town was built to accommodate the thousands of workers.

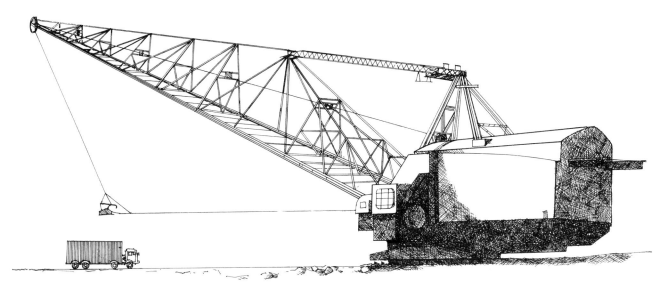

Above: A giant drag-line excavator such as is used in ironstone quarries today. It moves parallel to the rock face to be dug and removes the overburden, depositing it on surfaces where ore has already been extracted.

duced half a million tons of crude steel. Just after the war, the town's population was about 15,000 – ten times what it had been in 1920. With the development of Corby New Town, this figure more than doubled in the next ten years, and by 1960 it was producing nearly a million tons of pig-iron and over a million of steel per year, specializing in steel tubing and the rolled steel from which bicycles are largely made. Stewarts and Lloyds were the chief promoters of Corby's development, and they imported a large contingent of Scottish workers to boost the mushroom growth of the town during the depression, steel being, of course, 'man's work', unlike hosiery, boots and shoes and other East Midlands trades in which large numbers of women are employed.

Young couples came south to new homes and jobs on the Glasgow-Corby train that came to be called the 'honeymoon express', and Hogmanay and Burns Night became annual celebrations in this erstwhile North-amptonshire farming village where the only 'foreigner' to be seen at one time might have been a Jersey cow. Huge optimism was evident in the 1950's, when multi-million-pound expansion schemes were being an-nounced, and a population of a hundred thousand was confidently predicted for Corby by the end of the century.

Now all that has changed. Thirty years on, the British Steel Corporation is in dire straits, and Corby has become a place of dole queues and falling property prices. The bloom has gone out of its cheeks, and it remains to be seen what remains in store for Corby and the rest of the iron and steel industry in the Midlands.

Iron working had been carried on in other parts of the East Midlands on a less ambi-tious scale: for instance at Holwell in Leicestershire and in Lincolnshire. Again the tell-tale colour of the local cottages and churches, in what were once described as pretty villages, indicate the treasure below the soil. The iron deposits around Holwell were worked from the 1870's onwards, and produced 600,000 tons of ore a year at one time, with five blast furnaces in operation at Asfordby.

Where to go

Corby itself is the chief industrial monument of the steel industry in the East Midlands. It is best reached by road via Market Harborough leaving M1 at junction 20; or by A43 from A1 near Stamford.

Old ironstone workings can be seen at Hunsbury Hill, a couple of miles from Northampton to the south west.

If one travels the twenty-five miles or so from Corby to Northampton via Wellingborough and Kettering, instead of by the more direct route, one sees not only the depressing industrial landscape produced by the iron industry, but also the contrasting rural scene which it replaced.

Wales

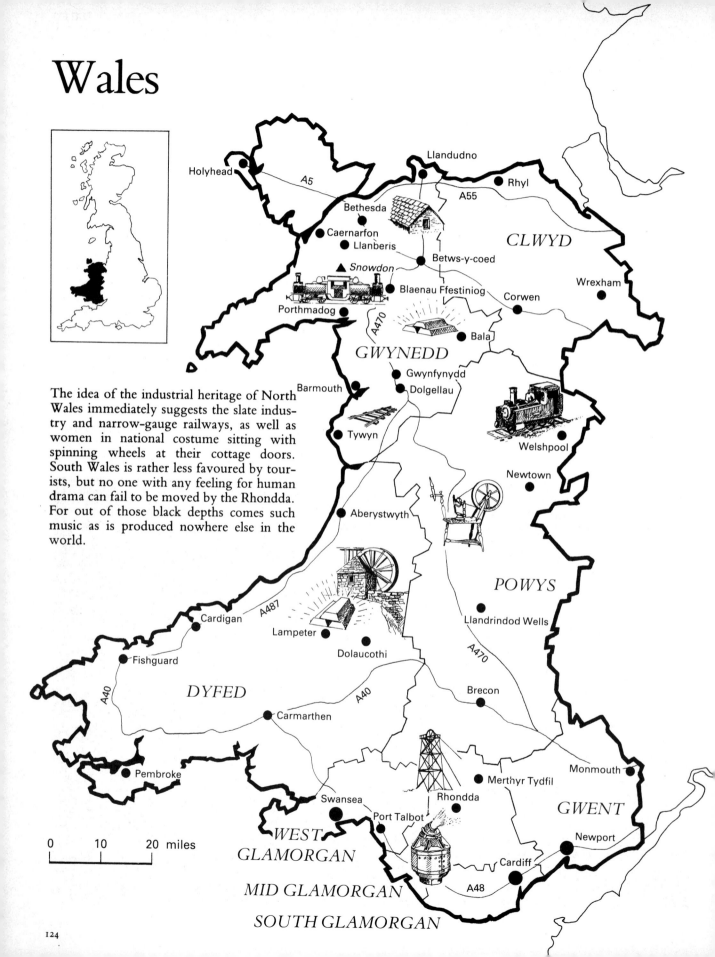

The idea of the industrial heritage of North Wales immediately suggests the slate industry and narrow-gauge railways, as well as women in national costume sitting with spinning wheels at their cottage doors. South Wales is rather less favoured by tourists, but no one with any feeling for human drama can fail to be moved by the Rhondda. For out of those black depths comes such music as is produced nowhere else in the world.

Holyhead

A5

Bethesda

Caernarfon

Llanberis

▲ Snowdon

Porthmadog

Llandudno

Rhyl

A55

Betws-y-coed

Blaenau Ffestiniog

Corwen

Wrexham

CLWYD

Bala

GWYNEDD

Gwynfynydd

Barmouth

Dolgellau

A470

Tywyn

Welshpool

Newtown

Aberystwyth

POWYS

Cardigan

A487

Lampeter

Dolaucothi

Llandrindod Wells

A470

Fishguard

A40

DYFED

A40

Brecon

Carmarthen

Pembroke

Merthyr Tydfil

Monmouth

Swansea

Rhondda

Port Talbot

GWENT

Newport

WEST GLAMORGAN

Cardiff

MID GLAMORGAN

A48

SOUTH GLAMORGAN

0   10   20 miles

Coal mining

The Rhondda valleys and neighbouring mining areas of South Wales form what is perhaps the most ravaged and tragic industrial landscape in Britain. Coal mining on a large scale was relatively late in coming to Wales, but when it did, its rapid transformation of the landscape was spectacular. No one alive now can remember how green were these valleys before the collieries came, and rows of terraced houses soon blanketed the steep hillsides.

The early miners in Wales descended the deep pit-shafts in cages to work long hours at the coal-faces with picks and shovels. They could not stand upright. They had no light except their Davy lamps. At one time they took children and ponies down to haul out the coal they dug, and canaries to give them warning of the presence of gas. They died relatively young from respiratory diseases if they were not killed even sooner in mine disasters. At the Ferndale Colliery in the Rhondda valley in 1867, 178 men died through the ignition of coal dust. 439 lives were lost at the Universal Colliery at Senghennydd, near Pontypridd, in 1913 – the worst disaster in British mining history. At Gresford, in North Wales, 265 men were entombed in 1934.

As advanced techniques were introduced and coal-cutting machinery eased the backbreaking labour of hacking away at solid rock, the miner's lot improved slightly, but men still died below ground in explosions or collapsing roadways. The noise of the machines meant that they no longer heard the tell-tale crack of timber which warned them of danger. And as lately as 1967, a generation of children died above ground when a tip slid down a hillside and buried a school at Aberfan.

The buried treasure

The stuff which primeval nature laid down beneath the Welsh rock and which justifies such sacrifice of life and limb is the relatively

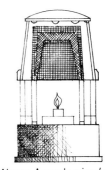

Above: An early miner's lamp. The open flame could ignite inflammable gases, causing serious explosions.

Below: Miners hacking coal with picks. Until the introduction of cutting machinery, this is how miners spent their working lives at the coal face, bent double beneath propped-up roofs.

scarce coking coal for blast furnaces and steam coal for ships' and locomotives' boilers. So colossal amounts of Welsh coal have been exported as well as being widely used in British industry.

Welsh coal had been mined on a small scale in Elizabethan days, and mining increased throughout the seventeenth century, so that Defoe, visiting Swansea, could remark that it has a 'very great trade for coals and culm, [anthracite dust] which they export to all the ports of Sommerset, Devon and Cornwall, and also to Ireland itself; so that one sometimes sees a hundred sail of ships at a time loading coals here; which greatly enriches the country, and particularly this town of Swanzey. ...' (It is worth adding here that the trade with Cornwall was a two-way process, for a great deal of tin and copper from the Cornish mines was shipped to South Wales for smelting.)

But the evils behind this mighty output were not seen by the casual observer. Before Lord Shaftesbury's act of 1842 forbade the employment of women and children in coal mines, youngsters of six or seven were taken down to work as carters, from six in the morning till six at night, hauling carts of coal along narrow passages where ponies could not be used, to add perhaps five pence a day to the family income. The housing put up by the mine-owners for their labourers was appalling. Cramped and insanitary, it was the cause of cholera epidemics through overcrowding, lack of ventilation and overflowing cesspools. Pigs and poultry were kept in three-room cottages in which three families might be living as well.

The mining boom

Darby's success in smelting iron with coke gave a great boost to the Welsh mining industry. Although it ran second for a long time to iron working, a huge export trade was developed with France, and in the second half of the nineteenth century a spectacular expansion took place.

The coal seams beneath the Rhondda valleys had been considered unworkable at one time, because they were so deep, but from 1865 onwards shafts of unprecedented depths were sunk, and it was not long before more than 20,000 men were packed into every square mile of the area, to dig the coal and make fortunes for the mine-owners. The coal was shipped from Swansea and Cardiff, Neath and Barry – the docks at Barry shipped a record of eleven millions tons of coal in 1911.

Stall-men – those who dug the coal – worked during the day, and other workers – repairers, rippers and timber-men – worked night shifts, so as not to interfere with production. Rippers were the men who removed the tops, or ceilings, of passages to

Right: The Lewis Merthyr Colliery at Porth, near Pontypridd – a typical Rhondda scene in which miners' houses cling to the hillside above colliery buildings and pithead winding gear.

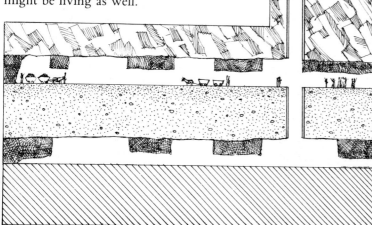

Left: Section through a mine shaft showing roads or galleries through coal seams some two hundred and fifty feet below the surface.

make way for ponies and wagons to pass through, and timber-men were those who erected props to support the roofs of the roadways. By around 1912, a collier could earn three or four pounds a week if he worked hard enough. His wages were paid according to his output, but the coal was screened for size, and any that was too small was not paid for.

At the end of his shift, the miner crawled from the coal-face to the pit-shaft and came up, naked from the waist up because of the heat, but coated with thick black dust. Leather pads would be strapped to his knees, and his back would be scarred where he had repeatedly crashed his spine against the roof in travelling bent double along the roadways. In this state, he trudged home in the dark to eat his meal before the long job of washing himself tolerably clean in small amounts of water heated by his wife in kettle or saucepan. Then he could relax and sleep for a few hours before setting off on his next shift. His weekend break was generally from two o'clock on Saturday afternoon until six o'clock the following morning.

Above: A miner with pit pony. Ponies were regularly used for underground haulage at one time, where the gradient of roads was fairly level and the galleries wide and high enough for the animals to move freely.

Exodus

After the First World War, the demand for coal from abroad fell drastically, and as unemployment rose steadily in South Wales, as elsewhere, the miners' unions gathered strength for the tragic period ahead, when the owners tried to enforce lower wages and longer working hours, and brought about the General Strike of 1926. Though the national strike itself lasted only nine days, the miners were out for six months. Many pits closed down, and men were reduced to living on lettuce, which they grew in their back gardens, and lamb, which they stole from the hill-farmers. A quarter of a million people left South Wales to seek jobs elsewhere. Many went abroad, never to return to their homeland.

The Second World War brought a further crisis to the coal industry, and under the National Coal Board, a great deal of re-organization and modernization has taken place, as well as restoration of some of the desecrated landscape. Large modern collieries take the places of many small and scattered pits of former days. Coal mining remains a vital part of Welsh life, and there is said to be enough coal to keep the industry going for another two hundred years. Perhaps by that time man's ingenuity will have devised means of getting the coal out of the ground without the necessity to send men deep into the earth to dig it.

Where to go
The Rhondda is a river with two branches (Afon Rhondda Fawr and Afon Rhondda Fach) rising west of Aberdare in Mid Glamorgan and flowing south east to join up near Pontypridd. The eastern branch flows through the town of Rhondda.

The valleys can be reached by A470 from Cardiff, or A465 from Abergavenny, passing Ebbw Vale and Merthyr Tydfil before branching off on A4059 or A4061 for the Rhondda valleys.

The National Museum of Wales at Cardiff has exhibits concerned with the coal mining industry, and the Welsh Industrial and Maritime Museum's collection of machines includes some from the mines.

Iron and steel

Iron working spread to Wales from Shropshire in the early eighteenth century, when Abraham Darby's fellow-Quaker Charles Lloyd used the new smelting process at Bersham in Denbighshire. Bersham became a specialist centre for cannon boring and cylinder making, and the Wilkinsons, who were largely responsible for Bersham's prosperity, extended their operations to South Wales in the area round a tiny hamlet called 'Merthyr Tudful'. By 1860, a thousand men were employed in extracting iron, and two hundred furnaces were employing two and a half thousand men.

Soon a huge industrial belt spread along the northern edge of the South Wales coalfield, from Carmarthenshire to Monmouthshire. Merthyr Tydfil grew rapidly into the biggest town in Wales, a position it maintained for a hundred years, during which time Wales was the largest iron-producing region in the world. The great Cyfarthfa ironworks at Merthyr developed by a London merchant, Anthony Bacon, was the first to use the improved puddling process by which the iron industry was revolutionized, and it came to be known as the 'Welsh method'.

Iron into Steel

In the later part of the nineteenth century, imports of high-grade iron ore from abroad set the Welsh industry back somewhat. The industry moved towards the coastal areas to meet the incoming ore. When ironworks evolved into steel plants, with the development of modern processes, it was in such places as Swansea and Port Talbot that they expanded, at the expense of the inland centres.

The production of Welsh steel on an industrial scale was made practicable by the Bessemer converter, introduced in 1856, and the Siemens open-hearth process, developed soon afterwards. Steel is basically an alloy of iron and carbon, and the proportion of carbon and method of production distinguish different forms of steel such as mild steel and stainless steel. In the Bessemer process, molten pig iron is converted to steel by blowing air at high pressure through the pear-shaped converter via holes in its base. The air removes excess carbon and other

Above: The Abbey Steel Works at Margam, near Port Talbot. The expanded works now have blast furnaces, continuous strip mill, coal and ore handling plant.

Above: An early blast furnace. The stone outer shell enclosed a stack into which ore was fed from above. The opening right was the tuyere arch, through which bellows blew air.

undesirable elements from the metal. The Siemens 'regenerative principle' uses preheated air to obtain a higher final temperature in the furnace.

The first commercial plant for producing steel by the Siemens method was built at Landore, just outside Swansea, in 1867, and the Siemens process eventually replaced the Bessemer converter altogether.

As the demand for steel increased, so the Welsh blast furnaces grew, and at Port Talbot, the smouldering cooling towers and belching chimneys of one of Europe's largest steel works spread for over four miles along the coastline against a background of hills, and employed a staggering total of nearly fourteen thousand people.

Where to go
The relatively new Welsh Industrial and Maritime Museum in Cardiff has exhibits from the iron and steel industries. The landscapes produced by iron and steel works are there for all to see at Port Talbot and Merthyr Tydfil. The former town is off M4 east of Swansea; the latter on A470 Cardiff-Brecon road.

Slate quarrying

The quarrying of slate – the only real industry in North Wales – began in the middle of the eighteenth century, and reached its peak about a hundred years later. Though it has been in decline since, it is a continuing activity, for the region has one of the biggest and best slate deposits in the world. The area where it is worked is around the Snowdon range, and since the industry began to be developed on a large scale around 1820, it has produced some bizarre effects on the local landscape.

Slate is a metamorphic rock. That is to say, it was once rock of a different structure which has been changed by extreme pressure under the earth's surface. Its chief characteristics are its hardness, fine grain and fissile nature, making it ideal for roofing purposes. What gave Wales such a huge industry was the fact that its slate was cheap to extract, and could be cleaved to make thin slates, light in weight.

Welsh slate has been both mined and quarried in the past. Mountain sides at Blaenau Ffestiniog were honeycombed with entrances to underground mines before open-cast quarrying was introduced, and around Llanberis and Bethesda huge craters testify to the enormous quantities of slate extracted. The Industrial Revolution made Welsh slate almost a universal roofing material for factories and houses throughout Britain, and slate was also exported to many parts of the world.

Blasting by gunpowder was used for dislodging slate from the rock face, and thereafter the slate was split and shaped by skilled men with the simplest of tools. The slate was taken from the rock face in terraced levels, called galleries, which eventually reached enormous depths – sometimes over a thousand feet. Some 16,000 men were working in the slate quarries in the middle of the nineteenth century. They were an isolated, industrious army, most of them speaking only Welsh, and some of them illiterate. (Not least among the quarries' products were writing slates for use in schools.) Their

Above: A roof of Welsh slate. In this drawing, slates of graded sizes are shown, increasing from the ridge downwards. Housing demand and mass production led to slates of uniform size (below).

Below: Dowlais, Glamorgan, in 1906.

Right: Slate quarry, Ffestiniog, Gwynedd.

Overleaf: The Rhondda Valley, Mid-Glamorgan. Disused coal mines at Tylorstown.

chief occupational hazard, not surprisingly, was lung disease caused by inhaling slate dust.

The industry gave the quarrying areas themselves dreary-looking grey towns and villages, each with its chapel, and little prosperity to the workers themselves, who often worked under conditions so near to slave labour that eventually the capitalist quarry-owners had on their hands what turned out to be the longest strike in British industrial history.

At the beginning of the nineteenth century 12,000 tons of slate a year were being sent by sea from the Penrhyn quarries to London alone, and five or six thousand men worked in that one quarry. At one time, the practice was to roof houses with the purple-grey or blue-grey slates in diminishing sizes from the ridge downwards, and the different sizes of slates acquired a curious, and perhaps psychologically telling nomenclature in the trade, derived from the female aristocracy. So there were standard 'duchesses', 'countesses' and 'marchionesses', as well as 'wide countesses' and 'narrow ladies'. Later slates of equal size were used for each roof, which did nothing to help the architectural poverty of urban housing.

Because the quarries were near the sea, a great deal of the slate was shipped to ports round the British coast as well as to destinations abroad, whilst inland transportation was by canal until the coming of the railways.

Eventually machine-cutting reduced the workforce needed to operate the quarries, and rival roofing materials reduced demand for Welsh slate, so that the quarry towns are now areas of high unemployment. Although slate is still produced, it is on a much smaller scale, and mechanization has virtually killed the craft of the slate quarryman.

The Dinorwic quarry, near Llanberis, is the biggest slate quarry in the world. It extends up the slopes of Elidir Fawr to a height of 2,300 feet in a great series of terraces. Its products were shipped from Port Dinorwic on the Menai Strait – now a yachting centre. The old quarry buildings now house the North Wales Quarrying Museum, where much of the trade's equipment and machinery can be seen.

Top: Splitting slate by hand. Exploiting the natural fissures in the material, skilled men dexterously split and dress it into thin and light roofing slates, relatively cheap to produce and to transport to all parts of Britain.

Above: A view of the Penrhyn slate quarries at Bethesda, showing the terraced progression of quarrying operations.

Where to go

The Llanberis Slate Museum is on an unclassified road on eastern slopes above Llyn Padarn, reached by A4086 from Caernarfon. Much machinery and equipment is exhibited there, and a fifty foot water-wheel of 1870 remains *in situ*.

The Penrhyn Quarries are to the north. Penrhyn Castle near Bangor (National Trust) was built from the huge quarrying profits of the first Lord Penrhyn. It has a museum of slate transport and industrial railways.

Near Blaenau Ffestiniog (A470 south west of Betws-y-Coed) are the Llechwedd Slate Caverns and Gloddfa Ganol Slate Mine. Visitors can tour the underground workings at the former, with their spectacular caverns, and see demonstrations of slate cutting. Open cast quarrying has replaced mining at the latter site, but visitors can see the sawing and dressing of slates, as well as the social background of the industry in restored quarrymen's cottages.

Narrow-gauge railways

The popularity of the narrow-gauge railways of North Wales is, like the similar sentiment for our inland waterways, among the triumphant conversions of defunct industrial transport into profitable tourist amenities. Both the trains and the routes they travel are picturesque, although they were built specifically for the haulage of industrial freight. They are also among the oldest railways in Britain, and therefore in the world; and very often where they led, the standard-gauge railways followed.

The two best known of the narrow-gauge railways, the Tal-y-llyn and the Ffestiniog, were both built for the slate industry. The Ffestiniog Railway was opened in 1836 to transport slate from the Blaenau Ffestiniog quarries to Porthmadog, whilst the Tal-y-llyn Railway, built in 1856, carried slate from the quarries below Cader Idris to the port of Tywyn.

Development of the narrow-gauge lines

The Ffestiniog's gauge is 1 foot 11½ inches, and the Tal-y-llyn's 2 feet 3 inches. Both eventually carried passengers as well as freight, and other lines were built too. The

Above: An early slate wagon of the Tal-y-llyn Railway. Each wagon could carry at least a ton of slate, and usually had an opening gate at one end to facilitate shovelling.

Below: A slate-workers' train on the Ffestiniog Railway around the turn of the century. The locomotive is the Double-Fairlie *Merddin Emrys* built in 1879.

North Wales Narrow Gauge Railways Company, incorporated in 1872, planned lines joining the Croesor and Porthmadog mineral line to Beddgelert and Betws-y-Coed, and from Dinas to Bryngwyn. Farther south the Glyn Valley Tramway was converted into a steam passenger service in 1888, whilst the Corris Railway took passengers into the mountains from Machynlleth, and was at one time intended to link up with the Tal-y-llyn. Another unique and famous line is the Snowdon Mountain Railway, climbing from Llanberis to the peak of Snowdon. This was opened in 1896, purely as a tourist railway. These lines had a wondrous assortment of gauges. The NWNGR gauge was 1 foot 11½ inches like the Ffestiniog's, and the Corris line, like the Tal-y-llyn's, was 2 feet 3 inches. The Snowdon gauge was 2 feet 7½ inches, and the Glyn Valley 2 feet 4½ inches.

The Snowdon Mountain Railway has the steepest gradient of any locomotive track in Britain – 1 in 5½ – and reaches a height of nearly three and half thousand feet at its summit. Its opening, however, was less than triumphant. It had been built privately,

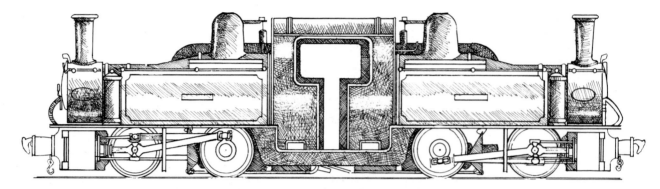

Above: The crest of the Ffestiniog Railway Co.

Top: A Double-Fairlie locomotive of the Ffestiniog Railway. An engine like this one was the last built for the line, in 1885.

Left: Boston Lodge works, the maintenance depot of the Ffestiniog line near Porthmadog.

based on Swiss rack-and-pinion models, and it set out on its maiden run in April 1896, but the engine jumped the rails and ran into a ravine. The carriages stayed on the track, but one man was killed when he jumped out. Modifications had to be made before operations could be resumed.

The Ffestiniog's maiden passenger run had been rather more respectable thirty-three years earlier. Two trains left the station at Porthmadog with about two hundred people on board. The engines puffed away up the slopes, scattering farm animals in the adjacent fields, and passing through a half-mile tunnel in which passengers suffered choking sooty fumes; but much of the journey was through beautiful scenery, the day was fine, and hundreds of quarrymen cheered the little trains into the terminus at Blaenau Ffestiniog after their haul of 13½ miles.

Although several rival lines of standard gauge were planned – and some actually built – by the big railway companies, the Welsh narrow-gauge lines did well enough out of the slate industry to keep ahead of the competition. The Ffestiniog was advertised to tourists as a 'toy train' carrying passengers

through 'fairyland', but it was also carrying about 140,000 tons of slate a year at the end of the nineteenth century. It had five 0–4–0 locomotives in operation, as well as four double-Fairlies, and began each working day with a train to take quarrymen to work at 5.25 a.m. It ran eight passenger trains each way as well as its freight duties every day. The slate trains came down from the quarries by gravity, and locomotives then hauled the empty wagons back up.

The great railway boom led to many ambitious plans for a whole network of narrow-gauge lines in the Welsh mountains, under the auspices of what came to be called Welsh Highland Railways, but most of them came to nothing.

Death and resurrection
By the 1920's, the Ffestiniog's slate load was only half what it had been twenty years before, and the Tal-y-llyn's story was similarly depressing. Economies in systems and repairs only led to unreliability and breakdowns, and road transport began to take away both freight and passenger trade.

In the Thirties many quarries closed

down, and freight traffic fell further. When the war came, quarrymen went into the services, tourists ceased to travel, and slate haulage fell to negligible levels.

This was the time, however, when nostalgia for the great railway age, now passing, produced a small army of die-hards whose enthusiasm extended to purchasing and preserving old railway stock and, in some cases continuing to operate the lines as going concerns. The Tal-y-llyn Railway Preservation Society stepped in in the nick of time and prevented that line from closing at all. It carries large numbers of passengers every year – most of them tourists – on the seven miles journey from Tywyn to Abergynolwyn and back.

The Ffestiniog Railway Society
The Ffestiniog line lay derelict for eight years after its closure in 1946, rusting, rotting and slowly sinking from sight beneath weeds and bushes. The Ffestiniog Railway Society was founded in 1951 to try to restore

Above: An open four-wheeled coach of the Ffestiniog line.

Below: A passenger train of the Tal-y-llyn line at Dolgoch station. The locomotive No. 4, *Edward Thomas*, originally belonged to the Corris Railway.

that line to working order as well. The problems were immense compared with those of the Tal-y-llyn. The Ffestiniog had closed down deep in debt, and its value as scrap metal was greater than its prospects of ever becoming a going concern again. Nevertheless, persistence and protracted negotiations led the Society to successful conclusions, and the huge task of recovering track and equipment from the undergrowth, and restoring the locomotives and rolling stock to working order, began with a keen army of volunteers. Within a few years, a passenger service was again running on the Ffestiniog line, though not along the whole length of its original route, for much work remained to be done, and a considerable diversion was necessary due to the creation of a reservoir for a hydro-electric power station. Completion of the rebuilding to the terminus at Blaenau Ffestiniog is imminent and a new station is being built there in co-operation with British Rail.

Where to go
There is an interesting Narrow-Gauge Railway Museum, run by the Tal-y-llyn Railway Society, at the Wharf Station at Tywyn (A493 from Dolgellau or Machynlleth). The Ffestiniog Railway Museum is at the railway's headquarters at Harbour Station, Porthmadog (A487 east of Criccieth).

Blaenau Ffestiniog is best reached via A5, then A470 south from Betws-y-Coed. A narrow-gauge railway centre is at the Gloddfa Ganol Mountain Tourist Centre.

The Tal-y-llyn and Ffestiniog lines are open most of the year, but Snowdon Mountain Railway does not operate during the winter months. Its terminus is at Llanberis (A4086 east of Caernarfon). The survival and popularity of these railways has led to the restoration of such lines as the Welsh Highland and the Welshpool and Llanfair Railways. The Welsh Highland Railway, a short stretch of which is now open, operates from its HQ adjacent to BR station at Porthmadog. The Welshpool and Llanfair operates from Llanfair Caereinion beside A458 nine miles west of Welshpool.

Gold mining

Not everything that has been taken out of the Welsh mountains by man has been as unattractive as coal, lead and iron ore. The presence of gold was well known to the Romans, but they had to overcome the natives before they could lay hands on it. Dolaucothi, north west of Llandovery in Dyfed (formerly Caermarthenshire) is where the Romans dug for gold with iron hammers. Gold ornaments have been found near the mines, as well as pottery, and there was a fort nearby in order to guard the imperial interest.

Needless to say, the mines were exploited by other prospectors after the Romans had departed, so their workings have been obscured by centuries of later interference, but it seems that both open-cast and underground mining were employed. Adit (approach) galleries reach a depth of eighty feet, and wooden water-wheels were used to drain them. The ore was crushed and washed at the site, using water brought by stone-lined aqueducts, one of which was over seven miles long. The village of Pumsaint nearby got its name from Carreg Pumsaint – 'stone of the five saints'. The stone in question is a roughly quadrangular rock with depressions in each face which are believed to have been made by pounding ore.

The Dolaucothi mine was reworked in this century, before the Second World War, but meanwhile gold had been discovered farther north in the hills around Dolgellau. Finds here in 1843 led to sporadic working right up to 1961. The Welsh gold rush soon produced a hundred and fifty shafts and trial of levels, and there were some rich strikes.

The Roman gold mine at Dolaucothi is now under the protection of the National Trust. It lies just east of the village of Pumsaint, on the road between Lampeter and Llandovery.

The largest gold mine in Britain is at Gwynfynydd, near Afon Mawddach about 6½ miles north of Dolgellau. The Morgan Gold Mining Company took £35,000 worth of gold from this mine within two years of discovering new deposits in 1888. Several surface remains can be seen at this mine, including a strong room near one of the adit entrances.

The yield of gold in Wales was always relatively small, but one of the traditions which grew out of its discovery and exploitation was that royal wedding rings are always made of Welsh gold. (One of the workings was called the Prince of Wales Mine.) Some say there is still plenty of gold to be got out of the Welsh mountains.

Above: The crushing mill of Vigra gold mine as it appeared in 1862. The overshot waterwheel was fed by a wooden launder (trough) at the top. A truck is seen entering the crushing house.

Where to go
Gwynfynydd is best reached by A470 north from Dolgellau, turning right at Rhiwgoch and following minor road south to the hamlet.

Several other gold mines are in the hills near Bontddu (A496 between Barmouth and Llanelltyd).

Pumpsaint is on A482, half way between Llandovery and Lampeter. An unclassified road leads east from the village to the Dolaucothi Estate.

Gold mining techniques are included among the exhibits at the Llywernog Mine Museum, Ponterwyd (A44 twelve miles east of Aberystwyth).

Weaving

The spinning and weaving of wool is a centuries-old traditional craft in Wales. But in place of the old woman in a tall black hat sitting at her cottage door with spinning wheel and spindle is a factory girl helping to produce machine-made blankets – a working mother as likely as not, who rushes home to get her children's tea when she clocks off.

In Elizabethan times, the wool from the Welsh mountain sheep was spun and woven into coarse cloth in cottages and farmhouses throughout the land. The rough cloth was taken to the weekly markets at Oswestry, and later to Shrewsbury, when an Act of Parliament gave the Shropshire county town a monopoly in trading in Welsh cloth. 'They speak all English in the town,' as one traveller remarked, 'but on a market-day you would think you were in Wales.' The weavers themselves were perhaps more inclined to reflect that the Welsh had the labour and the English the profit. Shrewsbury's finest half-timbered buildings were the homes of wealthy Tudor drapers.

It was not until the mid-eighteenth century that the English monopoly on Welsh woollens was broken. Some rough cloth was exported from Barmouth to the West Indies, where it was in demand for clothing slaves, and local markets began to deal in flannel and knitted stockings. By this time, machinery was making its appearance, and women moved from their cottage workrooms into mills, but a great deal of spinning was still done by women in their homes to supplement the meagre living made by their husbands on the land. Synthetic dyes were also introduced to replace the natural dyes obtained from bramble and bracken, heather and gorse.

The spinning of the wool, done on spinning wheels in the cottage industry, was done in the mills on a spinning 'mule' with as many as eighty spindles; and machine looms noisily but ingeniously reproduced the processes of hand weaving. The mills had to be sited beside rivers to drive the fulling and finishing processes, and the word 'pandy' in a place-name is a clue to the former presence of a fulling mill.

(See the sections on West Midlands and North East for further developments in the woollen industry.)

Top: The Esgair Moel woollen mill was built near Llanwrtyd around 1760, and was in operation until 1947. It was subsequently re-erected at St Fagans, Cardiff.

Above: A Welsh vertical spinning wheel of the type traditionally used in the cottage industry; now fetching high prices in antique shops.

Where to go

A Museum of the Woollen Industry was opened at Dre-fach Felindre, Dyfed, in 1976, as a branch of the National Museum of Wales. This occupies part of a working mill in the trade's most active area. The history of the industry is traced through machinery and other exhibits, and in the adjacent mill visitors can see weavers at work. The village is on an unclassified road south of A484 Cardigan–Carmarthen road, three miles east of Newcastle Emlyn. A water-powered mill from Llantwrtyd, Breconshire, has been re-erected at the Welsh Folk Museum, St Fagans, Cardiff, and can be seen in working order, along with many exhibits such as hand looms, spinning mules and so on.

At Machynlleth (A487 between Dolgellau and Aberystwyth) there is a permanent exhibition of Welsh crafts, including woollens, which was organised by the Council for Small Industries in Rural Areas.

North West England

Recent discoveries have shown that north west England was a thriving seat of industry far earlier than anyone had suspected. But with hindsight it hardly seems surprising that much of the region's industrial activity has ever since been concerned with exploiting nature's bounty. When the Industrial Revolution came, however, the men of the north west were more than equal to it, and textile manufacturing became a huge employer of local labour, and one of the great prides of Victorian Britain. Inventors such as Arkwright and Hargreaves have the sound of Lancashire in their names as well as the population of Lancashire in their debt, for they helped to build a wealthy industrial society and a proud and powerful nation.

The extrovert population of old Lancashire – now split up by contributions to Greater Manchester, Merseyside and Cumbria – has a huge capacity for enjoyment which it is glad to share with others, and Blackpool Tower stands as a monument to the tourist industry which, though it is not discussed here, is vitally important to the area.

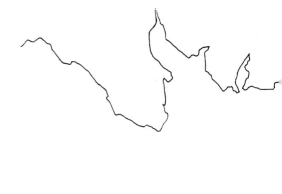

0   10   20 miles

CUMBRIA

A596

Carlisle

Workington

Keswick

A6

Penrith

Appleby

▲ Borrowdale

Shap

A595

▲ ▲ Langdale Pikes

Scafell Pike

Ravenglass

Windermere

Kendal

Finsthwaite

A66

A590

Barrow-in-Furness

Lancaster

LANCASHIRE

A6

Blackpool

Burnley

Preston

A583

Blackburn

Southport

A59

Bury

Rochdale

Wigan

Oldham

A6

Worsely

Manchester

MERSEYSIDE

St. Helens

Liverpool

Stockport

GREATER
MANCHESTER

Birkenhead

Cotton

Manchester and its satellite towns – Bolton, Oldham, Rochdale, Burnley, Bury, Chorley, Wigan, Blackburn – have been well known as 'Cottonopolis' since the beginning of the nineteenth century, when the great trade began its rise to become King Cotton, the pride and joy of Victorian England, and helped to civilize the Queen's subjects throughout the Empire by selling them cotton handkerchiefs to wave at Her Majesty's representatives on State occasions.

The origins of the industry go right back to the fourteenth century, when Edward III encouraged Flemish weavers to come to this country, and many of them settled in and around Manchester. From that time onwards, raw cotton became one of our most vital imports, and Liverpool grew to become one of the world's chief markets.

Process of cotton manufacture

Raw cotton has to go through many stages during its metamorphosis into garments, and the humid atmosphere of the Manchester area is an aid to some of the processes involved. The cotton arrives in bales of tightly packed and matted material, and is first released and stored so that the fibres regain their natural state and excessive moisture evaporates. Blending is then carried out to mix different qualities of fibre, to produce yarns for specific uses and quality.

The next process is 'scutching' by which the cotton is cleaned and formed into continuous rolls, ready for carding. This process combs out the twisted cotton into straight strands. After being further cleaned, the strands are drawn or stretched slightly, and twisted together to form cotton ready for winding on to bobbins. Spinning, sizing and weaving come next.

All these complicated procedures were carried out by hand before the Industrial Revolution by small concentrations of textile workers in various parts of the country. With the ingenious inventions, mostly by Lancashire men in the second half of the eighteenth century, which led to complete mechanization, all cotton manufacturing converged on the Manchester area, and grew

Right: Frosts' Mill at Macclesfield, Cheshire. Built in 1785, this is in fact a silk mill, but it is typical of the region's industrial architecture. Powered at first by water, it changed to steam power in 1811 and to electricity in 1914.

Below: Engraving showing carding, drawing and roving operations in an early Lancashire cotton mill. The carding machines at left (called 'scribblers') combed raw cotton into straight strands on a series of rollers, after which it was drawn out and twisted slightly into 'roves' (right).

into the great factory industry we can still recognize today in the Lancashire towns, despite its sad present state.

Inventions of local men

James Hargreaves, of 'spinning jenny' fame, was a poor weaver of Blackburn. John Kay of Bury invented the 'fly-shuttle'. Richard Arkwright who patented the spinning frame in 1764, was a barber, born in Preston. Samuel Crompton, a weaver from Bolton, combined the principles of Arkwright's frame and Hargreaves' jenny in his 'mule spinning frame'. It was a Midlands rector, Dr Edmund Cartwright, who invented the first primitive steam-powered loom, but William Horrocks of Stockport and Richard Roberts of Manchester brought the idea by stages to efficient realization.

These revolutions in cotton manufacturing did not pass into the industry without trouble. Textile workers feared that fast mass-production machines threatened their livelihoods. There was much rioting and machine-breaking in the troubled years of the Luddite Rebellion (see pages 106 – 109). But gradually the spinners and weavers

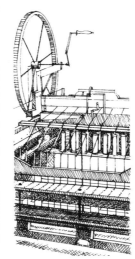

Above: A spinning jenny. Invented by Hargreaves in 1764, the mechanism, operated by the hand-wheel left, span cotton on multiple spindles. 'Jenny' is merely a corruption of 'engine'.

moved out of their cottages and small work-shops into huge mills, and a great export trade in cotton goods brought large profits to an industry which had a head start over all other textile-producing countries, thanks to home-grown ingenuity.

The factory system

Sir Richard Arkwright (as he became) is generally considered to be the father of the factory system in cotton manufacturing. Ironically, he set up his first mills in Nottinghamshire and Derbyshire, having been driven away from his native county by the workers' opposition to his machines; and in time he became High Sheriff of Derbyshire – not bad for a barber's apprentice.

Other men stayed at home, and to many of them we owe the familiar industrial appearance of towns like Bolton and Oldham and Wigan, with their tall brick mills standing like fortresses among the rows of terraced houses built to accommodate the vast armies of workers in the industry.

The cotton industry became a major employer of female labour. In the early days, before Robert Owen and Lord Shaftesbury,

it employed child labour, too. One such employer was William Douglas, whose demise was recorded by the local paper in 1810: 'highly respected and deeply lamented ... He bore a long and painful illness with the greatest fortitude and resignation; his last moments were tranquil and he died without a struggle.' Not so some of his unfortunate young slaves, though, taken from the workhouses at six or seven years old and worked for long hours during which they were so illtreated that some committed suicide and others became so deformed that Douglas's mill in Salford was known as the 'Cripple Factory'.

Nor were the adult workers much above slave labour in some cases. In hard times, when wages were low and the menfolk perhaps out of work, the women's wages were essential to the survival of the family, and if they became pregnant, it could be a disaster. How many women had self-induced abortions by primitive methods, and how many went back to the mills too soon after childbirth, for fear of losing their jobs, we shall never know.

Cotton's catastrophes

Among the crises of the Lancashire cotton industry – not least were the activities – for perfectly honourable reasons – of two great men on opposite sides of the world – Abraham Lincoln and Mahatma Gandhi.

British workers had hardly recovered from the hardships brought about by the Napoleonic Wars in Europe and disastrous harvests at home, before the American Civil War brought a famine of raw cotton which, by this time, was imported chiefly from the Confederate southern states. The rebel ports were blockaded by Federal ships. Half a million cotton workers in Lancashire were put on short time, then laid off, by the quarrel across the Atlantic. There was no unemployment pay in those days, and many went without bread. When the first shiploads of cotton arrived in Liverpool after a gap of two years, Lancashire men shed tears of gratitude.

Between the two world wars, a great part of the Far Eastern market was lost to India and Japan. India was probably the birthplace of cotton weaving. It had an export trade

Above: Cotton mills at Shaw, between Oldham and Rochdale. Victorian multi-storey mills and chimney stacks epitomize the Lancashire cotton industry. The old image of millgirls in clogs, pinafores and headscarves clattering along cobbled streets at dawn to the chorus of factory whistles is still not too distant for recall in such places.

Right: A spinning mule. This machine was invented by Samuel Crompton in 1779. It was driven by water-power, and originally had about thirty spindles, but more sophisticated versions had over a thousand.

three thousand years before Mahatma Gandhi did for cotton what Bernard Shaw did for Jaeger woollens. During the growing campaign for Indian self-rule, Gandhi made great efforts to revitalize cotton spinning throughout the sub-continent, and he succeeded in creating a demand for home-spun cloth which released India from its dependence on Lancashire. More than half of Britain's enormous cotton exports to India were lost in the ten years before the Second World War.

Other countries also entered the fight to win orders that Britain had once taken for granted. The half million cotton workers of the late twenties were reduced by a hundred thousand during the next decade, and a third of those remaining were out of work when the war started. The industry has never fully recovered from these setbacks.

After the war, the government had to advertise for people to go to Lancashire to work in the cotton mills, but the demand for labour was short-lived. The dole queues in Lancashire are today as long as anywhere in Britain.

Relics of the industry

Many old buildings survive from the early days of the cotton industry. Weaving sheds, houses with weavers' attics, early mills and machinery are among the industrial heritage of this corner of Britain.

The Swan Lane Mill at Bolton is a good example of a brick-built Victorian spinning mill. It was designed to accommodate nearly two hundred thousand mule spindles. At Littleborough (four miles north-east of Rochdale) Clough Mills is a stone-built factory of two storeys which was run on water power. Oldham once had more than a hundred mills in operation, and today these buildings of the late-nineteenth and early-twentieth centuries can be seen throughout the town.

James Hargreaves' cottage survives at Stanhill, near Oswaldtwistle, while an early steam-powered factory remains at Heaton Mersey, Stockport. This is the six storey Orrell's Mill built in the 1830's with cast iron columns and beams to support the weight of machinery.

At Macclesfield, Cheshire, several silk mills in Georgian style show distinctive textile architecture. One is now Slaters' carding factory; another Frosts' Yarns.

Where to go
The Lewis Textile Museum in Exchange Street, Blackburn, and the North Western Museum of Science and Industry in Manchester both have many exhibits of the local cotton industry. The Lewis Textile Museum displays working models of the 'spinning jenny' and the 'spinning mule'.

The Tonge Moor Textile Museum at Bolton also houses an important collection of machines and illustrates much of the history of cotton working.

The paintings of L.S. Lowry, of which the Art Gallery at Salford (Peel Park) has the largest public collection, vividly capture the social atmosphere of the cotton towns.

The Northern Mill Engine Society preserves a fine engine at Dee Mill, Shaw, which lies between Oldham and Rochdale.

Canals

The great network of canals throughout Britain, now chiefly the peaceful territory of boat-loving holiday-makers, began as an answer to the transport problems of growing industries in the eighteenth century. Britain was late to realize the virtues of canal transport. Canals had been constructed in Egypt and China long before the birth of Christ, and though they were probably invented originally for irrigation purposes, it was not long before their advantages for transport were realized. Locks were invented by Europeans – probably the Dutch – in medieval times, to cope with changes in water levels. Leonardo da Vinci worked on six locks in the fifteenth century to link the canals of Milan.

Beginnings of British canals

It was in the north west of England where British canals were pioneered, and once British industrialists – particularly coal-mine owners – had caught on to the enormous advantages of canal transport, no area did more to promote and further the interests of canal building.

The first *truly* industrial canal was financed mainly by Liverpool manufacturers to link the St Helens coalfield with the Mersey. It was opened in 1751. Much more famous, and often wrongly described as the 'first canal', was the Bridgewater Canal, which was opened ten years later. This was built by Francis Egerton, 3rd Duke of Bridgewater, who came to be called the 'Canal Duke' and the 'Father of Inland Navigation'. Its purpose was to link the duke's collieries at Worsley with Manchester, where most of the coal was sold. The duke's engineer was James Brindley, an illiterate genius, who is now often referred to as the 'Father of English Canals'. Part of the canal travelled underground from the coal mines, and it was carried across the valley of the River Irwell by means of a high aqueduct. Faint hearts regarded Brindley's proposals as crazy, and confidently predicted that this madman's ideas would never see the light of day. When they did, however, the great explosion of enthusiasm for canal building began.

Two less likely industrial heroes can scarcely be imagined. Brindley could neither read nor write, and worked out all his calculations in his head. The duke was better educated but more ignorant. He swore he would never speak to another woman after his fiancée walked out on him, and as far as I know, he never did. But the brains of the one and the money of the other came together to achieve an amazing engineering success.

The Worsley canal cut the price of coal in Manchester by half, and mine-owners, quarry-owners, chemical and other manufacturers quickly saw the advantages of carrying their heavy goods by canal barge instead of by pack-horse and other primitive means. Eager capitalists jumped on the bandwagon of the early promotors and engineers, and had visions of vast networks of canals linking the navigable rivers and forming waterway transports systems which would bring in huge profits in the growing industrial revolution.

Rise and fall

For a time they did. Canal owners became rich men almost overnight. Colossal armies of 'navvies' were recruited to dig canals throughout the industrial north and midlands. They terrorized towns and villages with their unruly behaviour, but they

Below: Construction of the Manchester Ship Canal. A photograph of about 1888 showing the Latchford cutting near Warrington with the railway viaduct crossing it. The original depth of the canal was 26 feet (it has since been made two feet deeper) and its narrowest width 120 feet. Tidal action ceases on the canal beyond Latchford, and it is fed by the rivers Mersey and Irwell from here to Manchester.

Above: The original aqueduct carrying the Bridgewater Canal over the River Irwell near Manchester. It was conceived by James Brindley and financed by Francis Egerton, 3rd Duke of Bridgewater and the so-called 'Father of Inland Navigation'. Built in 1761, the aqueduct was regarded at first as a crazy idea. It is difficult to see why. The Romans had built many such structures successfully. This aqueduct was demolished in 1869 to be replaced by the Barton Swing Aqueduct.

achieved incredible results. In a hundred years, more than four thousand miles of canals were built, and great engineers such as Telford and Jessop spent much of their working lives in canal construction.

Massive tonnages of freight were moved about the country on canals, and profitable amalgamations took place between independent companies. For example, the canals linking the Trent with the Thames were turned into a single waterway – the 280 mile-long Grand Union Canal.

The coming of the railways gradually brought an end to the dream, however. Industrialists discovered many advantages in rail transport, and although canals continued in use for many years afterwards (and indeed are still used to a limited extent in some places), the freight they carried fell year by year, and the great age of canal building was virtually over. Bankruptcy came to many of those who had become rich on water, and many canals were drained and left derelict.

One of the great surviving monuments to the canal age, however, is the Manchester Ship Canal. The first plan to link Liverpool and Manchester with a direct waterway was put forward in 1825, but it was not until sixty years afterwards that a much altered scheme got through Parliament, and the canal was finally opened officially by Queen Victoria in 1894. It had cost nearly twenty million pounds by the time it was completed, with docks, wharves, swing bridges and locks, but it turned Manchester from an inland city into a major port, and was of enormous benefit to Lancashire trade. It is still, of course, very much in operation.

Where to go

Brindley's masonry aqueduct across the Irwell valley was replaced in 1894 by the Barton Swing Aqueduct, which carries the Bridgewater Canal over the Manchester Ship Canal five miles west of Manchester. The steel trough, full of water (weighing 1450 tons) can be swung to allow the passage of large vessels on the Ship Canal. It was designed by the Ship Canal engineer, Sir E. Leader Williams.

Near St Helens (off A58 east of town) are the first staircase locks in Britain, built 1758 and known as Old Double Locks.

At Worsley Delph (B5211) entrances to the old underground canal system can still be seen. The narrow boats which operated on the underground canals were called 'starvationers'. They can be seen in Manchester's North Western Museum of Science and Industry (Grosvenor Street).

Slate quarrying

The quarrying of slate and granite has been among the most important industries of Cumbria for a very long period. Shap granite is used all over England except in the south west, which has its own deposits, but granite is not evident on a large scale in Cumbria itself, whereas slate, the older and more widespread product of this region, certainly is. So-called Westmorland Slate is in wide demand for roofing, and in the Lake District, practically every roof is of the local material, whilst quarry waste and rubble has been used for building local houses, farms and barns.

The colour of the slate is generally greeny-blue, and it is quarried at various sites on the fells which would once have seemed virtually inaccessible. In no modern industries except tin and coal mining have men had to work in such appalling conditions. On the Old Man of Coniston, on Honister Pass and at other mountain sites, the quarrymen of Cumbria have spent their lives battling with the elements to put roofs over the nation's heads since as far back as the Roman occupation, when the guardians of the Empire's northern frontier roofed their granaries with local slate.

Dangerous work

The quarrymen's journeys to work used to be so hard and hazardous that they left their cottages in the valleys on Monday mornings and did not return home until Saturday nights for their brief weekend breaks, though the actual distance from home to quarry might be small. Wordsworth leapt upon this practice in his romanticized account of Betty Yewdale, whom he claimed to have discovered one dark night standing at her cottage door holding a lamp aloft to light the way home for her husband Jonathan:-

Three dark mid-winter months pass
And I never see,
Save when the Sabbath brings it kind
  release,
My helpmate's face by light of day. He
  quits
His door in darkness, nor till dusk returns,
And through Heaven's blessing, thus we
  gain the bread
For which we pray.

The notorious Honister quarries were remarked on by many an unbelieving travel-

Above: A quarryman transporting rough slate from the Honister quarry to the workshops using a 'trail-barrow'. This was a highly dangerous operation.

Below: *A Cumberland Slate Quarry* by Nelson Wright, 1926. This painting, in Manchester City Art Gallery, shows a mine entrance in Borrowdale.

ler. Remote and isolated, they were not, strictly speaking, quarries at all, but mines, since the slate was brought out from underground. The more genteel visitors to the Lake District were often shocked by hardliving and hard-drinking quarrymen, but if they had tried to do the work themselves for a week, or even a day, they might have felt more tolerant. One of the most hair-raising operations at Honister, before roads, railways and machinery came to the industry's aid, was the job of getting the stone down the steep fellsides to sheds where the material was made into roofing slates.

The slate – a quarter of a ton at a time – was loaded on to a sort of wooden sledge called a 'trail-barrow' which had two long handles, called 'stangs'. A man stood between these like a horse between the shafts of a wagon, gripping them with his hands, and set off down the precipitous rock face with this huge weight behind him. The momentum of this great load lifted the man off his feet for yards at a time, threatening to career completely out of control, and there were many accidents. But some men became so skilled at sledging that they became local folk heroes. Samuel Trimmer is remembered for making fifteen such journeys in a day. Each time they reached the sheds, of course, they had to climb back up the hillside with the empty barrows – a half hour's journey.

When the slate had been docked, riven and dressed in the workshops, the finished product was conveyed by pack-horse to ports and river barges for transportation to its destinations. Nowadays, of course, modern transport has put an end to such dangerous ways of earning a living, but Lake District slate is still in demand, and much of the formerly hard and slow work is done by diamond-tipped power saws which cut through hard rock as if it were cheese.

Roofs of Westmorland slate can be seen everywhere in the Lake District, but two good places to see slate-stone used in wall construction are the villages of Troutbeck, north of Windermere, and Elterwater, in Great Langdale. At Chapel Stile, near the latter village, a footpath leads up past the church to some old workings known as Thrang Quarry.

Above: Dressing Shap granite at Threlkeld, near Keswick, around 1935. The workman is dressing rough granite into the squared blocks called 'setts' for road making.

Where to go
The Lake District Green Slate Company at Fence, near Burnley, Lancashire (A6068 south west of Nelson) makes slate quarried at Coniston and Elterwater into all manner of luxury goods. Visitors can see the workshops, including diamond-tipped saws, in operation on working days.

Troutbeck is beside the A592 Kirkstone Pass road from Windermere. B5343 from Skelwith Bridge leads through Great Langdale. Honister Pass is on B5289 between Buttermere and Derwent Water. The Old Man of Coniston rises behind Coniston, on A593 between Broughton-in-Furness and Ambleside.

Bobbin turning

Right: A typical woollen mill at Hebden Bridge, West Yorkshire.

Overleaf: Leeds and Liverpool Canal at Burnley, Lancashire.

The making of bobbins, or cotton reels, in and around the Lake District was at first a coppice industry given its *raison d'etre* by the rise of the cotton industry in Lancashire. The craftsmen who made them worked in woodlands, beside the fast-flowing becks which powered their machinery, and this occupation therefore made no great impact on the landscape, even when bobbin mills evolved in the eighteenth century.

The stronghold of bobbin making was the Furness district of what was then Lancashire, but bobbin mills were to be found here and there in Cumberland and Westmorland, too. Standards of local birch were used for the product until they ran out, and then foreign timber had to be imported. The wood was cut into lengths and 'blocked out' before passing through drying kilns; then the holes were bored through them for fitting on to spindles, and lathes turned them to the final shape. Finally the bobbins were dyed or waxed.

Advances in bobbin making

The invention of a bobbin-making machine by John Braithwaite gave further impetus to the industry which, by the mid-nineteenth century, was producing about half of all bobbins used in the textile trade, with more than fifty mills at work in the region. A finishing lathe could turn out on average two thousand bobbins an hour, and stacks of timber would be stored ready for use in barns or sheds attached to the mills.

Decline

When demand from the cotton mills was low, the bobbin factories could turn to other lines such as rollers for mangles, or pill boxes, but the decline of the cotton industry in this century gradually closed down the bobbin mills, which also faced increasing foreign competition. They were given their *coup de grace* by the introduction of plastic bobbins.

One of the last working mills was at Stott Park, Finsthwaite. It was built in 1835 and closed down in 1971, but it has been preserved by the Department of the Environment and can be seen complete with its barns, engines, and much nineteenth century equipment and drying racks.

Where to go

Bobbin makers' equipment can be seen at the Museum of Lakeland Life and Industry in Kendal (Abbot Hall).

Stott Park is at the southern end of Windermere near the western bank, and is most easily reached on the unclassified road from A590 at Newby Bridge, via Finsthwaite.

Although most bobbin mills were in what is now southern Cumbria, the most spectacular site is at Caldbeck in the north (B5299 south west of Carlisle). You can only reach the mill on foot, but the walk is worthwhile. From the south corner of the green, a wall sign indicates the way to The Howk, through farm gates. Cross the stile and walk along the path; then go through the gate on to another path along the river bank, bringing you into The Howk, a deep and eerie limestone gorge with swallow holes. You come to the threadbare ruins of an old bobbin mill in this most unlikely industrial site, where the rushing water powered the mill's machinery.

Above: Bobbins in use on a machine for doubling the thickness of cotton thread, in use at about the turn of the century.

Below: Part of a bobbin mill in the 1930's. Here, the bobbins have been turned on the lathe and are ready for finishing by waxing or varnishing.

Axe making

Scafell Pike, England's highest mountain, and the famous Langdale Pikes, are well-known to tourists for their distinctive appearance in the beautiful Cumbrian landscape, and by rock climbers for their challenging crags and peaks. Few, perhaps, would associate such an unspoiled part of the country with what was certainly one of the first of all British industries. Indeed, the preponderance of Scandinavian place-names in the region led to a general assumption, until recent times, that the Lake District had remained a virtually unpopulated wilderness until the Viking settlements of the tenth century. An occasional stone circle or burial mound might occur here and there, but these were usually assumed to be Bronze Age structures of nomadic origin, with no implications of permanent settlement or activity in the area.

Archaeological revelations

Archaeologists, on the other hand, began to find stone axes and other primitive tools, made of a fine-grained volcanic tuff which could only have come from the so-called Borrowdale Volcanic rocks of which the central fells of Cumbria are formed. The stone flakes when struck, and can be worked to a sharp edge, like flint. Axes from the same source have been discovered not only locally, but as far away as Dorset and Gloucestershire, Scotland and South Wales.

In 1947, the site of an axe-making factory was discovered at the top of the scree tumbling from Pike of Stickle to the valley floor. Neolithic craftsmen were at work on this bleak factory floor some four thousand years ago, probably roughing out tools from the abundant material here and carrying them by mountain tracks to settlements near the coast where the axes were finished by shaping and polishing. No polished axes have been found on the site itself, but the scree and terraces above have revealed many unfinished axes. Nearby is a small man-made cave in the rock face where the workers probably sheltered in rough weather two thousand feet up in the wettest part of England.

In 1959, another axe-making site was found near the summit of Scafell Pike, and one or two others are now known in the same locality. Clearly a thriving trade was in progress in these desolate and savage places long before

Top: The prehistoric factory site on Pike of Stickle, in Great Langdale, Cumbria. Stone Age men roughed out axes from the volcanic rock.

Above: Roughly shaped Neolithic axes made from volcanic tuff.

the Romans came to Britain, and the stone quarrying which has remained an important Lakeland industry for centuries, was actually begun thousands of years ago.

The Lake District fells can be dangerous places for the inexperienced – it is easier to see the factories' products in museums.

Where to go
Among the museums which have collections of locally made axes and other Neolithic tools and implements are the Museum and Art Gallery at Carlisle (Castle Street) and the Museum of Lakeland Life and Industry at Kendal (Abbot Hall, Kirkland). Unfinished roughouts can be seen as well as polished tools, found all over England except in the south east, where flint was preferred.

The major axe factories are on the south west side of Scafell Pike, just below the summit, and on the southern slopes of Pike of Stickle above the scree. The fells should not be climbed without expert guidance, however.

Wadd mining

At the time when the Klondike Gold Rush was at its height on the other side of the Atlantic Ocean, armed guards and an Act of Parliament were used to protect mines in what was then Cumberland, where smugglers were keen to get their hands on the precious metal hidden below the rocks of Borrowdale. It was not gold. It did not glitter. The locals called the stuff 'wadd', but there were other names for it: 'black lead', 'plumbago', 'black cawke', or to be more scientific, graphite.

Books on industry which mention wadd at all will generally tell you that it was 'discovered' in the eighteenth century. But the Borrowdale folk knew about it long before that. Local farmers used it to brand their Herdwicks, and old wives ground it to a paste and administered it in white wine as an infallible cure for a variety of ills. As it worked by causing sweating, vomiting and urinating, the mere anticipation of the cure was probably sufficient to dispel the disease.

Some said the wadd was soot from the fires of hell which had been forced up to the earth's crust during the volcanic upheavals that created Borrowdale. This theory seemed the more likely, no doubt, because the deposits were formed in vertical 'pipes', like chimneys, and the Lakeland geologist John Postlethwaite argued that it only needed slightly different geological circumstances to produce diamonds instead of black lead.

Be that as it may, it was not long before Borrowdale's buried treasure came to the notice of industrialists from outside, who found that these were the purest graphite deposits in the world, waiting to be exploited. The stuff was a preservative against rust, a fixing agent for blue dyes, good for glazing pottery and casting cannon balls, ideal for black-leading fire grates and as pencil lead. A famous pencil factory grew up at Keswick on the strength of it, and still exists, though it now uses imported lead.

The rush for wadd

When the capitalist landowners had realized the great value of the Borrowdale plum-

Right: An eighteenth-century map of part of the Lake District showing Borrowdale and the site of the Black Lead mines near Seathwaite. 'Keswick Water' is now Derwent Water. The village of Seathwaite is actually on the east side of the River Derwent, not the west as shown here.

Below: An early photograph of the wadd mines, showing spoil heaps and water-powered crushing mill. This rare photograph is believed to have been taken in about 1850–60 using a primitive pin-hole camera.

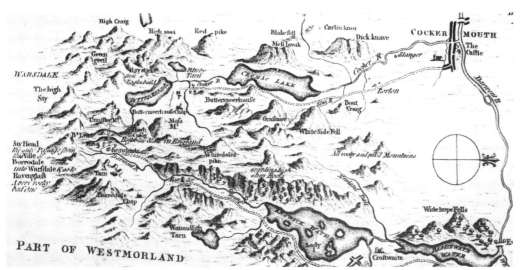

bago, they naturally wanted it all for themselves, but local folk realized they had been sitting on a fortune all these years and began illicit mining. The stuff was smuggled on pack-horse to the coast over Styhead Pass, or to Keswick, where the 'Bunch of Grapes' inn became a rendezvous for illicit traders.

In 1752 an Act of Parliament made it a felony, punishable by imprisonment with hard labour, to enter 'any mine or wad hole of black cawke, commonly called black lead, or unlawfully taking or carrying away any wad etc., therefrom, as also the buying or receiving the same. . . .' Armed guards were posted at mine entrances, and legitimate miners were searched as they left work each day. Armed escorts accompanied the pack-horses which carried the wadd from mines to customers. These precautions did not entirely succeed, however. Gangs of men attacked mine offices, or tunnelled underground to reach nearby mine workings, and there were occasional skirmishes. One visitor exploring upper Borrowdale in 1749 wrote: 'We had not ascended very far before we perceived some persons at a very great distance above us who seemed to be very busy, though we could not distinguish what they were doing. As soon as they saw us, they hastily left their work, and were running away. . . .' They had been digging with all kinds of implements among the spoil heaps, where they could find enough wadd to make a few shillings a day.

Meanwhile, the mine-owners were making huge profits. One deposit found in 1778 yielded graphite worth nearly £44,000, and another discovered in 1803 produced over £100,000 worth of wadd, most of which went to the pencil manufacturers, making and exporting what became known as the 'crayon d'anglais'.

By the late 1830's, however, the deposits were more or less exhausted, and when a group of miners worked for over a year without finding even a small amount of wadd, the owners called it a day and closed down. The mountains of Borrowdale were once more left to the sheep and the fell walkers.

Where to go
The old plumbago mines are about a thousand feet up the fells above Seathwaite and the infant River Derwent. The road through Borrowdale from Keswick branches off south from Seatoller before rising to the Honister Pass, and peters out when it reaches the tiny village of Seathwaite. The mines are 1000 feet up the fells to the west. Diminutive spoil heaps can be seen around the mine adits, but a hundred and fifty years of amateur geology and hopeful prospecting have sifted them to a fine powder unlikely to yield as much as a thimbleful of wadd.

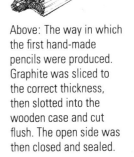

Above: The way in which the first hand-made pencils were produced. Graphite was sliced to the correct thickness, then slotted into the wooden case and cut flush. The open side was then closed and sealed.

Glass making

Although glass has been made by man for something like six thousand years, and we naturally take it very much for granted, it still seems to me one of the minor miracles of human industry that we can see through solid matter and let light into buildings without leaving them open to the elements.

After the departure of the Romans from Britain, the art of glass making was lost in these islands until two centuries later when, according to the Venerable Bede, Abbot Benedict 'sent messengers to Gaul to fetch makers of glass ... who were at that time unknown in Britain, that they might glaze the windows of his church ...' at Monkwearmouth (near Sunderland). Bede says that they also 'taught the English nation their handicraft'. This no doubt explains why glass making became so firmly established in the north of England and Scotland, although another more recent factor was the need for coal supplies after James I banned the use of wood to fuel glass furnaces because of the timber shortage.

Venice was the great centre of beautiful glassware for centuries, and it was not until relatively recent times that English glass won some notability, although it was made at many sites throughout the country. The finest glass used throughout the Middle Ages in England was imported.

Rise of British glass making

Between St Helens and Southport lie vast deposits of sand which is ideal for glass making. Largely for this reason, St Helens developed into a major centre of glass making on an industrial scale in the second half of the eighteenth century. Huge quantities of sand are still dug from beneath the topsoil after which the land is progressively restored to agricultural use.

The casting hall of the Ravenhead Glass Works, built in 1773 for the British Cast Plate Glass Company, was reputedly the largest factory under one roof in Britain at the time. Little of this now remains among the modern buildings of Pilkingtons' famous works, but it was built for the production of sheet glass by the modern process which was also introduced here from France. The huge demand for sheet glass created by the housing explosion of the Industrial Revolution

gave rise to other companies such as the Union Plate Glass Works and the St Helens Crown Glass Company.

Manufacturing techniques

Window and plate glass, which are the most matter-of-fact products of the glass makers, are produced by fusing sand, sodium carbonate and limestone. Other chemical ingredients are also used in specialised glass-making. The sand chosen has to be as free as possible of iron, otherwise the glass will turn green. The raw materials are melted in a tank furnace built of special clay blocks to withstand the high temperatures necessary. The mixture of raw materials is called 'frit' and it is melted at temperatures of up to 1600° C.

The fabrication of sheet glass was done until recently by pouring the molten glass through water-cooled rollers on to an 'annealing lehr' where it was cooled and toughened slowly to prevent crystallization. Then sheets were cut to size and transferred to tables where they were ground mechanically by a series of abrasives of reducing coarseness, and finally polished with felt. 'Nothing to it', one might think, but this streamlined mechanical process was the result of thousands of years of devoted

Left: Inside the casting hall of the old Ravenhead Glass Works, now part of the Pilkington group. The date 1773 can be seen on the arch. Sheet glass was made here by melting the raw materials in a high-temperature furnace and pouring the mixture on to annealing lehrs to cool and solidify. Factories such as this succeeded the many glass cones built in the area to exploit the ideal local sand, still dug for the purpose (below).

craftsmanship in making glass by hand for many purposes.

The older alternative 'pot' system took place in a glass 'cone' in which a coal furnace heated several clay pots or crucibles, from which melted glass passed on to a cooling gallery which opened into the wall of the cone.

The blowing iron by which blown glass vessels such as bottles and vases were made was evidently of Roman invention, and is still in use by individual craftsmen, although industrial manufacturers now duplicate the blowing process by mechanical means. The pipe is about five feet long, and is dipped into the molten glass and rotated to gather a quantity of glass on the pipe, which is then spun and swung about as the craftsman blows through it to form the glass into a rough shape before transferring it to a mould and blowing it to fit the pre-formed shape required. Flat glass was made by this method once, being blown in cylindrical form before

being cut through the length and flattened out. Coloured glass is made by adding metallic oxides to the basic ingredients, such as cobalt oxide for blue glass and manganese oxide for red.

Glass making today

Since 1959, the French method has been superseded here by the 'float glass' method developed by Sir Alistair Pilkington. In this process, instead of being poured on to a solid surface, the molten glass is floated across a bath of liquid tin, and the time-consuming processes of grinding and polishing have been eliminated by the automatic production of clear sheets of brilliant glass, putting Britain in the forefront of modern glass making technology.

The traditional method of blowing glass. The craftsman blows through the pipe to form the molten glass into the required shape.

Where to go

The Pilkington Glass Museum at St Helens, Merseyside (Prescot Road, off A58 Liverpool road one mile south west of town centre) shows the history of glass making in Britain as well as the many uses of glass. The manufacture of sheet glass can be seen by prior arrangement.

Makers of glass tableware in West Midlands (Stourbridge) demonstrate traditional glass blowing and hand cutting.

North East England

Apart from fishing, the industries discussed in this section may be classed as 'modern', although they are generally much older than the Industrial Revolution. The region is still very much a man's world, where the father of the family still rules the roost, Women's Lib and sex discrimination notwithstanding. The workers in heavy industry on land and dangerous work at sea derive their strength and character from the Brigantes and the Vikings who were such thorns in the flesh of Romans and Anglo-Saxons respectively.

The region has startling contrasts of landscape and activity, from the ugly industrial conurbations of Leeds/Bradford and Newcastle/Sunderland to the beautiful and sparsely populated areas of the Yorkshire Moors and Northumberland. But the growing industrialization of the north east in the eighteenth and nineteenth centuries brought pioneering minds to bear on the problems of development here, as elsewhere. Among the likeliest lads of the Victorian north east were the Father and Son of Tyneside, so to speak – George and Robert Stephenson, the latter rising from assistant builder of his father's world-famous *Rocket* to Member of Parliament for Whitby.

In a region which has grasped all its opportunities and led the way so often, it is perhaps not to be wondered at that power has tended to corrupt a little more often here, from George Hudson to more recent friends of Prime Ministers, but big prizes have been on offer for the adventurous, and Britain has benefited from those bold enough to take chances.

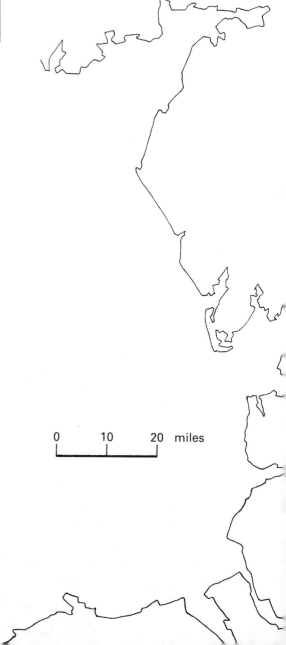

0   10   20   miles

Berwick-upon-Tweed

A1

Alnwick

NORTHUMBERLAND

Morpeth

North Shields

Newcastle

Hexham

South Shields

TYNE & WEAR

Sunderland

DURHAM

Durham

CLEVELAND

Hartlepool

Redcar

Darlington

Middlesbrough

Whitby

Richmond

A19

Northallerton

Hawes

NORTH YORKSHIRE

Pickering

Scarborough

Thirsk

A1

A64

Skipton

Harrogate

A65

York

HUMBERSIDE

Haworth

Bradford

Leeds

Selby

A63

Hull

WEST YORKSHIRE

Halifax

Heckmondwyke

Pontefract

Wakefield

Huddersfield

A19

Scunthorpe

Barnsley

Doncaster

A18

Grimsby

Rotherham

SOUTH YORKSHIRE

Sheffield

161

Wool

It was during the latter part of the eighteenth century that what was then called the West Riding of Yorkshire began its rise to supremacy in the wool textile industry. The widely scattered spinning and weaving centres of previous centuries, chiefly in the west of England, started to lose their leading positions with increased mechanization of the processes of woollen manufacturing, and Yorkshire was the beneficiary by virtue of its natural advantages.

Although it had not been dominant before the Industrial Revolution, Yorkshire had a long tradition of trading in wool and cloth; the Pennines had the right degree of humidity for spinning; adequate water-power was available to run increasingly large mills; Pennine water was of the right lime-free quality for washing, carding and combing; and when steam-power took over from water, Yorkshire had all the coal it needed close at hand. Last, but hardly least, it had plenty of its own sheep to provide the wool. With so much going for it, and its chief potential rival on the other side of the Pennines already deeply committed to cotton, west Yorkshire moved into a position of pre-eminence from which it has never looked back.

From cottage to factory

Halifax has the oldest claim to importance in the West Yorkshire wool trade. There were fullers and weavers here in the thirteenth century, and the town's prosperity rose on the backs of sheep as surely as that of the Cotswold towns.

As the wool industry spread, some specialization began to take place, with the result that Bradford and Keighley became known for worsteds, Leeds and Morley for woollens, Dewsbury and Batley for 'shoddy' (inferior cloth made from wool-waste and re-used wool). Worsteds use wool of long fibres or staple in which the fibres lie parallel to one another; woollens are made of short staple wool in which the fibres are not parallel. Yorkshiremen call them 'tops' and 'noils' respectively.

The growing army of workers moved out of their home workrooms and into the mills, where waterwheels turned the new machinery. Women and children worked long

hours in the mills, and sometimes slept in them rather than make the journey home and back again. But many were put out of work by mechanization, and when the Luddite riots broke out in the Midlands and north (see section on Hosiery in East Midlands chapter) there was a lot of damage and some bloodshed in the Yorkshire woollen industry. Charlotte Brontë used the rebellion as the background for her novel *Shirley*.

Yorkshiremen were in the vanguard of the movement to limit the crippling hours – sometimes fifteen a day – which children worked in the woollen and worsted mills. John Wood, a Bradford spinner, declared that factory children were worse off than the slaves of the West Indian sugar plantations, and it was Richard Oastler, a Leeds man,

Above: A scene inside a Yorkshire woollen mill in 1918. Note the good lighting conditions provided by the glass roof, contrasting with the primitive-looking machinery. The wool industry of Yorkshire was well behind the cotton industry of Lancashire in adapting itself to modern methods and factory organization. Hand-loom weaving survived the Industrial Revolution by over a hundred years.

thirties he had four mills of his own, and had experimented successfully with spinning the wool of the South American Alpaca goat, which his rivals had considered unusable. He set about building a big new factory just outside Bradford with a complete new village around it to house his workers, away from the heavy atmosphere of the town where the less fortunate were crammed into back-to-back houses with primitive sanitation and little self-respect.

Saltaire, as it was named, provided its new residents with school, hospital, laundry, church and fresh air, as well as work, and it stands there still, entirely stone-built, with a statue of Salt in the riverside park (looking not unlike Karl Marx). This model settlement preceded other famous industrial villages such as Bournville and Port Sunlight.

Below: Diagram of a typical old woollen mill, showing how water-power could be used to drive machinery on four floors. The wide waterwheel would be breastshot for maximum power. The overhead shafts turned pulleys to which the driving belts of machines were attached. This type of mill, using shafts of wrought iron turning at relatively high speeds, was in operation until the mid-nineteenth century, when steam-powered gears took over.

who led the campaign to have working hours for children under eighteen limited to ten a day. There is a statue of him in Bradford.

The mill-owners were often hard and occasionally cruel task-masters, but a great social upheaval like the Industrial Revolution was inevitably accompanied by much suffering, and better things were on the way. Poor working people asked the right questions with their rioting and their sacrifices, and sometimes with their blood, and the capitalists had to find sufficient answers.

Enlightened conditions

One who did produce answers was Sir Titus Salt. He was born at Morley and became his father's partner in a worsted manufacturing concern. By the time he was in his early

Rags to riches

By this time, steam power was taking over from water power, and the mill owners' operations were therefore no longer confined to the river valleys, so that places like Haworth up on the moors could take their share in the new industrial growth. Haworth is a visible monument to woollen textiles, as well as to the Brontë sisters. One of the most obvious differences between the cotton towns of Lancashire and the wool towns of Yorkshire is that while the mills of the former are built of brick, those of the latter are of stone, as were the old tall blocks of weavers' houses, with their long, high, mullioned windows.

Many of the early technical innovations of the textile industry were made in the Lancashire cotton operations, and are dealt with in that section, but the name of Samuel Lister, who became Lord Masham, is famous in the wool industry for several inventions, among which was a machine for combing the wool.

One of the more curious by-products of

Top: A Lister Comb, patented 1851, to comb long fibred wools, and below it, a Holden Comb for short fibre wools.

the wool industry is lanolin, extracted from the grease washed out of the raw wool, and used as the basis of ointments and in leather dressing. The wool trade also gave our language some of our most common everyday phrases: 'spinster', 'on tenterhooks', and 'spinning a yarn', among them.

Bradford soon became the world's largest and most famous wool market. Its population rose from thirteen thousand to over a quarter of a million during the course of the nineteenth century.

Leeds got the railway first, and grew rich on the rag trade, with a large population of Jewish immigrants from Europe helping to make it the ready-to-wear capital of Britain.

Wool towns and villages today

West Yorkshire is still a great stone-built monument to the wool industry, and almost every town and village one visits has its old preoccupations writ large in its buildings. One particularly rewarding site is the old market town of Hebden Bridge and its lofty

Above: John Marshall's Temple Works, Leeds – an eccentricity rare among Yorkshire's hard-headed businessmen. The architect went to Egypt to study the famous temple at Karnak.

Left: The neo-Gothic Wool Exchange in Bradford, another of the more flamboyant architectural monuments of the wool trade.

Left: A nineteenth-century engraving of Sir Titus Salt's riverside Alpaca wool mill at Saltaire, with houses built around it for the workers. The belching chimneys of Bradford are seen in the distance. The mill was conceived as a Renaissance palace by the architects, Lockwood and Mawson, and the village, with over five hundred houses by the 1860's, was a pioneer among industrial model housing estates.

tower. Saltaire village survives virtually unchanged, though now surrounded by outer suburbs on the Shipley side of the city, whilst Manningham Mills in Heaton Road is the huge and grand factory built by Lister for making velvet and plush. East of the city centre are the 'Little Germany' warehouses, built from 1853 onwards to supplement the Piece Hall, which was no longer adequate. The name comes from the flamboyant style of the buildings.

Halifax has the only surviving example of a Piece Hall in Horton Street, where cloth traders displayed their wares in more than three hundred separate rooms, built in three tiers round a quadrangle. It was completed in 1779 and is scheduled as an Ancient Monument. It now houses a museum of the textile industry, after having previously served as a vegetable market!

One of the more pretentious monuments of the industry's megalomania at one time is the Temple Works in Leeds (Marshall Street), where John Marshall built a flax mill in 1840 based on the Temple of Karnak in Egypt!

moorland neighbour Heptonstall. The town is in the valley, the village on the hill above it. The latter's winding streets and gaunt stone houses were the homes of the earlier cottage weavers, and the place is extremely interesting and even, in a rugged northern sort of way, picturesque. A surviving street sign in the vernacular announces 'Top oth town.' But when powered mills began to make their appearances, they were built down in the valley at Hebden Bridge, where the river provided power and the canal provided transport, so the town grew at the expense of the village.

In Bradford, as well as the nineteenth century mills, the great Wool Exchange stands overlooking Market Street, with St Blaise, patron saint of woolcombers, on its

Where to go

Saltaire is off A650 between Bradford city centre and Bingley to the north west. Hebden Bridge is at the junction of A646 and A6033 west of Halifax, and a minor road leads north from the town up to Heptonstall.

Armley Mills in Canal Road, Leeds, houses the city's industrial museum, whilst Bradford has a similar establishment at Moorside Mills and Moorside Road. Much textile machinery is on display there, including a working water-wheel and working machines which convert raw wool into worsted cloth. In Huddersfield, the Tolson Museum has fascinating exhibits on the industry's history.

Visitors to the Brontës' home at Haworth can combine a visit to 'Brontë Tapestries' at Ponden Hall, Stanbury (minor road two miles west of Haworth), where hand loom weaving is demonstrated in the building which Emily put into *Wuthering Heights* as Thrushcross Grange.

Fisheries

The North Sea was a scene of industry many centuries before gas and oil were found beneath it, but its industry is not one which seduces the industrial archaeologist, for fishing has not left its history in derelict buildings and rusting machinery – only in the headstones of seaport churchyards and the long memories of trawlermen and lifeboat crews. Hull and Grimsby, Whitby and North Shields are only the larger and better-known places among those north east coastal towns and villages whose harbours have sent men out in search of fish.

Religion and the rise of cod

British North Sea fisheries were already well established by the Norman Conquest, when boats went out as far as the Arctic to satisfy the market for fish largely created by the growth of Christianity, which enjoined its followers to fast on Wednesdays and Fridays. Fish was an acceptable substitute for the meat and other foods which the Church saw as self-indulgent. (Religion thus helped the Cheshire salt industry, too, since fish was preserved in salt before refrigeration became universal.) The fast day or 'fish day' subsequently came to be practised only on Fridays, and when the Reformation came, it badly hit the fishing industry. Ironically enough, the government of Elizabeth I, so frantically concerned to oppose Catholicism, tried to help the fishing industry by making it unlawful for anyone, whether Catholic or Protestant, to eat flesh on specified fish days.

In Shakespeare's 'King Lear', the Earl of Kent recommends himself to the king by undertaking, among other things, 'to eat no fish.' The phrase was the Elizabethan Protestant's way of denying that he was a Papist.

Drifters and trawlers

Cod, plaice and sole were the chief catches in the deep sea fishing grounds off the north east coast, but of course men from these parts went much further afield – to the Faroes, Iceland and the Baltic – and as steam began to power their vessels, fresh impetus

Below: The trawler *Kingston Jade* at the quayside in St Andrew's Dock, Hull, in the late 1950's. Men and women can be seen working on the quay to prepare the unloaded catch for market, whilst other trawlers are also seen tied up in the background.

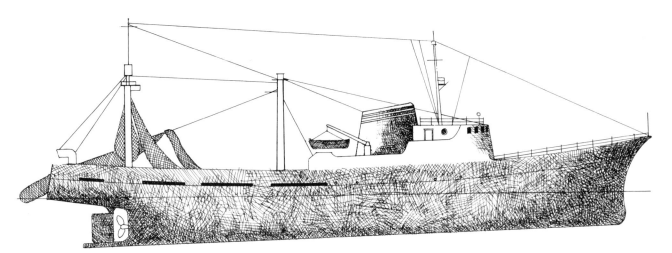

was given to the industry by its greater speed and capacity. The main methods of fishing were by drifting and trawling. Drifters work closely together dragging a series of vertical nets between them to catch fish such as herring and mackerel which swim near the surface.

The North Sea fisheries thrive on so-called 'ground fish', however, and for these the familiar trawler was introduced to north east ports in the mid-nineteenth century. It operates by dragging a wide-mouthed net along the sea floor. The hardest part of the trawlermen's work before mechanization was dragging the loaded nets on board. They spent a lot of time, too, in mending nets damaged by obstacles on the sea floor.

By the late 1930's, British fishermen, of whom there were over forty thousand, were landing more than a million tons of fish a year, of which by far the largest proportion was the trawlermen's haul of cod. Aided by storage of their fish in ice, they could make longer trips and the market was increased by the ability to deliver fresh fish to every inland part of the country.

Danger and depression
Trawling in the North Sea has always been a dangerous business, and every fishing community, large or small – Scarborough, Filey and Bridlington, Redcar, Staithes and Robin Hood's Bay, as well as Hull and Grimsby – has its tale of tragedy. Fishing fleets could be held up for many days by storms in winter, or prevented from entering harbour when they returned, sometimes having to be led to safety by lifeboats.

Modern navigational aids have eased the trawlerman's lot to a considerable extent, and the appearance of factory trawlers and the location of shoals by echosounder have

Top: A modern North Sea trawler. Science and technology are at the service of modern fishermen to help in a difficult and dangerous job.

increased the efficiency of the industry, but one of the consequences is the vexed modern problem of over-fishing.

The recent Cod War and Common Market restrictions do nothing to help an ancient British occupation which has gone hand-in-hand with the national seafaring tradition, but as long as there are fish in the North Sea, it is safe to suppose that the men of the Yorkshire and Northumbrian coasts will strive to earn a living by catching them.

Above: The scene at Grimsby's fish market, said to be the world's largest, where over half of all plaice and nearly all the turbot landed in England used to come to the docks in the oldest chartered town in the country. But the recent 'cod war' with Iceland has seriously affected the port's activity.

Where to go
Grimsby's Fish Dock is said to be the world's biggest fish market, whilst Hull has the country's largest trawler fleet. In Hull's Queen Victoria Square is the Town Docks Museum devoted to whaling, shipping and fisheries. Whitby, from where whaling vessels once sailed to Greenland, is still a busy fishing port. The *Cod and Lobster* at Staithes is a public house with a name typical of the region.

Steel making

With its large deposits of coal and iron ore, the north east was predestined to become important in the steel industry. From Sheffield and Rotherham in South Yorkshire to Middlesbrough and the Tees-side towns of Cleveland, up to Consett in Durham (much in the news at the time of writing) great steel works have cast a pall of smoke over the landscape since the Industrial Revolution made iron and steel the raw materials of manufacture of everything from spoons and razor blades to ships and bridges.

Whereas the more northerly works produce bulk steel for car bodies, ship and boiler plates, railway lines, bridge girders and so on, the Sheffield industry is famous for its narrower specialization, and it is with this that we are concerned in this section.

Sheffield's growth

In *The Canterbury Tales* Chaucer describes the Trumpington miller in the Reeve's Tale as bearing a 'Sheffield thwitel' (a large knife) in his hose, so by the fourteenth century the town was already noted for its knives. By Elizabethan times it was famous for all manner of cutlery. It had all the natural advantages for the growth of the industry – iron ore, coal and the carboniferous rock from which grindstones were made.

One of those who aided Sheffield in its successful progress through the Industrial Revolution was a Doncaster clock-maker, Benjamin Huntsman. He was dissatisfied with the imported steel from which his springs and pendulums were made, and moved to Sheffield to try to improve its uniformity, which he did by means of the 'crucible' technique. Crucible steel was made at Sheffield into the present century, when it was replaced by more sophisticated methods of high-quality steel production.

Stainless steel

Sheffield grew into a vast smoky forge, making knives and axes, saws and sickles, scythes, shears and scissors, and the Cutlers' Company, established in 1624, assumed control of the quality of all goods bearing the trade mark 'Sheffield Steel'. The Master Cutler would ceremoniously destroy, in Paradise Square, any product which was considered unworthy of the town.

Left: The Cutlers' Hall, Sheffield. The classical facade, with its Corinthian columns, cannot have pleased Ruskin, the champion of Gothic architecture, who thought that Sheffield might become a world art centre.
Below: A battery of five crucible furnaces in which high quality steel was made at Abbeydale Industrial Hamlet.

Below: An early view of the Cyclops Steel and Iron Works at Sheffield. Conical cementation furnaces can be seen in the middle distance, left. The cementation process made steel by packing bars of high-quality iron in charcoal, which was then raised to high temperatures for some days until the iron absorbed carbon and became steel.

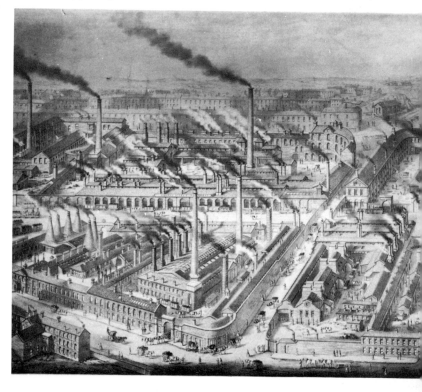

Above: The tilt forge at Abbeydale Industrial Hamlet. Built in 1785, the forge was powered by an 18 foot diameter breastshot water-wheel which drove the tilt hammers seen here. Scythes and other agricultural edge tools were made, using crucible steel made on the site. Other water wheels drove blowing cylinders, and grinding and boring machinery.

damage, and with plans for a prosperous future, though it still lives under the pall of smoke which has given it a doubtful environmental distinction since the Industrial Revolution. The story of its industry is well told in a number of survivals from its earlier days.

The largest remaining crucible steel shops, dating from 1898, are in the Balfour works in Broughton Lane, whilst the British Iron and Steel Research Association in Hoyle Street houses on its premises the country's only remaining cementation furnace. In Church Street, the nineteenth century Cutlers' Hall stands behind a classical facade.

The Abbeydale Industrial Hamlet is a unique industrial museum which was originally a late eighteenth century scythe works with stone-built workers' cottages and manager's house. This was a water-driven factory, and its waterwheels survive – one drove the blowing cylinders and another the tilt-hammers. This mill continued in production until 1933, and was opened as a fully restored museum in 1970. The spread of the city has rather destroyed the rural environment the workers used to enjoy, but once inside this fascinating tiny industrial estate you soon forget the modern housing estates outside, and can follow the making of edged tools through all the processes from start to finish.

The Sheffield City Museum has many interesting exhibits of local industry. Among other things, it owns an early nineteenth century water-powered grinding shop in Endcliffe Park, a little way outside the city on the west side. It has much equipment inside as well as its restored overshot waterwheel.

Every year the Cutlers' Company held its Cutlers' Feast, which it still does, one of the traditional courses being 'brewis', a concoction almost as mysterious as the Scots' haggis. It formed the chief item of diet for apprentices in poorer days.

Stainless steel came into use in the present century with the addition of nickel to the alloy, which increased tensile strength and gave resistance to corrosion. Later, chromium and nickel became the most usual additions, combining hardness and strength with the ability to withstand both heat and corrosion.

Sheffield today

Sheffield today is a modern city, much rebuilt after Second World War bomb

Where to go

The Abbeydale Industrial Hamlet lies on A621 at the south west edge of Sheffield not far from the Derbyshire border. The Shepherd Wheel and grinding shop are in Hangingwater Road (open Wednesday to Sunday only).

A new Industrial Museum is scheduled to open at Kelham Island, Sheffield, during 1982.

Water mills

Before steam power began to turn the wheels of the Industrial Revolution, those areas which were not flat enough to use the wind as their source of power had to rely on water running down from the hills. The north was especially favoured in this respect, with high rainfall feeding the fast streams flowing from the Pennines. Waterwheels, which had since ancient times been used only for driving the grind-stones of corn mills, gradually came into use for a wide variety of early industries, and by the Elizabethan age were the chief source of power throughout Europe. They drove fulling mills, bellows and hammers for the iron industry, pumping equipment and saw mills and other machinery, as well as continuing their important function in corn milling.

Types of waterwheel

The earliest types of waterwheel in use in Britain were those called 'Norse mills' and 'Vitruvian mills', which names adequately imply their origins. The Norse mill was a very primitive wheel driven horizontally to turn a vertical shaft. The Vitruvian wheel was an early version of the 'overshot' wheel which the Romans came to use.

There have been a great many refinements and variations in waterwheel design and operation since this form of power became more widely used, but generally speaking, waterwheels fell into three categories – undershot, breastshot and overshot.

The undershot wheel stood above a fast-flowing stream and was driven by the impulse of the water against the blades or paddles of the wheel. Its power was in proportion to the speed and volume of the water, the size of the blades and the wheel's radius. It did not generate a great deal of energy, however, and the breastshot wheel was much more efficient, being driven by water which fell down an artificial waterfall and thus struck the blades with more force on its downward motion. The overshot wheel was one in which water falling on to the wheel from above it was caught in buckets or compartments instead of striking flat blades, and thus the wheel was driven round by gravity. These latter types of wheel were soon found to generate the most power, and as the design of waterwheels

improved, mills could soon be run on as much as a hundred horse-power. Not least of the advantages of the overshot wheel was the fact that it did not depend on a continuously running stream. Water could be stored by the construction of a dam, and the mill-owner could turn it on to run the wheel just when he wanted it.

The great engineer Sir William Fairbairn was one of those who studied mill workings and achieved notable improvements in the efficiency of waterwheels. Lightweight metal replaced heavy timber for their construction, and waterwheels continued to be built for many years after the introduction of steam power, largely because they were cheap to install and cheap to run, compared with the new engines. A few waterwheels are still in operation today.

Surviving waterwheels

Yorkshire has a considerable number of the country's remaining waterwheels, and in Leeds, of all places, was one of the last mills to use them regularly. This was the Thwaite Putty Mill, in Thwaite Lane, Hunslet, where until recently two breastshot iron waterwheels ran machinery which ground chalk for making putty.

Above: The larger of the two breastshot iron waterwheels at Thwaite Mills, Hunslet. It is 17 feet 10 inches in diameter and 14 feet 4 inches wide, and was built in 1825 to drive grinding machinery for crushing flint used in glazing pottery. Subsequently the mill made linseed oil putty, for which the machinery was used to grind chalk. This mill's two wheels were driven by the River Aire.

Left: Consett steel works, Durham. A steel furnace in the town where iron has been smelted since about 1840, now a casualty of the world recession.

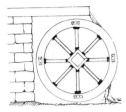

Overshot wheel

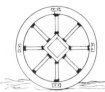

Undershot wheel

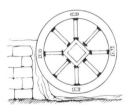

Breastshot wheel

Above: The operation of (top to bottom) overshot, undershot and breastshot waterwheels.

Sheffield has a working waterwheel in the Sharrow Snuff Mill – an overshot wheel which powers mills for the powdering of tobacco. Another overshot wheel worked until recently at the Low Matlock Rolling Mill outside the city.

At Skipton, in North Yorkshire, two waterwheels are preserved in the private museum of a restored watermill at Chapel Hill, known as High Mill.

Dale End Mill at nearby Lothersdale, originally a corn mill and later a silk spinning mill, has a huge wheel built of iron in 1862. It has a diameter of 45 feet and a width of five feet, with 162 'buckets'.

At Pateley Bridge, north west of Harrogate, the Foster Beck Mill has a breastshot wheel 35 feet in diameter.

Above: Worsbrough Mill, near Barnsley. Parts of this stone-built corn mill date from 1625. The three-storey building is a nineteenth-century extension. The original mill was powered by a cast iron overshot waterwheel of 14 feet 4½ inches diameter, driven by a leat. It turned three pairs of millstones. The mill has been restored to full working order and is maintained as a museum, off A61 south of Barnsley.

Where to go

As well as water wheels mentioned in above text, several water-driven mills are mentioned in various other sections of this book (and see Wool and Steel making in this section).

A curiosity of northern mills is that the wheels are usually incorporated in the interior of the buildings, unlike those in the south.

A working mill grinding meal and flour can be visited by arrangement at Alvingham, Lincolnshire (unclassified road north east of Louth.)

Britain's largest water-wheel is the 'Laxey' wheel on the Isle of Man.

Coal mining

The coal deposits of north eastern England have provided the modern foundations of the country's most concentrated industrial activities. They stretch from Nottingham to Leeds and from the Tees to the Coquet. Many of those towns whose very names evoke grim black images of slag heaps and pit-head winding gear and smoking chimneys were founded on coal – Barnsley and Doncaster, Wakefield and Pontefract, Durham and Newcastle.

Extraction and transportation

Some open-cast mining of coal was done along the banks of the Tyne and Wear river banks as early as the twelfth century, but it was not until Elizabethan days that coal began to replace timber as the most important fuel, and by that time it was being exploited by mining, mainly in the form of drifts and bell-pits. Drifts were horizontal galleries cut into hillsides along the coal seams. Bell-pits were small shafts cut through to the shallow seams and then widened beneath the surface.

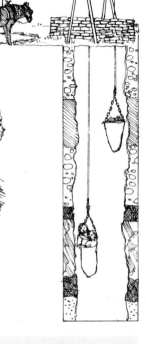

Right: A simple horse gin lowers working children down a mine shaft in one basket, coal being raised in another by the same operation. The baskets, made of hazel, were called 'corves'.

Above: A child hauling with chain and girdle. The corf might hold half a ton of coal, and colliers expected twenty hauls in each shift.

Below: A nineteenth century engraving which graphically captures the industrial scene in its view of Percy Pit, Percy Main Colliery, at North Shields.

In 1606, Huntington Beaumont, a member of a great Leicestershire family that owned mines in the north east, demonstrated a borehole technique to locate worthwhile coal seams more cheaply and easily than by the laborious process of sinking trial shafts, and shaft mining developed rapidly from this time onward. Beaumont is also believed to have operated a primitive wooden railway to carry coal from his mines to the river barges.

The Northumberland and Durham coalfield in due time became the biggest in the country. Coal was being shipped regularly from Newcastle to London and the Continent in large quantities, and the growing shipyards of Tyneside and Sunderland were kept busy building fleets of colliers for transportation of the fuel which the whole country was demanding on an increasing scale. Boats called keels brought coal downriver to the ports for loading on to the colliers. Four hundred ships were constantly carrying coal to the east coast ports in the seventeenth century.

Darkness at noon

Underground, the story was a grim one by the time of the Industrial Revolution. Women and children were employed in the mines. Sometimes women hewed coal alongside the men, both sexes naked to the waist in the insufferable heat. Chiefly, however, women and girls acted as 'drawers' or 'hurriers', crawling on all fours to haul loads of coal along the pit roads by means of ropes or chains attached to their waists and passing between their legs. Sometimes they had to crawl through water in flooded passages.

Boys also worked with the men extracting coal when they were considered old enough, but even from the age of six they were employed as 'trappers', going down the mines early in the morning and spending long days squatting in darkness, opening 'trap-doors' for the ventilation of the pits and the passage of men and coal.

The Yorkshire mine-owners were worst for their remorseless use of child labour, but the Northumberland and Durham pits were the worst for mine accidents. Explosions were frequent, even after the introduction of the Davy lamp. It was the disaster at the

Above: A north eastern colliery with vertical winding gear. The Northumberland and Durham coalfield introduced this variation on the horizontal winding engine, which became a regional distinction in the nineteenth century.

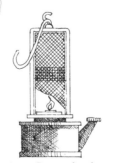

Above: Davy safety lamp. Invented by Humphrey Davy in 1816, the flame is enclosed by fine wire mesh to prevent the escape of fumes at temperatures high enough to ignite gases.

Felling Colliery near Gateshead in 1812, when ninety-two men and boys were killed, which led to the formation of the Society for Preventing Accidents in Coal Mines at Sunderland, and to Humphrey Davy's investigation into the dangerous methane gas which miners called 'firedamp'.

The modern coal industry of the north east has been built on foundations of misery, disease and death, and it is hardly surprising that it is associated with militant trade unionism. The Durham Miners' Gala is an annual event which never fails to make the national news, providing as it does an ideal platform for major speeches by Labour politicians.

Where to go
The North of England Open Air Museum at Beamish, Durham (A693 between Stanley and Chester le Street) is a major information source for the industry of the north east. Vertical winding gear, peculiar to this region, can be seen, as well as rebuilt interiors of pitmen's cottages, and the only remaining coal-drop, brought from the harbour at Seaham.

Railways

Nearly every part of Britain has made some important contributions to railway development, so that it might seem invidious to single out particular areas for discussion, but no one could deny that the north east is entitled to a leading place in the story of railway progress. Newcastle-upon-Tyne is said to have had the first system of transport that could reasonably be called a railway, as early as the reign of Charles I, although Huntington Beaumont had used the basic principle of rail transport even earlier at his Northumberland mines. The Stephensons were Newcastle men and George Hudson ('the Railway King') a Yorkshireman. Doncaster was to become one of the great railway workshops, and the National Railway Museum is now established at York. (Also worth visiting at York is the station, which is of some architectural merit, with its roof of glass and cast iron.) At Doncaster, still one of British Rail's main locomotive works, were made some of the great LNER locomotives, including *Flying Scotsman* and *Mallard*.

The most decisive factor in the north east's claim to be in the forefront of railway progress, however, was the opening in 1825 of the Stockton and Darlington Railway, the first public line on which steam locomotion was brought into use – though the first trains to run on it were horse-drawn. The great expansion of railway building got its impetus from this. With the exception of the Enclosure Acts, nothing has had a greater impact on the whole British landscape. Within twenty-five years, approval had been given for more than 12,000 miles of track, though not all of that planned was actually built. A quarter of a million men – popularly known as 'navvies' after the navigators of the canal age – were employed in building railways.

The pioneers

Railways came into use originally as the easiest and cheapest method of moving coal from the mines to the canals and rivers which carried it to its destinations. They were initially trains of wagons propelled along rails by gravity or horse-power, and the use of mobile steam-power did not come until 1802 with Trevithick's experiments at

Above: The opening of the Stockton and Darlington Railway, 1825. A contemporary artist's impression showing George Stephenson's *Locomotion* hauling thirty-two wagons at 10 m.p.h.

Below: Stephenson's High Level Bridge across the Tyne at Newcastle. The double-decked bridge carries three railway tracks on top and a roadway with footpaths below.

Coalbrookdale in Shropshire. Twenty-three years later, George Stephenson's locomotive pulled a train between Stockton and Darlington, and it was not long before the general form of the steam locomotive became established, to remain unchanged until well over a century later, when steam locomotives were retired from service with British Railways.

The standard gauge of 4 feet 8½ inches appears to have been adopted from the width between horse-drawn tram wheels in use at the time. It was believed to have been the distance between the wheels of an ancient Roman chariot.

The men who built the railways – the

years between 1830 and 1860, some 25,000 railway bridges were built, many of them masterpieces of design and engineering which remain with us today. The oldest surviving railway bridge is the Causey Arch at Tanfield, County Durham. It was built as long ago as 1727, and is among the largest masonry bridges built for a railway in Britain. Other notable railway bridges in the north east include the seven-arch Victoria Bridge across the Wear in Sunderland, built in 1838 for the Durham Junction Railway, and the High Level Bridge built by George Stephenson in 1849 across the Tyne at Newcastle.

When George Hudson became a dictator of railway speculation in the north and Member of Parliament for Sunderland, he began that amalgamation of local railways which led to the North Eastern Railway, the earliest regional monopoly in the railway industry. The NER controlled all railways between the Humber and the Scottish border, and between the Pennines and the North Sea, and was the first step on the road to a national railway network. The later company, the London and North Eastern Railway, achieved the highest speed then attained by a steam locomotive in 1938 when the 167 ton *Mallard* recorded 126 m.p.h., this world record still stands today.

'navvies' – were gangs of labourers thrown together in a great industrial enterprise which brought unprecedented changes to the towns, villages and countryside they worked their way through. They were hard workers who risked life and limb, and in consequence were a law unto themselves, violent and quarrelsome. Their language output and their liquor intake were equally shocking to much of the population of Victorian Britain, and everywhere they went they terrorized the local women. But their achievements were of a magnitude we easily overlook now, as we take the railways so much for granted.

Railway landscape
Because railways could not work efficiently if they encountered steep gradients or sharp bends, the object of the planners was always to make the lines as straight and as level as possible, and to this end, entire hills had to be moved, cuttings and embankments made, rock had to be tunnelled through, and river valleys crossed. The work was on a scale the world had hardly seen since the building of the pyramids or the Great Wall of China, and the landscape was changed for ever by the vast earthworks that were undertaken.

Perhaps the most obvious additions to the landscape were the bridges. In the thirty

Top: A 4-2-2 locomotive of the Great Northern Railway, built at Doncaster.

Above: The LNER's A3 Pacific class locomotive *Flying Scotsman* also built at Doncaster. The streamlining of this class from 1935 led to the world record speed for a steam locomotive.

Above: The amalgamation of a number of smaller railway companies led in 1863 to the first regional monopoly, the North Eastern Railway, whose crest is shown.

Where to go
The National Railway Museum at York is now the chief centre of railway history, covering a century and a half of the industry. It has an unequalled collection of locomotives, including diesel and electric as well as steam. The LNER's *Mallard* is among them.

At the Darlington Railway Museum, at North Road Station, Darlington, is Stephenson's *Locomotion*, built for the Stockton and Darlington Railway in 1825. Industrial locomotives can also be seen at Beamish (see Coal mining).

Among preserved steam railways of the region are the Keighley and Worth Valley Railway (Keighley); the North York Moors Railway (Pickering); and the Bowes Railway (Springwell, near Gateshead).

Scotland

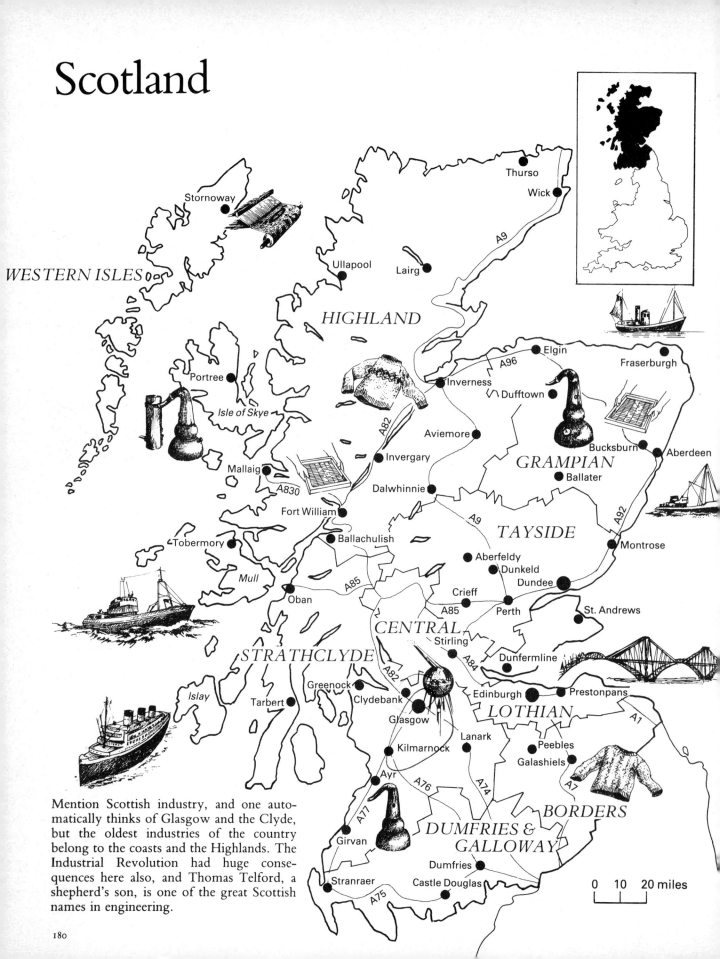

WESTERN ISLES

Stornoway

Thurso
Wick

Ullapool
Lairg
A9

HIGHLAND

Portree
Isle of Skye

Elgin
Inverness
A96
Dufftown
Fraserburgh

Mallaig
A830
Invergary
Aviemore
GRAMPIAN
Bucksburn
Aberdeen
Ballater

Fort William
Dalwhinnie
A9
TAYSIDE
A92
Montrose

Tobermory
Ballachulish
Aberfeldy
Dunkeld
Dundee

Mull
Oban
A85
Crieff
Perth
A85
St. Andrews

CENTRAL
Stirling
Dunfermline

STRATHCLYDE
A82
A84

Islay
Greenock
Clydebank
Edinburgh
Prestonpans
LOTHIAN
A1
Tarbert
Glasgow
Lanark
Peebles
Galashiels
BORDERS
A7

Kilmarnock

Ayr
A76
A74
DUMFRIES &
GALLOWAY
A77

Girvan
Dumfries
Stranraer
Castle Douglas
A75

Mention Scottish industry, and one automatically thinks of Glasgow and the Clyde,
but the oldest industries of the country
belong to the coasts and the Highlands. The
Industrial Revolution had huge consequences here also, and Thomas Telford, a
shepherd's son, is one of the great Scottish
names in engineering.

0   10   20 miles

Paper making

The paper making industry has grown in Scotland since wood pulp began to be used for manufacturing cheaper paper. Industry's colossal demand for newsprint and other papers is being met in part by manufacturing from wood pulp instead of from the more expensive rags and esparto grass. Scotland's softwood forests supply the substitute for linen and cotton rags which are becoming increasingly scarce as synthetic fibres replace them. The country has the necessary water supplies for the industry, as well as the timber, and the Forestry Commission's conifer plantations will ensure supplies of paper far into the future.

Paper from pulp

The basic principles of paper making are explained in the chapter on South East England, but the pulping process is of two types. In one, logs of coniferous trees are ground down to produce a cellulose fibre for what is known as mechanical wood pulp, which is used to make cheaper papers such as newsprint.

Other papers are known as wood-free, but they still contain wood pulp, which is made in this case by chemical processing. It removes all those impurities which are allowed to remain in mechanical wood pulp, and thus results in a purer quality of paper. Various additives are mixed with the pulp according to the type of paper required, but the chief ingredient is water.

The biggest concentration of paper mills in Scotland is in and around Edinburgh, along the streams and rivers which flow into the Firth of Forth. The Scottish capital has been an important publishing centre for centuries, and its demand for paper is very considerable. Mills in the area produce a fifth of all Britain's fine papers, using pulp from Canada and Europe, and esparto grass from North Africa. Glasgow and Aberdeen are among other centres of the paper industry, whilst paper-making machinery is built at Dalkeith.

The Wiggins Teape Group is one of the country's largest paper-making concerns, and among its ten mills is Stoneywood Mill on the River Don near Aberdeen, where up to forty thousand tons of paper a year can be produced for a world-wide market.

Top: Wiggins Teape's pulp and paper mill at Corpach, during construction in the Sixties. This mill at the narrow neck of Loch Eil was intended to exploit Scotland's coniferous timber and provide much-needed employment in the Highlands, but the pulping operation proved unprofitable and has since been closed down. The paper mill is still in production, using imported pulp.

Above: The Stoneywood Mill near Aberdeen. The production lines of this huge mill can produce over forty thousand tons of paper a year, ranging from fine writing and printing papers to security papers and coated papers for other special purposes.

Where to go

Members of the public can visit Stoneywood Mill (Bucksburn – A96 north west of Aberdeen) by prior arrangement.

At Corpach (north west of Fort William) Wiggins Teape opened a pulp mill in 1966. This has been closed recently, but the firm's paper mill there is still in operation.

Chemicals

Chemicals and associated light industries, such as plastics and glass making, have been 'introduced' to Scotland in the present century to relieve the country's hazardous dependence on heavy industries such as shipbuilding and steel making. But 'introduced' is a misleading term, for Scotland – and Glasgow in particular – has been familiar with chemical working for a long time.

Prestonpans, near Edinburgh, takes its name from the salt pans used by monks as long ago as the twelfth century to extract salt from sea-water. The town supplied salt to eastern Scotland for centuries, until the Act of Union enabled English salt to be sold in Scotland, but it was not until 1959 that the local business ceased.

Industrial chemicals

The textile industries gave Glasgow an early interest in bleaching and dyeing processes. Charles Tennant set up the St Rollox works there in 1799 to manufacture bleach from chlorine and lime. The process used sulphuric acid, and Glasgow became one of the chief centres of producing the acid by the 'lead chamber' process. In this process, sulphur and potassium nitrate were burned and the fumes condensed on to water held in a lead container, because lead was impervious to the resulting acid.

It was a Glasgow chemist, Charles Macintosh, who discovered in 1823 the technique of dissolving rubber, and coating fabrics with the solution in order to make garments waterproof. Although we now use plastics instead of rubber to keep the rain off, we still keep his name alive in calling the modern equivalent a 'plastic mac'. Macintosh also started Scotland's first alum works.

Another important Scottish chemical industry, which might be regarded with hindsight as a portent, was the extraction of oil from shale by a distillation process. This industry was begun in the mid-nineteenth century by Dr James Young, who had been associated with Michael Faraday and the afore-mentioned Charles Tennant. He mined the shale and refined paraffin from it, and the industry expanded rapidly in the Lothians, where Britain's largest deposits of oil shale were found. These were given the name Torbanite, after Torbane where

Below: Aerial view of the St Rollox chemical works at Springburn, Glasgow, about 1930. This complex, founded in 1799 to manufacture bleaching powder, has now been demolished. The chimney, top centre, reputedly the world's largest, was built to disperse unpleasant fumes over a wide area and avoid excessive pollution in the immediate vicinity. The method of producing bleach gave Glasgow a lead in making sulphuric acid.

Young began his exploitation. Oil shale was also called Boghead Coal. A refinery was built at Pumpherston, and in due course Scotland came to supply ninety per cent of the world's shale oil output, but the industry came to an end about twenty years ago.

At Ardeer, Strathclyde (between Irvine and Ardrossan) Imperial Chemical Industries have their explosives factory, where most of Britain's industrial explosives are now made, for use in mines, quarries and civil engineering works.

Where to go
The area of Lothian west of Edinburgh was the site of the shale oil industry.

Pumpherston is between M8 and A71, and just north of the motorway is Broxburn, once an important centre of the industry.

Torbane is near Bathgate, farther west near the motorway.

The most obvious remains of the shale oil industry are the mining waste heaps, called 'bings'.

Shipbuilding

Although boatyards had existed on the Clyde for hundreds of years, it was not until the nineteenth century that shipbuilding became a major industry there. Little more than a century ago, much of the river bank where huge shipyards now stand was fertile agricultural land. However, the availability of local steel and the coming of steam power provided Glasgow with the incentive to dredge and widen the river in order that big ships could be built and launched there.

The Clyde is tidal and navigable as far as Glasgow, and its wharves and shipyards stretch westward from the Govan and Clydebank districts of the city towards the estuary as far as Port Glasgow and Greenock. Glasgow began its colossal industrial growth after the Act of Union, and from the middle of the nineteenth century its population rocketed to make it Britain's third largest city, and one of the world's chief ports and shipbuilding centres.

The demand for merchant vessels for trading across the Atlantic was one of the main reasons for the growth of Clyde shipbuilding. The first sea-going ship with a steam engine, Henry Bell's *Comet* – forty feet long and capable of six miles an hour – was launched at Port Glasgow in 1812; and the first ocean-going vessel built of steel was launched at Dumbarton in 1879. Turbine engines were first used on passenger steamers on the Clyde, and were first used in transatlantic ships in 1905. By the First World War, Clyde yards were producing nearly eight hundred thousand tons of shipping a year, including oil tankers and other merchant ships of increasingly colossal size, as well as a large part of the Royal Navy's fleet. The best known of the Clyde ships, however, were the ocean liners.

The crossing of the Atlantic Ocean was

Below: The Cunard White Star liner *Queen Mary* being launched at John Brown's shipyard, Clydebank, on a wet day in September 1934. Her Majesty Queen Mary performed the naming ceremony, but legend has it that the ship was so named through a misunderstanding between Cunard's chairman and King George V. After fitting out, the famous liner made her first voyage across the Atlantic in 1936, and is now used as a convention centre in California.

one of the greatest adventures in the traveller's world at the turn of the century. The sea
which separated Britain and Europe from
the New World could, of course, be crossed
only by ship. It was a voyage of several days,
and the big shipping companies such as
Cunard were anxious to assure passengers
that the Atlantic Ocean, which is never
exactly as calm as a millpond, could be
crossed in perfect comfort. They built what
were virtually floating towns, with everything aboard that would be expected of a
first class hotel on land, as well as all the
machinery and fuel necessary to drive the
vessel to its destination. Soon luxury liners
advertised as 'floating palaces' were crossing
the ocean on regular schedules, and they
remain among the greatest monuments to
man's engineering skill and ingenuity.

The advent of the luxury liner
The building of a ship is a complicated
combination of architectural and engineering
skills, and the larger the vessel, the greater
the problems become. A ship is subject to
stresses resulting from its great weight and
the pressures of water against its bulk. Its
structure 'settles' after launching like the
foundations of a building on land, and all
these factors must be allowed for in the
design and building, whilst at the same time
the shipping company which has commissioned the ship demands speed and efficiency
as well as good looks in the vessel.

As long ago as 1888, Sir William Pearce of
the Fairfield shipyard on the Clyde had
designed a ship that he claimed would cross
the Atlantic in five days. Pearce did not live
to see his plan realised, but from this time
onwards, the liners equipped with sail to get
them home in the event of mechanical failure
were on their way out, and on the horizon
were the first of the mammoth liners,
Cunard's *Mauretania* and *Lusitania*.

Mauretania was built in England, and
Lusitania at Clydebank, in a yard whose
world-famous speciality was to be luxury
liners – John Brown's. *Lusitania* was a ship of
31,000 tons with four raked funnels. She
made her maiden voyage in 1907, crossing
the Atlantic in five days. In 1915, she was
sunk by one torpedo fired from a German
U-boat, and over a thousand lives were lost.

Cunard suspended transatlantic passenger
operations for the duration of the war, and
after it, French and German liners competed
for superiority in size and speed. Nevertheless, by the beginning of the thirties, John
Brown's shipyard had an order on the stocks
for Cunard which was to be the largest ship
afloat. To the men who were busy building
her, she was Job No. 534. To the world at
large, she was to be known as the *Queen
Mary*.

The Clydebank *Queens*
The *Queen Mary* was launched in September
1934. She had a gross tonnage of 81,235, a
total length of over a thousand feet, and a

Below: Shipyards on the
Clyde at Glasgow. Along-
side the shipbuilding
industry, marine
engineering has
developed, as well as
repairing and refitting.
Engines, cranes and other
equipment are built, not
only for the local
shipyards, but for
overseas docks and ship
builders, whilst large
graving docks are
equipped to repair
the largest ships afloat.

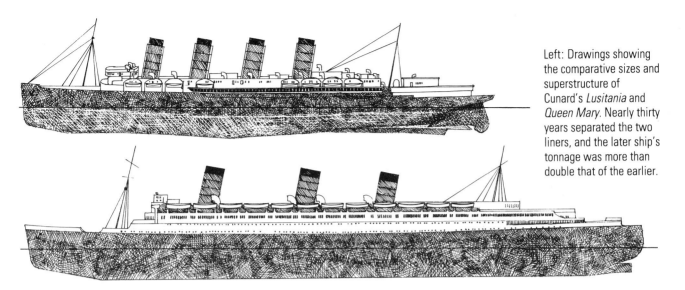

Left: Drawings showing the comparative sizes and superstructure of Cunard's *Lusitania* and *Queen Mary*. Nearly thirty years separated the two liners, and the later ship's tonnage was more than double that of the earlier.

top speed of twenty-eight knots. She was propelled by four screws which alone weighed thirty-five tons each. Even while she made her maiden voyage to New York in 1936, John Brown's had an even bigger ship under construction, the *Queen Elizabeth*.

The new ship had fourteen decks, and accommodation for over two thousand passengers, and she cost nine million pounds. No wonder a cartoonist of the time drew a gigantic Cunard liner with the name RMS *Megalomania*.

Queen Elizabeth was launched in 1939 but remained on the Clyde during the early months of the Second World War, hardly fitted out and painted troopship grey, until she got secret orders to sail direct to New York. Both she and the *Queen Mary* served as troopships, and came into passenger service after the war until the sixties, when John Brown's built and delivered the *Queen Elizabeth 2*, to be ever afterwards known simply as 'QE2'. She cost nearly thirty million pounds.

The story goes that Cunard wanted to engage the Beatles to play a specially composed tune at the ship's launching, but John Rannie, the boss of Brown's, told Cunard that she was not their ship until delivered, and as the last great liner slid down the slipways into the Clyde, a band played 'Scotland the Brave'. John Rannie, like William Pearce of Fairfields, had risen from the ranks, as it were, starting work at John Brown's as an apprentice boilermaker.

Below: A modern ship under construction at the Govan shipyard, Glasgow. The Clyde yards still build a wide range of ships – tankers, bulk carriers and naval vessels as well as cruise liners. Much of their activity nowadays is concerned with North Sea Oil, and the yards build drilling platforms and support vessels for Britain's most important new industry.

Meanwhile, the redundant Queens Mary and Elizabeth were sold to American entrepreneurs. *Queen Mary* was to be used as a floating convention centre in California, and *Queen Elizabeth* eventually came to rest in Hong Kong Harbour, where she was to be a unique maritime university, but her life ended when she was gutted by fire.

As well as the famous 'Queens', Brown's shipyard also built the royal yacht *Britannia*. By this time, however, passenger aircraft, each carrying several hundred passengers, were crossing the Atlantic in about seven hours, whilst liners were still taking five days, as they had since 1907.

Shipyard reorganisation

Changes in fortune over the century since heavy industry grew on the Clyde have made the shipbuilders among the most militant of modern workers. The lightning growth of Glasgow's population gave the city the worst slums in the kingdom, with wages often behind those elsewhere.

As foreign competition challenged the supremacy of British shipbuilders (who had produced a third of all the world's ships as late as 1950) the industry went through economic crisis after crisis, and the Clyde shipyards underwent drastic changes. Some closed down altogether, and others formed major combines like Govan Shipbuilders.

Where to go

The Clyde's industrial landscape can be seen from A814 which passes through Clydebank and Dumbarton on the north bank of the river from Glasgow, whilst A8 passes through Govan and goes to Port Glasgow and Greenock on the south bank of the Firth of Clyde.

Glasgow's Museum of Transport (Albert Drive) has a large collection of model ships, and the McLean Museum at Greenock also has exhibits on the shipping industry.

Tweeds and woollens

Weaving and knitting are among the very few occupations which have to some extent remained as cottage industries in parts of Scotland, virtually untouched by the Industrial Revolution. On the mainland, knitting is an important Scottish factory industry, but on the islands, world-famous tweeds and woollen goods are still made in the traditional way.

Hebridean tweeds

The crofts on the island of the Outer Hebrides (or Western Isles) known as Lewis (of which Harris is the southern peninsular end) date from the domination of the islands from the seventeenth century by clans such as the Seaforth Mackenzies, who allowed their tenants to farm the land and engage in cottage industries. From this time the origins of Harris tweed are dated.

The name 'tweed' is a corruption of 'twill', the word for cloth with parallel diagonal lines in the weave. One tweed is eighty yards long, and one man can weave

about two and a half tweeds in a working week.

Today the wool is spun and dyed in mills at Stornoway, the 'capital' of the island's tweed industry, but it is still woven on hand looms by the Gaelic-speaking crofters in their cottages. One can sometimes see the

Left: A loom used in the manufacture of Harris tweed in a crofter's cottage in the Western Isles. Hand loom weaving still thrives on the islands round the Scottish mainland.

Below: A self-employed weaver is seen at work in the Orkney Islands. Hand looms are still made of traditional hardwoods in Scotland, for cottage weaving is a successful business with a big export trade. All Harris tweed is hand-woven, but spinning, dyeing and finishing processes are carried out in mills at Stornoway, Lewis.

tweed piled up at the roadsides awaiting collection by the mills – a testimonial to its hard-wearing qualities as well as its genuine origin. In turn, the mills deliver yarn daily to all the villages where weaving is carried on.

The trade-mark of Harris Tweed is given only to tweed which is hand-woven, as well as spun, dyed and finished, in the Outer Hebrides from 'pure virgin wool', and attempts by mainland concerns to break into the profitable use of the name have consistently failed. The industry consumes about a third of all Scottish-grown wool, and the bulk of the finished cloth is exported, much of it to the United States.

Fair Isle and Shetland woollens
Fair Isle is Britain's most remote inhabited island, but its name is well known throughout the world for the garments which its women knit by hand in highly complicated traditional patterns. It is probable that Fair Isle patterns are of Norse origin, for all these northern islands were Viking strongholds during a long period of their development.

The Shetland woollen industry is much more diverse. It is still carried on by individual knitters, but machinery from the mainland has also given rise to several hosiery and

Above: Gloves knitted with typical Fair Isle patterns. Fair Isle knitwear is traditionally made with intricate designs of dyed wool, whereas Shetland knitwear is in the natural colour of the wool.

Below: Trow Mill near Hawick. Tweeds, blankets and travel rugs are among the products of this mainland mill, where the processes of weaving are demonstrated during guided tours.

knitwear mills in and around Lerwick employing a hundred or more people.

Mainland knitwear
The factory textile industry in Scotland is widespread, but one of its main and best known centres is Hawick and the surrounding area south of Edinburgh. Before the Industrial Revolution, small mills were established along the streams and rivers, and although steam-power relieved manufacturers from this imperative location, the pattern of growth of the textile industry has tended to remain in the vicinity of the River Tweed and its tributaries.

Huge amounts of woollen goods are produced by Hawick's mills and factories, which employ more than half the town's workers, with other concentrations in Peebles, Selkirk, Galashiels and other local centres, and there is a big export trade in products which again are world-famous, largely because Scottish producers were forced – by overwhelming competition from Yorkshire during its industrial growth – into specialising in high-quality and expensive fashion knitwear. Cashmere shawls were among Scotland's most coveted products.

Where to go
Lewis can be reached by regular ferry between Ullapool and Stornoway. Ferries also operate from Uig, on Skye, to Tarbert on Harris.

Fair Isle is half way between the Orkney and Shetland Islands, and a weekly boat service operates between it and the Shetland port of Gruntness.

Sea and air services carry passengers to the Shetlands from Aberdeen.

Hawick is on A7 Carlisle–Edinburgh road. Two and a half miles north east of the town on A698, Trow Mill stands, a picturesque building where visitors can see round the works.

The Holm Mills of James Pringle Ltd are at Inverness. Parts of the building date from 1780, and visitors can see processes involved in the manufacture of the firm's famous lambswool garments.

Bridge building

The great Scottish civil engineer Thomas Telford was called by the poet Southey 'the Colossus of Roads'. It was an apt pun, but we are inclined to remember Telford today for his more spectacular engineering feats – the bridges which carry his roads across rivers and valleys.

The building of the Iron Bridge in Shropshire in 1779 (see West Midlands) heralded a new age in bridge building, and Telford, who was appointed County Surveyor for Shropshire in 1788, became one of its earliest and greatest exponents. In 1803, he was commissioned to improve communications throughout the Scottish Highlands, and in the course of making nearly a thousand miles of new roads, he also built no less than 1117 bridges.

All fixed bridges are based on one of three principles or a combination of them. These are the 'beam' principle, of which the most primitive form is a tree trunk across a stream; the 'arch' principle, in which the structure is supported by the mutual pressure of the stones or blocks which create its shape; and the 'suspension' principle, in which the bridge is held by chains or cables anchored to towers of steel or masonry.

Scotland had some notable bridges, of course, before Telford arrived on the scene. Many a Scottish village and hamlet is named after the ancient crossing of the local stream. The Brig o' Balgownie over the River Don at Aberdeen was built by Robert the Bruce in the fourteenth century, and is still standing, a graceful Gothic arch of stone referred to by Byron in *Don Juan*.

Of five bridges crossing the Nith at Dumfries, one with six arches called Devorgilla's Bridge dates from 1426. The Old Bridge crossing the River Almond at Cramond, near Edinburgh, is where James I of Scotland was warned by a sooth-sayer to proceed no further, prior to his murder at Perth.

Below: Thomas Telford's bridge across the River Spey at Craigellachie, completed in 1815. The graceful arched bridge of cast iron is terminated by castellated masonry towers at each end, the total length of the span being 150 feet. The apparent fragility of this bridge shows Telford's complete mastery of ironwork – most of his bridges were strictly functional and solid. The function of this bridge has now been taken over by the much uglier box girder bridge in the background.

Right: Forth Bridge, Scotland. The cantilever railway bridge, linking Fife and Lothian, was opened in 1890 to carry trains across the mile-wide Firth of Forth.

Telford's first bridge in Scotland was the Tongueland Bridge crossing the River Dee at Kirkudbright (A755). It is a masonry bridge with a single arch of 112 feet span, and was built in 1806. It was unusual in two respects. It did not rise to the crown of the arch, which had always been the practice to ensure that rainwater would run off a bridge quickly; and it had hollow spandrels, giving a deceptive appearance of lightness to the structure. Spandrels are the spaces between the curves of the arches and the structure the arches support, and they had always previously been filled in or faced with stone so as to appear solid.

Many other arched bridges followed this one, crossing the Dee at Ballater (B976); the Tay at Dunkeld (A9); the Spey at Craigellachie (A95) and so on. The Dunkeld bridge was the largest of Telford's stone bridges, with seven arches. The Craigellachie's main arch is an elegant span of cast iron between two pairs of castellated stone towers.

Among the most dramatic of Telford's bridges is the Cartland Crags Bridge, crossing the gorge of Mouse Water just north west of Lanark (A73). Completed in 1822, it crosses the stream 129 feet below by means of three stone arches.

Telford's last stone bridge in Scotland was the Broomilaw Bridge spanning the Clyde at Glasgow, but this was demolished at the end of last century, and we must look to Edinburgh for one of his last surviving great works, the Dean Bridge crossing the Water of Leith, completed in 1831.

Another notable Scottish bridge builder was John Rennie, who built the Kelso bridge across the Tweed (A698), and who was later responsible for three famous crossings of the Thames – the London, Waterloo and Southwark bridges. The London bridges have all been replaced, but the Tweed bridge still stands at Kelso with its five elliptical arches.

Railway bridges

The coming of the railways presented new challenges to bridge builders in Scotland, especially in crossing the wide estuaries of the Tay and the Forth. The first Tay Bridge was completed in 1878, thirty-four years after Telford's death. It was designed by Thomas Bouch, a prodigious bridge-builder. Twenty men were killed during the construction, but it was the longest bridge in the world, one of the greatest prides of Victorian engineering, and the queen soon knighted Bouch for his achievement. The honour proved premature.

Above: The present Tay railway bridge, with Dundee in the background. The remaining stumps of the old bridge can be seen on the right. After the disaster of 1879, the new bridge was built of wrought iron lattice girder construction like the old, but much scientific and engineering experience went into ensuring that the new bridge would withstand lateral wind pressure. It was completed in 1887, and is Britain's longest railway bridge.

Left: Scotch whisky, Carron, Grampian. A warehouse of the Imperial Distillery, showing oak casks of whisky being stored for maturing before bottling.

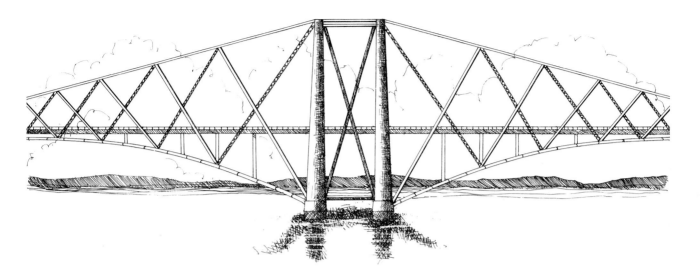

On the evening of 28th December in the following year, a train started to cross the bridge during a frightful gale. The high girders in the centre of the great structure collapsed and fell into the raging firth, taking the train with them, and the seventy-five people on board all lost their lives. A thousand and sixty yards of the bridge disappeared in a few seconds, when twelve iron columns and the thirteen spans they supported gave way in the pressure of the storm. The last casualty of the disaster was Sir Thomas Bouch himself. His design had been faulty, and his supervision of the engineering work negligent. He died a broken man four months after the tragedy.

The present Tay Bridge was opened eight years later. It is of wrought iron lattice girder construction like its predecessor, but proper allowances were made this time for lateral wind pressure. It is the longest railway bridge in Britain at just over two miles, linking Dundee with Fife.

The Forth Bridge was an even greater engineering achievement. Thomas Bouch had already begun construction of a suspension bridge across the Forth when the Tay disaster occurred, and not surprisingly, the Forth project came to a sudden halt. New engineers were appointed, and work eventually got under way on a steel cantilever bridge – a combination of the beam and suspension principles. It took eight years to

Above: Part of the Forth Bridge, showing its cantilever construction.

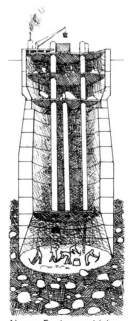

Above: Engineers driving piles into the bed of the Firth of Forth to support the structure.

build and cost three million pounds and the lives of fifty-seven men. It was at the time the largest cantilever bridge in the world, with its two main spans each nearly a third of a mile long, carrying a double railway track a hundred and fifty feet above water level.

In recent years both the Tay and the Forth railway bridges have been joined by major road bridges. The Forth road bridge was opened in 1964 and is a mile-and-a-half long suspension bridge with a central span of 1100 yards. The Tay toll bridge, of similar length, was opened two years later. Until recently, the Tay crossing was the longest road bridge over a river in Britain, and the Forth crossing the country's longest suspension bridge, but both these records have now been exceeded by the new Humber Bridge near Hull.

Where to go

Telford's Dean Bridge became a popular spot with suicides until the parapet was heightened, but is otherwise as Telford left it, an unorthodox design of four arches.

The Forth road bridge carries A90 across the estuary between North and South Queensferry, with the railway bridge down-river to the east.

Fisheries

It is hardly possible to over-estimate the importance of fishing to the Scottish economy over the centuries. The seafaring traditions of a people heavily influenced by the Vikings helped to create a vital herring industry on the east coast before the Norman Conquest, and for hundreds of years the entire male populations of many villages have been engaged in catching herring and haddock in the North Sea, whilst the men of Shetland have sought ling and cod in more distant waters.

Herring

In the eighteenth century, herring fisheries were seen as one answer to the problems of unemployment which were leading to depopulation in Scotland, and new fishing centres were developed. By the middle of the nineteenth century, five hundred boats were sailing from Wick alone. The men shot their drift nets by hand, and east coast harbours were soon landing more than a million barrels of herring a year for curing. The herring catches were gutted, sorted and packed into barrels by teams of girls, and three experienced girls could handle twenty thousand fish in a day.

It was George Leslie of Shetland who first used an aeroplane to search for shoals of herring and direct the fishing fleets to them, and this method was used until the introduction of echo-sounding equipment made it obsolete.

Above: Women packing herrings at the turn of the century. Women have traditionally found employment at the quayside in this important industry.

Below: A steam powered drifter of around 1930, as used for herring fishing. By this time, herring were by far the biggest catch of the Scottish fisheries. The fish swim near the surface, and are caught in nets which are kept vertical by weights at the bottom and floats at the top. The nets are kept at right angles to the direction of the shoals.

Some Scottish fishermen maintain that herring catches are poorer on moonlit nights, and it has been argued that fish can see the nets in the clear northern waters. However that may be, overfishing has become the chief problem of the herring industry in recent years.

Haddock

Haddock was the mainstay of inshore fishermen, and there were important fisheries all round the mainland coasts as well as in Orkney, Shetland and the Hebrides. The trade in smoked haddock was a development of the coastal area between Aberdeen and Stonehaven in the early nineteenth century, and Findon, a village roughly half way between the two, gave its name to the well known 'Finnan Haddock' in which the fish is split open, soaked in brine and smoked in a kiln over a wood fire.

The fishermen of Shetland suffered much hardship at one time. The local lairds, who gave them the means to earn a living by providing larger boats and better equipment, owned their entire property and abused this power by exploitation. Further difficulties came at the end of the nineteenth century when new steam trawlers from Aberdeen began to operate around the northern coasts and regularly fished close in to land. This led to a civil 'haddock war' long before international 'cod wars' captured national headlines. In 1907, thirteen Aberdeen skippers ap-

peared in court at Lerwick on charges of infringing the three-mile limit, and many a crofter-fisherman was forced to emigrate by trawlers poaching in shallow waters. Half a century later, however, particularly big catches of haddock helped the economic revival of the Shetlands before the discovery of North Sea Oil.

Commercial fishing today

From Tarbert and Oban and Mallaig in the west, round to Fraserburgh and Aberdeen and Stonehaven in the east, and from scores of smaller harbours in between, hundreds of boats put out to sea for herring and white-fish, or into shallower waters for lobster and prawns, in what is still a multi-million-pounds Scottish industry despite current difficulties.

Aberdeen, the 'granite city', is the most important of the east coast fishing ports. Visitors can see the catches being auctioned in the fish market if they are up early enough – auctions begin at 7.30. Fish from many

Above: Aberdeen's Fish Market. The fish are packed in ice at sea, the catches being winched ashore and displayed in boxes.

Below: Smoking haddock. The fish are hung by the tails in the kiln, to be smoked over wood fires.

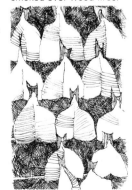

smaller harbours all round the Scottish coast are brought here for canning and kippering.

Mallaig is the chief west coast harbour, and indeed is one of the major herring and shellfish ports of Britain, with fifty herring boats operating from it and a huge annual lobster catch, which is auctioned on the quay on Saturday mornings. Kippering kilns and an ice factory are among the essential adjuncts of the harbour's fishing programme.

Where to go

The Scottish Fisheries Museum at Anstruther, Fife, is a first class museum with model fishing vessels, fisherman's cottages, etc. Anstruther is reached from Edinburgh by the Forth Bridge and coast road, or from Dundee by the Tay bridge and coast road through St Andrews.

A new Maritime Museum at Aberdeen is due to join museums at Stonehaven and Dundee which also have seafaring exhibits.

Whisky distilling

The word 'whisky' is a derivation from the Gaelic *uisge beatha* – water of life – but the actual origins of the fiery spirit are lost in Highland myths – or mists. It may, in fact, have been an Irish invention, for the Irish were producing (and consuming) whiskey (as they spell it there) when Henry II invaded the island in the twelfth century. At any rate, the making of whisky was a thriving business in Scotland by the sixteenth century. Before it became a national industry, distilling was done in the winter months as part of the annual cycle of farmwork in the areas which had been provided by nature with peat and clear streams, and by man with barley.

The first process in making whisky is the malting of the barley grain. (For this process, see under Eastern England – the only difference between malting for beer and malting for whisky is that the malt is traditionally dried, at least partly, over burning peat in Scotland, which imparts to whisky some of its unique flavour.)

The dried malt is ground and then mashed in hot water and the liquid drained off has yeast added to it for the brewing process, when fermentation takes place and converts sugar into alcohol. So far, the procedure is not very different from that involved in brewing ale, but what we have at this stage is neither ale nor whisky, but a clear liquid which distillers call the 'wash'.

Distillation

The basic process of converting 'wash' into whisky is merely one of evaporation and condensation. The wash goes up in smoke, so to speak, and comes down as one of the finest beverages ever invented by man.

The wash is first transferred to a copper still of pear shape, called a 'wash still', in which it is distilled, and then into another called a 'low wines still' in which it is distilled again. The colourless liquid which is collected from this is proof spirit, though it is not yet Scotch whisky. Spirit of proof strength is defined scientifically nowadays as that which at a temperature of 51° Fahrenheit weighs exactly twelve thirteenths of an equal volume of distilled water at the same temperature. In the old days they used to test its strength by damping gunpowder with it and

Above: The Dalwhinnie Distillery near the northern end of Loch Ericht, in the Scottish Highlands. In this part of the complex the germinating barley is dried over burning peat, while ventilators at the top draw hot air through the barley. The smoke imparts a peaty flavour to the malt and is a vital part of the whisky making process.

seeing if it still ignited!

The next procedure is to put the whisky into wooden casks to mature for a minimum legal period of three years before bottling – eight years is a more usual period. The casks are of oak, and the best casks are not new, but old ones which have previously held sherry. The colourless liquid acquires a pale tint from the sherry which seeps into it from the wood. During maturing, the whisky which goes into the casks as a rough and coarse spirit becomes smooth and mellow.

What has been produced by the method described so far is pure malt whisky. It may appear a straightforward business, but in fact it is an art perfected only with long experience and fine judgment on the part of

maltsters, brewers and distillers alike.

In 1826, a process was invented for the rapid distillation of grain whisky by means of a 'patent still', and John Haig of Fife was one of the first to use it. The modern adaptation of the invention produces the grain whisky which is blended with malt whiskies to give us the most widely known brands of 'Scotch' today.

In the grain whisky method, crushed cereal of unmalted barley or maize with a little malted barley is cooked and mixed with ground malted barley and hot water, and fermented. Evaporation and condensation of the 'wash' are achieved by a different process from the 'pot still' method, and permit a faster, cheaper and continuous production process. The maturing also takes less time. The result is a lighter and less flavoured drink than malt whisky, but as it is drunk only when blended with malt whisky, this fact is relatively academic.

Each individual company's blend remains a highly secret recipe, despite agitation from some quarters for the proportions of malt and grain to be revealed. Many different whiskies may be used in the bottled blend. Some blenders put their malt and grain whiskies in casks to mature together; others only introduce the 'malts' to the 'grains' at the bottling stage. The whisky is also diluted slightly with pure water to render it about 70° proof. Caramel is also added at this point to give the whisky its familiar straw colour.

Left: A peat kiln being loaded with malt for drying and, right, a traditional warehouse at Lagavulin Distillery, Port Ellen, on Islay, Strathclyde. Here, single malt whisky is stored in sherry casks for several years to mature.

The whisky boom

A great increase in the popularity of whisky occurred in Scotland in the eighteenth century, and the consumption of beer dropped there as a result. This led to the industrial development of whisky production, though it did not replace the cottage distilleries altogether, and repeated attempts by the British government (such as the malt tax) to make capital out of the Scotsman's pleasures, made smuggling and illicit stills a commonplace, taxing the wits of excisemen as well as the products of legitimate distilleries.

It was not until the Spirits Act of 1860, however, that Scotch whisky was allowed to be exported to England in bottles. Shortly afterwards, several grain distillers formed themselves into the Distillers Company, and they and others began marketing whisky on a large scale in England and elsewhere. By a happy coincidence, their efforts to make Scotch popular in England took place at the same time as the great boom in tourism, when all things Scottish were in fashion.

By the end of the nineteenth century, there were more than a hundred and fifty legitimate distillers in Scotland, and 'Scotch' had become as famous a drink throughout the civilized world as Cognac had been for centuries. A huge export drive developed trade with the United States, where Americans mix the stuff with ice and soda and call it a 'highball'.

It was a cargo of Haig whisky bound for the States during the Second World War that went down with a wrecked ship in the Outer Hebrides and gave Compton Mackenzie the theme for his famous comic novel *Whisky Galore*. The retail price of a bottle of blended whisky in England at that time was about twelve shillings and sixpence!

The world-wide demand for whisky has meant that Scotland can no longer grow sufficient barley for its needs, and a great deal of English barley goes to Scotland

Left: The stillhouse at Ord Distillery, near Muir of Ord, west of Inverness. The liquid called 'wash' is heated in copper stills to vapourize the alcohol, which is then condensed and distilled once again before being transferred to the spirit vat as a colourless and fiery liquid, ready for dilution and storage.

without in any way altering the final product. What *does* affect the outcome is the quality of Scottish water and the peat kilns – attempts in various foreign parts to produce whisky by exact duplication of traditional methods have failed dismally.

Generally speaking, pot-still malt whisky is of Highland origin; patent-still blended whisky of Lowland origin. The Lowlands are the scene of famous blended-whisky names like Bells and Dewar, Grants and Haig, Teachers and White Horse. The Leith district of Edinburgh became a whisky 'capital' in the nineteenth century, whilst at Kilmarnock, the Johnny Walker whisky bottling plant is the largest in the world. But the Highland centre of pot-still distilleries is Speyside, where famous single-malt brands such as Glenfiddich, Glenlivet and Dalwhinnie have their origins.

As the duty on whisky continues to increase, the industry naturally fears for the consequences to the trade, but it is pleasant to be able to end this book on a note of industrial optimism, for nothing surely has a more secure future than 'Scotch', and no words could form a more satisfying conclusion than the traditional invitation at the end of a long day: 'Will ye have a wee dram?'

Where to go

Although 'Scotch' is produced at over a hundred widely scattered sites, including Islay and Kintyre, the greatest concentration of the industry is along the River Spey and its tributaries. Not all distilleries are open to the public, but Grants and Glenfiddich (both founded by William Grant), John Walker & Sons and John Dewar & Sons all offer guided tours. The Glenfiddich Distillery also has a Scotch Whisky Museum.

Grants is in Girvan, Strathclyde (A77 coast road twenty-two miles south of Ayr). Glenfiddich is on A941 by the River Fiddich north of Dufftown, Grampian (A96 and A920 from Aberdeen or A96 and A941 from Inverness). 'Johnny Walker' is at Kilmarnock (off A77 Ayr–Glasgow road), and Dewars at Inveralmond (A9 one mile north of Perth).

Museums

SOUTH WEST ENGLAND

Camborne
Cornish beam engines, East Pool Mine, (National Trust). Two complete beam engines of late 19th C. Daily, April to October.

Exeter
Maritime Museum, The Quay. 0392 58075. Claims to be world's largest collection of working boats. Open daily throughout year.

St Austell
Wheal Martyn Museum, Carthew. 0726 850362. Open-air museum of china clay industry in restored works. April to October.

Wookey Hole
The Paper Mill. 0749 72243. Demonstrations of paper making by hand. Open throughout year except Christmas Day.

CENTRAL SOUTHERN ENGLAND

Beaulieu
Maritime Museum, Bucklers Hard. 059 063 203. Models and exhibits of local shipbuilding. Open throughout year.

Portsmouth
Royal Naval Museum, Naval Base. 0705 22351. Naval history. HMS Victory adjacent. Open throughout year, including Sunday afternoons.

Reading
Museum of English Rural Life, Whiteknights Park. 0734 85123. (University of Reading). Agriculture and social history. Tuesday to Saturday except Bank Holidays.

Southampton
Maritime Museum, Bugle Street. 0703 23941. Museum of shipping in 14th C. wool store. All year except Mondays.

Swindon
Great Western Railway Museum, Faringdon Road. 0793 26161. Locomotives and railway history. Open throughout year, including Sunday afternoons.

GREATER LONDON AND NORTHERN HOME COUNTIES

High Wycombe
Chair and Local History Museum, Castle Hill. 0494 23879. Chairs (especially Windsor), Bucks lace, tools etc. All year except Wednesdays and Sundays.

London
The Museum of London, London Wall. 01-600 3699. Social and industrial history of London. Open all year except Mondays and Christmas.

National Maritime Museum, Romney Road, Greenwich. 01-858 4422. Maritime history, models, charts and paintings, etc. Open throughout year except some Bank Holidays.

Science Museum, Exhibition Road, South Kensington. 01-589 3456. Engineering, transport and industry through history. Open all year except some Bank Holidays.

Luton
Luton Museum & Art Gallery, Wardown Park. 0582 36941. Straw hat and lace industries and social history. Open all year except holidays and Sundays in December and January.

SOUTH EAST ENGLAND

Amberley
Chalk Pits Museum, Houghton Bridge. 079 881 370. Open air museum of south east industry, including iron founding. Easter to October: closed Mondays and Tuesdays.

Wye
Agricultural Museum, Court Lodge Farm, Brook. (University of London). Agricultural implements and machinery. May to September: Wednesday afternoons, and Saturdays in August.

EASTERN ENGLAND

Bressingham
Steam Museum. 037 988 386. Steam power on farm, road and railway. Sundays and Thursdays, May to September (afternoons only). Wednesdays in August and spring and summer Bank Holidays.

Fakenham
Thursford Collection, off A148. 032 877 238. Includes steam agricultural engines. Easter to October daily, and Sundays and Bank Holidays throughout year.

Gressenhall
Norfolk Rural Museum. 036 286 563. New museum of local rural life and agriculture. Mid-May to mid-September, every day except Mondays.

WEST MIDLANDS

Acton Scott
Working Farm Museum. 069 46 306/7. Animals and machinery in use at turn of century demonstrated April to October daily.

Birmingham
Museum of Science and Industry, Newhall Street. 021 236 1022. Wide coverage of industry and science, including small arms. Open all year except some Bank Holidays.

Burton on Trent
The Bass Museum, Horninglow Street. 0283 42031. History of local brewing and brewery transport. Open throughout year except certain Bank Holidays.

Dudley
Black Country Museum, Tipton Road. 021 557 9643. Canals, chain making, mining exhibits, etc. April to October except Saturdays.

Hereford
Museum of Cider, Ryelands Street. 0432 6411. Complete story of cider industry, with cooper's shop. All year except Tuesdays and Christmas Day.

Stoke on Trent
Gladstone Pottery Museum, Uttoxeter Road. 0782 319232. Bottle ovens, old workshops, and pottery being made. Open throughout year except winter Mondays and Christmas Day.

Chatterley Whitfield Mining Museum, Tunstall. 0782 813337. Actual coal mine, with visits underground. No children under 12. Every day except Mondays.

Styal
Quarry Bank Mill. Hand spinning and power loom weaving, and early development of cotton industry. Highly complicated opening arrangements – enquire of National Trust.

Telford
Ironbridge Gorge Museum. 095 245 3522. Extensive open air museum of mining, iron working and unique industrial monuments, plus Coalport china works. Open throughout year.

EAST MIDLANDS

Leicester
Museum of Technology, Corporation Road. 0533 61330. New museum with knitting machinery, beam engines, transport etc. Open throughout year.

Matlock Bath
Peak District Mines Museum, South Parade. 0629 3834. Open throughout year except Christmas Day.

Northampton
Museum of Leathercraft, Bridge Street. 0604 34881. Use of leather throughout history, in centre of boot and shoe industry. Weekdays throughout year.

Nottingham
Industrial Museum, Wollaton Park. 0602 284602. Hosiery, lace making, chemicals, printing, machinery etc. Every day April to September; Thursdays, Saturdays and Sunday afternoons October to March, except Christmas.

Stoke Bruerne
Waterways Museum. 0604 862229. Social and industrial history of canals. Open throughout year except winter Mondays.

WALES

Cardiff
Welsh Industrial and Maritime Museum. New development of National Museum of Wales. 0222 371805. Open throughout year, including Sunday afternoons, but not certain Bank Holidays.

Dre-Fach Felindre
Museum of Woollen Industry. 0559 370453. History of industry and textile machinery in working mill premises. Every day April to September except Sundays and May Day Bank Holiday.

Llanberis
North Wales Quarrying Museum. 028 682 630. Machinery, equipment and history of slate quarrying. Every day Easter to September except May Day Bank Holiday.

Porthmadog
Ffestiniog Railway Museum, Harbour Station. History of the narrow-gauge railway. Open daily during train service hours.

Swansea
Maritime and Industrial Museum, South Dock. 0792 55006. Woollen mill, transport and other local industry. Open throughout year.

Tywyn
Narrow Gauge Railway Museum, Wharf Station. Locomotives etc. and history of railway. Easter to October during operating hours.

NORTH WEST ENGLAND

Blackburn
Lewis Textile Museum, Exchange Street. 0254 667130. Development of cotton industry and machines of Arkwright, Hargreaves, Crompton etc. Open throughout year except Sundays.

Carnforth
Steamtown Railway Museum, Warton Road. 052 473 4220. British and foreign steam locomotives. Open throughout year daily.

Kendal
Museum of Lakeland Life and Industry, Abbot Hall. 0539 22464. Exhibits of local industry include bobbin making equipment. Open all year except weekend mornings and certain Bank Holidays.

Liverpool
Merseyside Maritime Museum, Pier Head. 051 236 1492. Extensive new open air museum illustrating history of dockland, with docks, cranes, warehouses, boats, etc. Every day from Spring to late Autumn.

Manchester
National Paper Museum, Grosvenor Street (part of North Western Museum of Science and Industry). 061 273 6636. History of paper making, machines, etc. Open throughout the year except Sundays.

St Helens
Pilkington Glass Museum, Prescot Road. 0744 28882. History of glass making. Open throughout year but afternoons only at weekends. Closed Christmas and New Year.

Salford
Museum of Mining, Eccles Old Road. History and technology of coal mining. Open throughout year.

NORTH EAST ENGLAND

Beamish
North of England Open Air Museum. 0207 31811. Social and industrial history of North, including coal mining and railways. Open throughout year except winter Mondays.

Bradford
Industrial Museum, Moorside Road. 0274 631756. Local industry and transport, including woollen and worsted industry. All year except most Mondays and some Bank Holidays.

Halifax
Industrial Museum, The Piece Hall. History and machinery of local textile industry. Open throughout year including Sunday afternoons.

Darlington
Railway Museum, North Road Station. 0325 60532. Restored Stockton and Darlington Railway station with locomotives and rolling stock. All year except winter Sundays.

Hartlepool
Maritime Museum, Northgate. 0429 72814. Social and industrial exhibits of fishing and shipbuilding, etc. All year except Sundays and certain Bank Holidays.

Hull
Town Docks Museum, Queen Victoria Square. 0482 223111. Whaling, fishing, trawling etc. Open throughout year including Sunday afternoons.

Newcastle on Tyne
Museum of Mining Engineering, Queen Victoria Road. 0632 28511. History and equipment of mining industry. Mondays to Fridays throughout year.

Sheffield
Abbeydale Industrial Hamlet, Abbeydale Road South. 0742 367731. 18th C. scythe works with furnace, tilt hammers etc. Open all year including Sundays.

Stocksfield
Hunday National Tractor and Farm Museum, Newton. 066 15 2553. Water-wheels, smithy, tractors and agricultural engines, etc. Open throughout year including Sundays.

York
National Railway Museum, Leeman Road. 0904 21261. History and sociology of British railway development, with locomotives etc. Open all year including Sunday afternoons, but closed some Bank Holidays.

SCOTLAND

Anstruther
Scottish Fisheries Museum, Harbourhead. 0333 310628. All aspects of local fishing industry. Open all year but afternoons only in winter, and not Tuesdays.

Dufftown
Glenfiddich Whisky Museum. 034 02 375. Private museum of distilling etc. Open all year except Christmas and New Year.

Index

Acknowledgements

The sources of information I have relied on in writing this book have been so varied and numerous that to list them would require far more space than is available. In a wide-ranging book of this nature, such a list would prove of little value to the general reader as a guide to further reading. Sources have included biographies and books on art, religion and social history as well as on industry and topography, and even one or two on 'industrial archaeology'.

I have also been most grateful for literature sent to me by particular industrial concerns; for information provided during personal visits; and for the high standard of helpfulness and courtesy from the staffs of several museums and reference libraries.

I would like to thank my friends Julian Holland and Philip Clark, designer and editor of the volume. Their constant cooperation gave me healing ointment for the writer's cramp I got through their eager encouragement.

My wife's help, not to mention her patience and understanding, has contributed more than a little to the making of the book. All authors' wives, I suspect, ought to appear on title pages alongside their husbands, but egotists that we are, we like to claim the lion's share of credit for ourselves, and toss them a morsel now and then to keep them going.

Photo credits

National Railway Museum **5**; Ironbridge Gorge Museum **6**; St Bride Printing Museum **8**; Central Electricity Generating Board **9**; County Museum, Truro **16**; John Cornwell **17**; Brian Hawkes **18**; John Cornwell **20**; H.M. Prison, Dartmoor **22**; The Times **25**; City of Bristol Museum and Art Gallery **26**; Aerofilms Ltd **28**; Dorset County Library **32**; Kingston Minerals Ltd **33**; Picturepoint **35**; Kenneth Scowen **36–37**; Kenneth Scowen **38**; The Stone Firms Ltd **39**; Vosper Hovermarine Ltd **40**; Hugh McKnight **42**; British Rail/Oxford Publishing Co **44**; Hulton Picture Library **45**; A.F. Kersting **46**; Richard E. Early **47**; St Bride Printing Library **49**; Aerofilms **50**; P.L.A. Collection, Museum of London **51**; Southwark Libraries **52**; Wycombe Chair Museum **54**; Ercol Ltd **55**; Adrian Hawkes **56**; The Design Council **57**; Hitchin Museum **58**; Aerofilms **60**; London Brick Company Ltd **61**; The Faversham Society **63**; National Maritime Museum **65**; The Faversham Society **66**; Sussex Archaeological Society **67**; Barcham Green and Company Ltd **68**; Barcham Green and Company Ltd **69**; Norfolk County Library and Eastern Daily Press **71**; Spectrum **73**; Kenneth Scowen **74**; A.F. Kersting **75**; Alec's Photique, Stowmarket **78**; Department of the Environment **80**; Cambridgeshire Libraries **81**; Donald O.F. Monk **82**; Salt Museum, Northwich **86**; Birmingham Museum and Art Gallery **87**; Ironbridge Gorge Museum (Elton Collection) **89**; Spectrum **91**; Rita Bailey **92–93**; Ironbridge Gorge Museum **94**; Ironbridge Gorge Museum **95**; The Trustees of the Wedgwood Museum, Barlaston, Staffs **96**; Albion Galleries, Stoke-on-Trent **98**; Shropshire County Council **100**; Bass Ltd **101**; Lionel F.J. Walrond AMA, FSA **102**; Leicester Museum **106–107**; Corah Ltd **108**; Kenneth Scowen **111**; Sefton Photo Library **112–113**; Taylors Ltd **114**; Leicester Museums **115**; John Cornwell **116**; Taylors Ltd **118**; Industrial Museum, Nottingham **120**; British Steel Corporation **122**; John Cornwell **125–126**; Aerofilms Ltd **128**; National Museum of Wales (Welsh Folk Museum) **129**; Spectrum **131**; Picturepoint **132–133**; Julian Holland **134**; National Library of Aberystwyth **135**; Festiniog Railway Company/N. Gurley **136**; Manchester Public Libraries **142**; Oldham Evening Chronicle **144**; Hugh McKnight **146**; City Art Gallery, Manchester **148**; Abbot Hall Art Gallery, Kendal **149–150**; Colin Poole **151**; Hugh McKnight **152–153**; Trevor Wood **154**; T.H. McK. Clough **155**; Rexel Ltd **156**; Hulton Picture Library **157**; Pilkington Brothers Ltd **158–159**; James Drummond & Sons Ltd and Bradford Central Library **162**; The Mansell Collection **164**; Town Docks Museum, Hull **166**; Sheffield Central Library **168**; Martin Watts **170**; R.C. Green **171**; National Railway Museum **172–173**; Spectrum **174**; National Museum of Wales **176**; City of Newcastle-upon-Tyne, City Engineer's Dept **178**; Darlington Museum **178**; Wiggins Teape Ltd **181**; Strathclyde Regional Archives **182**; Hulton Picture Library **183**; Govan Shipbuilders Ltd **184**; Govan Shipbuilders Ltd **186**; W.G. Lucas, Hebridean Press Service **187**; Tom Weir **189**; D.C. Thompson & Co Ltd **190**; Brian Hawkes **191**; The Distillers Co Ltd **192**; Tom Weir **195**; The Distillers Co Ltd **196**; The Distillers Co Ltd **198**.

Holland & Clark would also like to thank the following for their help:
Belinda Allen; Avon County Central Library; Bass Museum, Burton on Trent; Bath Local Studies Library; Bradford Central Library and Industrial Museum; Chair and Local History Museum, High Wycombe; Cheshire County Council Libraries and Museums; Dorchester Library; Charles Early; Farmland Museums, Haddenham; Framework Knitters Museum, Ruddington; SS *Great Britain*; Industrial Museum, Wollaton Park, Nottingham; Leeds Local Studies Library; Leicester Art Gallery and Museum of Technology; Ann Mallinson, Selborne Bookshop; Master of Clipper Ship *Cutty Sark*; Museum of Lakeland Life and Industry; National Motor Museum, Beaulieu; National Museum of Wales; National Railway Museum, York; P. Pickford, Alton; Pilkington Glass Museum; Brian Render; Barbara Rogers; Salt Museum; Scottish Fisheries Museum; Sheffield Art Gallery, Museums and Local Studies Library; St Austell China Clay Museum; John Taylor & Co Ltd; Trow Mill, Hawick; HMS *Victory*; West Country Studies Library; Wiggins Teape Ltd.